P9-AGK-276

Fodor's
THIRD New EDITION

Florence, Tuscany & Umbria

"When it comes to information on regional history, what to see and do, and shopping, these guides are exhaustive."

—*USAir Magazine*

"Usable, sophisticated restaurant coverage, with an emphasis on good value."

—Andy Birsh, *Gourmet Magazine* columnist

"Valuable because of their comprehensiveness."

—*Minneapolis Star-Tribune*

"Fodor's always delivers high quality...thoughtfully presented...thorough."

—*Houston Post*

"An excellent choice for those who want everything under one cover."

—*Washington Post*

Reprinted from *Fodor's Italy*

Fodor's Travel Publications, Inc.
New York • Toronto • London • Sydney • Auckland
http://www.fodors.com/

Fodor's Florence, Tuscany & Umbria

Editor: Fionn Davenport

Editorial Contributors: Steven Amsterdam, Robert Andrews, Barbara Walsh Angelillo, Mary Ellen Schultz, M. T. Schwartzman, Dinah Spritzer, George Sullivan

Creative Director: Fabrizio La Rocca

Cartographer: David Lindroth

Cover Photograph: Antonio Sferlazzo

Text Design: Between the Covers

Copyright

Third Edition

ISBN 0–679–03219–3

Special Sales

Fodor's Travel Publications are available at special discounts for bulk purchases for sales promotions or premiums. Special editions, including personalized covers, excerpts of existing guides, and corporate imprints, can be created in large quantities for special needs. For more information, contact your local bookseller or write to Special Markets, Fodor's Travel Publications, 201 East 50th Street, New York, NY 10022. Inquiries from Canada should be directed to your local Canadian bookseller or sent to Random House of Canada, Ltd., Marketing Department, 1265 Aerowood Drive, Mississauga, Ontario L4W 1B9. Inquiries from the United Kingdom should be sent to Fodor's Travel Publications, 20 Vauxhall Bridge Road, London SW1V 2SA, England.

PRINTED IN THE UNITED STATES OF AMERICA

10 9 8 7 6 5 4 3 2 1

CONTENTS

Maps

ON THE ROAD WITH FODOR'S

WE'RE ALWAYS THRILLED to get letters from readers, especially one like this:

It took us an hour to decide what book to buy and we now know we picked the best one. Your book was wonderful, easy to follow, very accurate, and good on pointing out eating places, informal as well as formal. When we saw other people using your book, we would look at each other and smile.

Our editors and writers are deeply committed to making every Fodor's guide "the best one"—not only accurate but always charming, brimming with sound recommendations and solid ideas, right on the mark in describing restaurants and hotels, and full of fascinating facts that make you view what you've traveled to see in a rich new light.

About Our Writers

Amid the shops along Rome's Via Condotti, inside the trattorias of Trieste, and at the latest art exhibitions in Venice, you'll find Barbara Walsh Angelillo, Robert Andrews, and Giuliano Davenport studying the sights and looking for all the world like undercover agents. They won't be searching for signs of foul play, but rather for signs of excellence, innovation, and expertise. Their purpose: To track down the best of Italy—and eliminate the worst—to help our readers enjoy the trip of a lifetime.

The first time that **Barbara Walsh Angelillo** arrived in Rome, she was traveling on a tight schedule; still, she had time to fall in love with both the city and a dark-eyed Italian—simultaneously. Well aware that this was one of the hazards of touring Italy, she kept to her schedule and left Rome after only three days. Within a year, however, Barbara said *arrivederci* to her native New York City to settle, marry, and raise three children in Italy. As a freelance travel writer and editor, she loves to share her expertise about Italy with readers, and she has been doing so—mostly covering the regions of Rome, Florence, Tuscany, Liguria, and Piedmont—for Fodor's for more than 30 years. She also is associate editor of the glossy, bimonthly, English-language magazine, *Italy Italy,* which is published in Rome and distributed in the United States and elsewhere. To unwind, Barbara vacations in what she calls "two of Italy's most special places," Umbria and the Amalfi Coast.

The history, art, and architecture of European cities have been freelance writer **George Sullivan's** favorite subject since he spent a college summer in London many years ago. Having authored our exploring tour of Florence, he is currently working on an architectural guidebook on Rome. He now knows the city so well he's on a first-name basis with its entire population of stray cats.

Robert Andrews has familial roots in Sicily and has been wedded to Italy (the south of the country in particular) for most of his life. Though based in Bristol, England, where he pursues a parallel career as an anthologist of quotations, Robert visits the old boot annually and leaves ever more perplexed and exhilarated. In addition to covering Emilia-Romagna, Umbria, Campania, Apulia, Sicily, and Sardinia for us, he has written for many publications and coauthored books on Sardinia and Sicily.

Editor **Fionn Davenport** has, like his brother Giuliano, mixed Irish–Italian roots. His love affair with Italy has been a lifelong passion, and from his small apartment on New York's Lower East Side he dreams of owning a rustic cottage on a hill overlooking the sun-warmed vineyards and olive groves of the Tuscan countryside. Art and architecture *do* make Italy beautiful, but he reserves his greatest affections for the Italians themselves: In the words of E.M. Forster, Fionn advises travelers not to "go with that awful idea that Italy's only a museum of antiquities and art. Love and understand the Italians, for the people are more marvelous than the land."

What's New

A New Design

This year we've reformatted our guides to make them easier to use. Each chapter of *Florence, Tuscany & Umbria* begins with brand-new recommended itineraries to help you decide what to see in the time you have; a section called When to Tour points out the optimal time of day, day of the week, and season for your journey. You may also notice our fresh graphics, new in 1996. More readable and more helpful than ever? We think so—and we hope you do, too.

On the Web

Also check out Fodor's Web site (http://www.fodors.com/), where you'll find travel information on major destinations around the world and an ever-changing array of travel-savvy interactive features.

How to Use This Guide

Organization

Up front is the **Gold Guide.** Its first section, **Important Contacts A to Z,** gives addresses and telephone numbers of organizations and companies that offer destination-related services and detailed information and publications. **Smart Travel Tips A to Z,** the Gold Guide's second section, gives specific information on how to accomplish what you need to in Italy as well as tips on savvy traveling. Both sections are in alphabetical order by topic.

The Florence chapter begins with an Exploring section, which is subdivided by neighborhood; each subsection recommends a walking or driving tour and lists sights in alphabetical order. Each regional chapter is divided by geographical area; within each area, towns are covered in logical geographical order, and attractive stretches of road and minor points of interest between them are indicated by the designation *En Route.* Throughout, Off the Beaten Path sights appear after the places from which they are most easily accessible. And within town sections, all restaurants and lodgings are grouped together.

To help you decide what to visit in the time you have, all chapters begin with recommended itineraries; you can mix and match those from several chapters to create a complete vacation. The A to Z section that ends all chapters covers getting there, getting around, and helpful contacts and resources.

Icons and Symbols

★	Our special recommendations
✕	Restaurant
🏠	Lodging establishment
✕🏠	Lodging establishment whose restaurant warrants a detour
☾	Good for kids (rubber duckie)
☞	Sends you to another section of the guide for more information
✉	Address
☎	Telephone number
☯	Opening and closing times
✇	Admission prices (those we give apply only to adults; substantially reduced fees are almost always available for children, students, and senior citizens)

Numbers in white and black circles—② and ❷, for example—that appear on the maps, in the margins, and within the tours correspond to one another.

Dining and Lodging

The restaurants and lodgings we list are the cream of the crop in each price range. Price charts appear in the Pleasures and Pastimes section that follows each chapter introduction.

Hotel Facilities

We always list the facilities that are available—but we don't specify whether they cost extra: When pricing accommodations, always ask what's included.

Assume that hotels operate on the **European Plan** (EP, with no meals) unless we note that they use the **Full American Plan** (FAP, with all meals), the **Modified American Plan** (MAP, with breakfast and dinner daily), or the **Continental Plan** (CP, with a Continental breakfast daily).

Restaurant Reservations and Dress Codes

Reservations are always a good idea; we note only when they're essential or when they are not accepted. Book as far ahead as you can, and reconfirm when you get to town. Unless otherwise noted, the restaurants listed are open daily for lunch and dinner. We mention dress only when men are required to wear a jacket or a jacket and tie. Look for an overview of local habits under Dining in Smart Travel Tips A to Z and in the Pleasures and Pastimes section that follows each chapter introduction.

Credit Cards

The following abbreviations are used: **AE,** American Express; **DC,** Diners Club; **MC,** MasterCard; and **V,** Visa.

Don't Forget to Write

You can use this book in the confidence that all prices and opening times are based on information supplied to us at press time; Fodor's cannot accept responsibility for any errors. Time inevitably brings changes, so always confirm information when it matters—especially if you're making a detour to visit a specific place. In addition, when making reservations be sure to mention if you have a disability or are traveling with children, if you prefer a private bath or a certain type of bed, or if you have specific dietary needs or any other concerns.

Were the restaurants we recommended as described? Did our hotel picks exceed your expectations? Did you find a museum we recommended a waste of time? If you have complaints, we'll look into them and revise our entries when the facts warrant it. If you've discovered a special place that we haven't included, we'll pass the information along to our correspondents and have them check it out. So send your feedback, positive *and* negative, to the Italy Editor at 201 East 50th Street, New York, New York 10022—and have a wonderful trip!

Karen Cure
Editorial Director

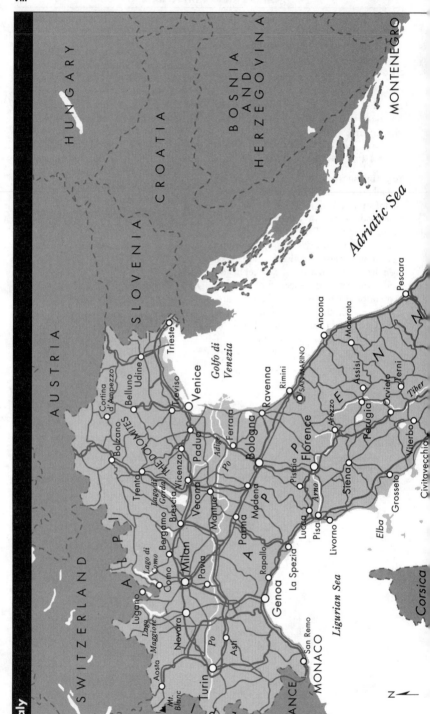

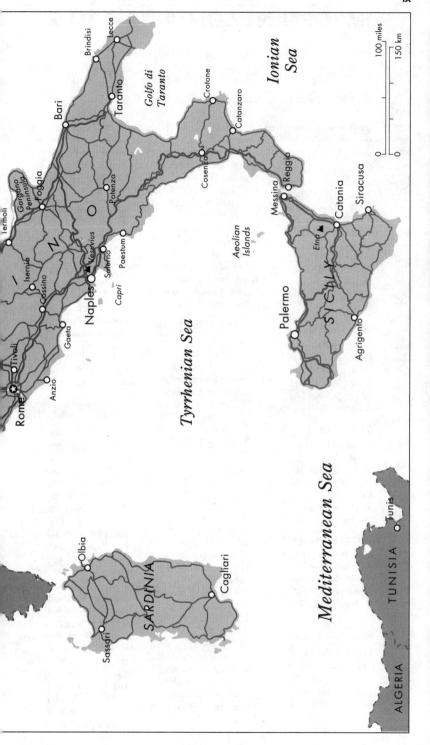

Rome

Tivoli

Anzio

Gaeta

Tyrrhenian Sea

Iermoli

Gargano
Peninsula

Foggia

Isernia

Cassino

Naples

Vesuvius

Salerno

Paestum

Capri

Potenza

Bari

Taranto

Golfo di
Taranto

Brindisi

Lecce

Crotone

Catanzaro

Cosenza

Reggio

Messina

Aeolian
Islands

Etna

Palermo

SICILY

Catania

Siracusa

Agrigento

Ionian
Sea

Olbia

Sassari

SARDINIA

Cagliari

Mediterranean Sea

Tunis

TUNISIA

ALGERIA

100 miles

150 km

IMPORTANT CONTACTS A TO Z

An Alphabetical Listing of Publications, Organizations, and Companies that Will Help You Before, During, and After Your Trip

A

AIR TRAVEL

International gateways to Florence, Tuscany, and Umbria include Rome's **Leonardo da Vinci Airport,** better known as Fiumicino after its location (☎ 011–39–6/659–53640), and Milan's **Malpensa Airport** (☎ 011–39–2/380–11172).

FLYING TIME

Flying time to Italy is 8½ hours from New York, 10–11 hours from Chicago, and 12–13 hours from Los Angeles.

CARRIERS

To ROME➤ Contact **Alitalia** (☎ 800/223–5730), **Continental** (☎ 800/525–0280), **Delta** (☎ 800/241–4141), and **TWA** (☎ 800/892–4141).

To MILAN➤ Contact **Alitalia, American Airlines** (800/624–6262), **Continental, Delta, TWA,** and **United** (☎ 800/241–6652).

FROM THE U.K.

Contact **Alitalia** (☎ 0171/602–7111 or 0345 212–121 outside London) and **British Airways** (☎ 0181/897–4000 or 0345/222–111 outside London).

COMPLAINTS

To register complaints about charter and scheduled airlines, contact the U.S. Department of Transportation's **Aviation Consumer Protection Division** (✉ C-75, Washington, DC 20590, ☎ 202/366–2220). Complaints about lost baggage or ticketing problems and safety concerns may also be logged with the **Federal Aviation Administration (FAA) Consumer Hotline** (☎ 800/322–7873).

CONSOLIDATORS

For the names of reputable air-ticket consolidators, contact the **United States Air Consolidators Association** (✉ 925 L St., Suite 220, Sacramento, CA 95814, ☎ 916/441–4166, FAX 916/441–3520). For discount air-ticketing agencies, *see* Discounts & Deals, *below.*

PUBLICATIONS

For general information about charter carriers, ask for the Department of Transportation's free brochure **"Plane Talk: Public Charter Flights"** (✉ Aviation Consumer Protection Division, C-75, Washington, DC 20590, ☎ 202/366–2220). The Department of Transportation also publishes a 58-page booklet, **"Fly Rights,"** available from the Consumer Information Center (✉ Supt. of Documents, Dept. 136C, Pueblo, CO 81009; $1.75).

For other tips and hints, consult the Consumers Union's monthly **"Consumer Reports Travel Letter"** (✉ Box 53629, Boulder, CO 80322, ☎ 800/234–1970; $39 1st year).

B

BETTER BUSINESS BUREAU

For local contacts in the hometown of a tour operator you may be considering, consult the **Council of Better Business Bureaus** (✉ 4200 Wilson Blvd., Suite 800, Arlington, VA 22203, ☎ 703/276–0100, FAX 703/525–8277).

C

CAR RENTAL

The major car-rental companies represented in Florence are **Avis** (☎ 800/331–1084; in Canada, 800/879–2847), **Budget** (☎ 800/527–0700; in the U.K., 0800/181181), **Hertz** (☎ 800/654–3001; in Canada, 800/263–0600; in the U.K., 0345/555888), and **National InterRent** (sometimes known as Europcar InterRent outside North America; ☎ 800/227–3876; in the U.K., 01345/222–525). Rates in Rome begin at $54 a day and $211 a week for an economy car with unlimited mileage. This does not include tax on car rentals, which is 19%. Many companies impose mandatory theft insurance on all rentals.

Coverage costs $10–$15 a day.

RENTAL WHOLESALERS

Contact **Auto Europe** (☎ 207/828–2525 or 800/223–5555), **Europe by Car** (☎ 800/223–1516; in CA, 800/252–9401), or the **Kemwel Group** (☎ 914/835–5555 or 800/678–0678).

Recent Italian legislation now permits certain rental wholesalers, including Auto Europe, to drop the VAT tax.

CHILDREN & TRAVEL

FLYING

Look into **"Flying with Baby"** (✉ Third Street Press, Box 261250, Littleton, CO 80163, ☎ 303/595–5959; $4.95 includes shipping), cowritten by a flight attendant. **"Kids and Teens in Flight,"** free from the U.S. Department of Transportation's Aviation Consumer Protection Division (✉ C-75, Washington, DC 20590, ☎ 202/366–2220), offers tips on children flying alone. Every two years the February issue of *Family Travel Times* (☞ Know-How, *below*) details children's services on three dozen airlines. **"Flying Alone, Handy Advice for Kids Traveling Solo"** is available free from the American Automobile Association (AAA) (✉ send stamped, self-addressed, legal-size envelope: Flying Alone, Mail Stop 800, 1000 AAA Dr., Heathrow, FL 32746).

KNOW-HOW

Family Travel Times, published quarterly by

Travel with Your Children (✉ TWYCH, 40 5th Ave., New York, NY 10011, ☎ 212/477–5524; $40 per year), covers destinations, types of vacations, and modes of travel.

LODGING

The Luxury Collection of **ITT-Sheraton** Hotels (☎ 800/221–2340 for reservations) has more than 20 properties in Italy, all of which welcome families.

TOUR OPERATORS

Contact **Grandtravel** (✉ 6900 Wisconsin Ave., Suite 706, Chevy Chase, MD 20815, ☎ 301/986–0790 or 800/247–7651), which has tours for people traveling with grandchildren ages 7–17; and **Families Welcome!** (✉ 4711 Hope Valley Rd., Durham, NC 27707, ☎ 919/489–2555 or 800/326–0724).

CUSTOMS

IN THE U.S.

The **U.S. Customs Service** (✉ Box 7407, Washington, DC 20044, ☎ 202/927–6724) can answer questions on duty-free limits and publishes a helpful brochure, **"Know Before You Go."** For information on registering foreign-made articles, call 202/927–0540 or write U.S. Customs Service, Resource Management, 1301 Constitution Ave. NW, Washington DC, 20229.

COMPLAINTS➤ Note the inspector's badge number and write to the commissioner's office (✉ 1301 Constitution Ave. NW, Washington, DC 20229).

CANADIANS

Contact **Revenue Canada** (✉ 2265 St. Laurent Blvd. S, Ottawa, Ontario K1G 4K3, ☎ 613/993–0534) for a copy of the free brochure **"I Declare/Je Déclare"** and for details on duty-free limits. For recorded information (within Canada only), call 800/461–9999.

U.K. CITIZENS

HM Customs and Excise (✉ Dorset House, Stamford St., London SE1 9NG, ☎ 0171/202–4227) can answer questions about U.K. customs regulations and publishes a free pamphlet, **"A Guide for Travellers,"** detailing standard procedures and import rules.

D

DISABILITIES & ACCESSIBILITY

COMPLAINTS

To register complaints under the provisions of the Americans with Disabilities Act, contact the U.S. Department of Justice's **Disability Rights Section** (✉ Box 66738, Washington, DC 20035, ☎ 202/514–0301 or 800/514–0301, FAX 202/307–1198, TTY 202/514–0383 or 800/514–0383). For airline-related problems, contact the U.S. Department of Transportation's **Aviation Consumer Protection Division** (☞ Air Travel, *above*). For complaints about surface transportation, contact the Department of Transportation's **Civil Rights Office** (✉ 400 7th St., SW, Room 10215, Washington DC, 20590 ☎ 202/366–4648).

ORGANIZATIONS

TRAVELERS WITH HEARING IMPAIRMENTS➤ The **American Academy of Otolaryngology** (✉ 1 Prince St., Alexandria, VA 22314, ☎ 703/836–4444, FAX 703/683–5100, TTY 703/519–1585) publishes a brochure, **"Travel Tips for Hearing Impaired People."**

TRAVELERS WITH MOBILITY PROBLEMS➤ Contact **Mobility International USA** (✉ Box 10767, Eugene, OR 97440, ☎ and TTY 541/343–1284, FAX 541/343–6812), the U.S. branch of a Belgium-based organization (☞ *below*) with affiliates in 30 countries; **MossRehab Hospital Travel Information Service** (☎ 215/456–9600, TTY 215/456–9602), a telephone information resource for travelers with physical disabilities; the **Society for the Advancement of Travel for the Handicapped** (✉ 347 5th Ave., Suite 610, New York, NY 10016, ☎ 212/447–7284, FAX 212/725–8253; membership $45); and **Travelin' Talk** (✉ Box 3534, Clarksville, TN 37043, ☎ 615/552–6670, FAX 615/552–1182), which provides local contacts worldwide for travelers with disabilities.

TRAVELERS WITH VISION IMPAIRMENTS➤ Contact the **American Council of the Blind** (✉ 1155 15th St. NW, Suite 720, Washington, DC 20005, ☎ 202/467–5081, FAX 202/467–5085) for a list of travelers' resources or the **American Foundation for the Blind** (✉ 11 Penn Plaza, Suite 300,

New York, NY 10001, ☎ 212/502–7600 or 800/232–5463, TTY 212/502–7662), which provides general advice and publishes **"Access to Art"** ($19.95), a directory of museums that accommodate travelers with vision impairments.

IN THE U.K.

Contact the **Royal Association for Disability and Rehabilitation** (✉ RADAR, 12 City Forum, 250 City Rd., London EC1V 8AF, ☎ 0171/250–3222) or **Mobility International** (✉ rue de Manchester 25, B-1080 Brussels, Belgium, ☎ 00–322–410–6297, FAX 00–322–410–6874), an international travel-information clearinghouse for people with disabilities.

PUBLICATIONS

Several publications for travelers with disabilities are available from the **Consumer Information Center** (✉ Box 100, Pueblo, CO 81009, ☎ 719/948–3334). Call or write for its free catalog of current titles. The Society for the Advancement of Travel for the Handicapped (☞ Organizations, *above*) publishes the quarterly magazine **"Access to Travel"** ($13 for 1-year subscription).

The 500-page *Travelin' Talk Directory* (✉ Box 3534, Clarksville, TN 37043, ☎ 615/552–6670, FAX 615/552–1182; $35) lists people and organizations who help travelers with disabilities. For travel agents worldwide, consult the *Directory of Travel Agencies for the*

Disabled (✉ Twin Peaks Press, Box 129, Vancouver, WA 98666, ☎ 360/694–2462 or 800/637–2256, FAX 360/696–3210; $19.95 plus $3 shipping).

TRAVEL AGENCIES & TOUR OPERATORS

The Americans with Disabilities Act requires that all travel firms serve the needs of all travelers. That said, you should note that some agencies and operators specialize in making travel arrangements for individuals and groups with disabilities, among them **Access Adventures** (✉ 206 Chestnut Ridge Rd., Rochester, NY 14624, ☎ 716/889–9096), run by a former physical-rehab counselor.

TRAVELERS WITH MOBILITY PROBLEMS➤ Contact **Flying Wheels Travel** (✉ 143 W. Bridge St., Box 382, Owatonna, MN 55060, ☎ 507/451–5005 or 800/535–6790), a travel agency specializing in European cruises and tours; **Hinsdale Travel Service** (✉ 201 E. Ogden Ave., Suite 100, Hinsdale, IL 60521, ☎ 708/325–1335), a travel agency that benefits from the advice of wheelchair traveler Janice Perkins; and **Wheelchair Journeys** (✉ 16979 Redmond Way, Redmond, WA 98052, ☎ 206/885–2210 or 800/313–4751), which can handle arrangements worldwide.

TRAVELERS WITH DEVELOPMENTAL DISABILITIES➤ Contact the nonprofit **New Directions** (✉ 5276 Hollister Ave., Suite 207, Santa Bar-

bara, CA 93111,
☎ 805/967–2841).

TRAVEL GEAR

The **Magellan's** catalog
(☎ 800/962–4943,
FAX 805/568–5406),
includes a section
devoted to products
designed for travelers
with disabilities.

DISCOUNTS & DEALS

AIRFARES

For the lowest airfares
to Italy, call 800/FLY–
4–LESS.

CLUBS

Contact **Entertainment
Travel Editions** (✉ Box
1068, Trumbull, CT
06611, ☎ 800/445–
4137; $28–$53, de-
pending on destination),
Great American Traveler
(✉ Box 27965, Salt
Lake City, UT 84127,
☎ 800/548–2812;
$49.95 per year), **Mo-
ment's Notice Discount
Travel Club** (✉ 7301
New Utrecht Ave.,
Brooklyn, NY 11204,
☎ 718/234–6295;
$25 per year, single or
family), **Privilege Card
International** (✉ 3391
Peachtree Rd. NE,
Suite 110, Atlanta, GA
30326, ☎ 404/262–
0222 or 800/236–9732;
$74.95 per year), **Travel-
ers Advantage** (✉ CUC
Travel Service, 49 Music
Sq. W, Nashville, TN
37203, ☎ 800/548–
1116 or 800/648–4037;
$49 per year, single or
family), or **Worldwide
Discount Travel Club**
(✉ 1674 Meridian Ave.,
Miami Beach, FL
33139, ☎ 305/534–
2082; $50 per year for
family, $40 single).

HOTEL ROOMS

For hotel room rates
guaranteed in U.S.

dollars, call **Steigen-
berger Reservation
Service** (☎ 800/223–
5652).

PASSES

See Train Travel, *below.*

STUDENTS

Members of Hostelling
International–American
Youth Hostels (☞
Students, *below*) are
eligible for discounts on
car rentals, admissions
to attractions, and
other selected travel
expenses.

PUBLICATIONS

Consult **The Frugal
Globetrotter**, by Bruce
Northam (✉ Fulcrum
Publishing, 350 Indiana
St., Suite 350, Golden,
CO 80401, ☎ 800/
992–2908; $16.95 plus
$4 shipping). For publi-
cations that tell how to
find the lowest prices
on plane tickets, *see* Air
Travel, *above.*

Also see Fodor's **Afford-
able Europe** (available
in bookstores, or ☎
800/533–6478; $18.50
plus $4 shipping).

DRIVING

AUTO CLUBS

The main organization
is the **Automobile
Club of Italy** (✉ ACI,
Via Marsala 8, 00185
Rome, ☎ 06/499–
82389, FAX 06/499–
8234; also has offices
in many cities through-
out Italy).

BREAKDOWNS

ACI Emergency Service
(✉ Servizio Soccorso
Stradale, Via Solferino
32, 00185 Rome, ☎
06/44595) offers 24-
hour road service. Dial
116 from any phone,
24 hours a day, to reach
the nearest ACI service
station.

E

EMERGENCIES

**Important emergency
numbers in Italy** are 112
for 24-hour access to
Carabinieri; 113 for
Police; 115 for Fire;
116 for the Italian
Automobile Club; 118
for medical emergency
and ambulance (this
number is not yet
operational in all areas;
alternatively call 113).

G

GAY & LESBIAN TRAVEL

ORGANIZATIONS

The **International Gay
Travel Association** (✉
Box 4974, Key West,
FL 33041, ☎ 800/448–
8550, FAX 305/296–
6633), a consortium of
more than 1,000 travel
companies, can supply
names of gay-friendly
travel agents, tour
operators, and accom-
modations.

The national gay and
lesbian association in
Italy is **ARCIGAY** (✉
Via Acciaresi 7, 00157
Rome, ☎ 06/417–
30752).

PUBLICATIONS

The 16-page monthly
newsletter **"Out &
About"** (✉ 8 W. 19th
St., Suite 401, New
York, NY 10011, ☎
212/645–6922 or 800/
929–2268, FAX 800/
929–2215; $49 for 10
issues and quarterly
calendar) covers gay-
friendly resorts, hotels,
cruise lines, and airlines.

TOUR OPERATORS

Atlantis Events (✉ 9060
Santa Monica Blvd.,
Suite 310, West Holly-
wood, CA 90069,
☎ 310/281–5450 or

THE GOLD GUIDE / IMPORTANT CONTACTS

800/628–5268) and **Toto Tours** (✉ 1326 W. Albion Ave., Suite 3W, Chicago, IL 60626, ☎ 312/274–8686 or 800/565–1241, FAX 312/274–8695) offer group tours to worldwide destinations.

TRAVEL AGENCIES

The largest agencies serving gay travelers are **Advance Travel** (✉ 10700 Northwest Fwy., Suite 160, Houston, TX 77092, ☎ 713/682–2002 or 800/292–0500), **Club Travel** (✉ 8739 Santa Monica Blvd., W. Hollywood, CA 90069, ☎ 310/358–2200 or 800/429–8747), **Islanders/Kennedy Travel** (✉ 183 W. 10th St., New York, NY 10014, ☎ 212/242–3222 or 800/988–1181), **Now Voyager** (✉ 4406 18th St., San Francisco, CA 94114, ☎ 415/626–1169 or 800/255–6951), and **Yellowbrick Road** (✉ 1500 W. Balmoral Ave., Chicago, IL 60640, ☎ 312/561–1800 or 800/642–2488). **Skylink Women's Travel** (✉ 2460 W. 3rd St., Suite 215, Santa Rosa, CA 95401, ☎ 707/570–0105 or 800/225–5759) serves lesbian travelers.

H
HEALTH

FINDING A DOCTOR

For its members, the **International Association for Medical Assistance to Travellers** (✉ IAMAT, membership free; 417 Center St., Lewiston, NY 14092, ☎ 716/754–4883; ✉ 40 Regal Rd., Guelph, Ontario N1K 1B5, ☎ 519/836–0102; ✉

1287 St. Clair Ave. W., Toronto, Ontario M6E 1B8, ☎ 416/652–0137; ✉ 57 Voirets, 1212 Grand-Lancy, Geneva, Switzerland, no phone) publishes a worldwide directory of English-speaking physicians meeting IAMAT standards.

MEDICAL ASSISTANCE COMPANIES

The following companies are concerned primarily with emergency medical assistance, although they may provide some insurance as part of their coverage. For a list of full-service travel insurance companies, *see* Insurance, *below*.

Contact **International SOS Assistance** (✉ Box 11568, Philadelphia, PA 19116, ☎ 215/244–1500 or 800/523–8930; ✉ Box 466, Pl. Bonaventure, Montréal, Québec H5A 1C1, ☎ 514/874–7674 or 800/363–0263; ✉ 7 Old Lodge Pl., St. Margarets, Twickenham TW1 1RQ, England, ☎ 0181/744–0033), **Medex Assistance Corporation** (✉ Box 5375, Timonium, MD 21094, ☎ 410/453–6300 or 800/537–2029), **Near Travel Services** (✉ Box 1339, Calumet City, IL 60409, ☎ 708/868–6700 or 800/654–6700), **Traveler's Emergency Network** (✉ 1133 15th St. NW, Suite 400, Washington DC, 20005, ☎ 202/828–5894 or 800/275–4836, FAX 202/828–5896), **TravMed** (✉ Box 5375, Timonium, MD 21094, ☎ 410/453–6380 or 800/732–5309), or **Worldwide Assistance Services** (✉ 1133 15th St. NW,

Suite 400, Washington, DC 20005, ☎ 202/331–1609 or 800/821–2828, FAX 202/828–5896).

I
INSURANCE

IN CANADA

Contact **Mutual of Omaha** (✉ Travel Division, 500 University Ave., Toronto, Ontario M5G 1V8, ☎ 800/465–0267(in Canada) or 416/598–4083).

IN THE U.S.

Travel insurance covering baggage, health, and trip cancellation or interruptions is available from **Access America** (✉ 6600 W. Broad St., Richmond, VA 23230, ☎ 804/285–3300 or 800/334–7525), **Carefree Travel Insurance** (✉ Box 9366, 100 Garden City Plaza, Garden City, NY 11530, ☎ 516/294–0220 or 800/323–3149), **Tele-Trip** (✉ Mutual of Omaha Plaza, Box 31716, Omaha, NE 68131, ☎ 800/228–9792), **Travel Guard International** (✉ 1145 Clark St., Stevens Point, WI 54481, ☎ 715/345–0505 or 800/826–1300), **Travel Insured International** (✉ Box 280568, East Hartford, CT 06128, ☎ 203/528–7663 or 800/243–3174), and **Wallach & Company** (✉ 107 W. Federal St., Box 480, Middleburg, VA 22117, ☎ 540/687–3166 or 800/237–6615).

IN THE U.K.

The **Association of British Insurers** (✉ 51 Gresham St., London EC2V 7HQ, ☎ 0171/600–3333) gives advice by phone and publishes the free pamphlet **"Holiday Insurance and Motoring Abroad,"** which sets out typical policy provisions and costs.

L
LODGING

For information on hotel consolidators, *see* Discounts, *above.*

APARTMENT & VILLA RENTAL

Among the companies to contact are **At Home Abroad** (⊠ 405 E. 56th St., Suite 6H, New York, NY 10022, ☎ 212/421–9165, ℻ 212/752–1591), **Europa-Let/Tropical Inn-Let, Inc.** (⊠ 92 N. Main St., Ashland, OR 97520, ☎ 541/482–5806 or 800/462–4486, ℻ 541/482–0660), **Hometours International** (⊠ Box 11503, Knoxville, TN 37939, ☎ 423/690–8484 or 800/367–4668), **Interhome** (⊠ 124 Little Falls Rd., Fairfield, NJ 07004, ☎ 201/882–6864, ℻ 201/808–1742), **Property Rentals International** (⊠ 1008 Mansfield Crossing Rd., Richmond, VA 23236, ☎ 804/378–6054 or 800/220–3332, ℻ 804/379–2073), **Rental Directories International** (⊠ 2044 Rittenhouse Sq., Philadelphia, PA 19103, ☎ 215/985–4001, ℻ 215/985–0323), **Rent-a-Home International** (⊠ 7200 34th Ave. NW, Seattle, WA 98117, ☎ 206/789–9377 or 800/488–7368, ℻ 206/789–9379, rentahomeinternational@msn.com), **Vacation Home Rentals Worldwide** (⊠ 235 Kensington Ave., Norwood, NJ 07648, ☎ 201/767–

9393 or 800/633–3284, ℻ 201/767–5510), **Villas and Apartments Abroad** (⊠ 420 Madison Ave., Suite 1003, New York, NY 10017, ☎ 212/759–1025 or 800/433–3020, ℻ 212/755–8316), and **Villas International** (⊠ 605 Market St., Suite 510, San Francisco, CA 94105, ☎ 415/281–0910 or 800/221–2260, ℻ 415/281–0919). Members of the travel club **Hideaways International** (⊠ 767 Islington St., Portsmouth, NH 03801, ☎ 603/430–4433 or 800/843–4433, ℻ 603/430–4444, info@hideaways.com; $99 per year) receive two annual guides plus quarterly newsletters and arrange rentals among themselves.

HOME EXCHANGE

Some of the principal clearinghouses are **HomeLink International/Vacation Exchange Club** (⊠ Box 650, Key West, FL 33041, ☎ 305/294–1448 or 800/638–3841, ℻ 305/294–1148; $78 per year), which sends members five annual directories, with a listing in one, plus updates; and **Loan-a-Home** (⊠ 2 Park La., Apt. 6E, Mount Vernon, NY 10552, ☎ 914/664–7640; $40–$50 per year), which specializes in long-term exchanges.

HOTELS

Among the best-known chains operating in Italy are: **ITT-Sheraton/The Luxury Collection** (⊠ 745 5th Ave., New York, NY 10151, ☎ 800/221–2340, ℻ 212/421–5929), which has more than 20 Italian properties, almost all five-star deluxe; **Jolly**

(☎ 800/247–1277 in New York state, 800/221–2626 elsewhere, 800/237–0319 in Canada), with 32 four-star hotels in Italy; **Atahotels** (⊠ Via Lampedusa 11/A, 20141 Milano, ☎ 02/895261 or toll-free in Italy 1678/23013, ℻ 02/8465568; some bookable through E&M Associates, ☎ 212/599–8280 or 800/223–9832), with 20 mostly four- and five-star hotels; and **Starhotels** (⊠ Via Belfiore 27, 50144 Florence, ☎ 055/36921, ℻ 055/36924, or book through 800/448–8355), with 14 mainly four-star hotels. **Space Hotels** (toll-free in Italy ☎ 1678/13013; or book through Supranational, ☎ 416/927–1133 or 800/843–3311) has about 50 independently owned four- and five-star (some three-star) hotels. **Italhotels** (toll-free in Italy ☎ 1678/01004) also has about 50 independently owned four- and five-star hotels.

AGIP Motels (☎ 06/444–0183 reservations in Italy) is a chain of about 50 mostly four-star motels on main highways; the motels are commercial, functional digs for traveling salesmen and tourists needing forty winks, but they—and the Jolly hotels—can be the best choice in many out-of-the-way places. **The Forte** group has taken over some top-of-the-line AGIP properties throughout Italy. **Best Western,** an international association of independently owned hotels, has some 75 mainly three- and four-star hotels in Italy (☎

THE GOLD GUIDE / IMPORTANT CONTACTS

800/528–1234 for reservations or to request the *Europe and Middle East Atlas* that lists them).

Family Hotels (✉ Via Faenza 77, 50123 Florence, ☎ 055/217975, FAX 055/238–1905), grouping about 75 independently owned, family-run two- and three-star hotels (some one-star), offers good value. For information in Italy, contact the address above (it's not a central booking service, however). A spin-off of this group, the **Sun Rays Pool** comprises three- and four-star hotels (information and reservations ☎ 055/462–0080).

M
MONEY

ATMS

For specific foreign **Cirrus** locations, call 800/424–7787; for foreign **Plus** locations, consult the Plus directory at your local bank.

CURRENCY EXCHANGE

If your bank doesn't exchange currency, contact **Thomas Cook Currency Services** (☎ 800/287–7362 for locations). **Ruesch International** (☎ 800/424–2923 for locations) can also provide you with foreign bank notes before you leave home and publishes a number of useful brochures, including a "Foreign Currency Guide" and "Foreign Exchange Tips."

WIRING FUNDS

Funds can be wired via **MoneyGram℠** (for locations and information in the U.S. and Canada, ☎ 800/926–9400) or **Western Union** (for agent locations or to send money using MasterCard or Visa, ☎ 800/325–6000; in Canada, 800/321–2923; in the U.K., 0800/833833; or visit the Western Union office at the nearest major post office).

P
PACKING

For strategies on packing light, get a copy of *The Packing Book,* by Judith Gilford (✉ Ten Speed Press, Box 7123, Berkeley, CA 94707, ☎ 510/559–1600 or 800/841–2665, FAX 510/524–4588; $7.95 plus $3.50 shipping).

PASSPORTS & VISAS

IN THE U.S.

For fees, documentation requirements, and other information, call the State Department's **Office of Passport Services** information line (☎ 202/647–0518).

CANADIANS

For fees, documentation requirements, and other information, call the Ministry of Foreign Affairs and International Trade's **Passport Office** (☎ 819/994–3500 or 800/567–6868).

U.K. CITIZENS

For fees, documentation requirements, and to request an emergency passport, call the **London Passport Office** (☎ 0990/210410).

PHOTO HELP

The **Kodak Information Center** (☎ 800/242–2424) answers consumer questions about film and photography.

The ***Kodak Guide to Shooting Great Travel Pictures*** (available in bookstores; or contact Fodor's Travel Publications, ☎ 800/533–6478; $16.50 plus $4 shipping) explains how to take expert travel photographs.

S
SAFETY

"Trouble-Free Travel," from the AAA, is a booklet of tips for protecting yourself and your belongings when away from home. Send a stamped, self-addressed, legal-size envelope to Trouble-Free Travel (✉ Mail Stop 75, 1000 AAA Dr., Heathrow, FL 32746).

SENIOR CITIZENS

CLUBS

Sears's **Mature Outlook** (✉ Box 10448, Des Moines, IA 50306, ☎ 800/336–6330; annual membership $14.95) includes a lifestyle/travel magazine and membership in ITC-50 travel club, which offers discounts of up to 50% at participating hotels and restaurants. (☞ Discounts & Deals *in* Smart Travel Tips A to Z).

EDUCATIONAL TRAVEL

The nonprofit **Elderhostel** (✉ 75 Federal St., 3rd Floor, Boston, MA 02110, ☎ 617/426–7788), for people 55 and older, has offered inexpensive study programs since 1975. Courses cover everything from marine science to Greek mythology and cowboy poetry. Costs for two- to three-week international trips—including room, board, and transportation from the United States—range from $1,800 to $4,500.

Interhostel (✉ University of New Hampshire, 6 Garrison Ave., Durham, NH 03824, ☎ 603/862–1147 or 800/733–9753), for travelers 50 and older, has two- to three-week trips; most last two weeks and cost $2,000–$3,500, including airfare.

ORGANIZATIONS

Contact the **American Association of Retired Persons** (✉ AARP, 601 E St. NW, Washington, DC 20049, ☎ 202/434–2277; annual dues $8 per person or couple). Its Purchase Privilege Program secures discounts for members on lodging, car rentals, and sightseeing.

STUDENTS

GROUPS

The major tour operators specializing in student travel are **Contiki Holidays** (✉ 300 Plaza Alicante, Suite 900, Garden Grove, CA 92640, ☎ 714/740–0808 or 800/266–8454) and **AESU Travel** (✉ 2 Hamill Rd., Suite 248, Baltimore, MD 21210-1807, ☎ 410/323–4416 or 800/638–7640).

HOSTELING

In the United States, contact **Hostelling International–American Youth Hostels** (✉ 733 15th St. NW, Suite 840, Washington, DC 20005, ☎ 202/783–6161, FAX 202/783–6171); in Canada, **Hostelling International–Canada** (✉ 205 Catherine St., Suite 400, Ottawa,

Ontario K2P 1C3, ☎ 613/237–7884); and in the United Kingdom, the **Youth Hostel Association of England and Wales** (✉ Trevelyan House, 8 St. Stephen's Hill, St. Albans, Hertfordshire AL1 2DY, ☎ 01727/855215 or 01727/845047). Membership (in the U.S., $25; in Canada, C$26.75; in the U.K., £9.30) gives you access to 5,000 hostels in 77 countries that charge $5–$40 per person per night.

ORGANIZATIONS

A major contact is the **Council on International Educational Exchange** (✉ mail orders only: CIEE, 205 E. 42nd St., 16th Floor, New York, NY 10017, ☎ 212/822–2600, FAX 212/822–2699, info@ciee.org). The **Educational Travel Centre** (✉ 438 N. Frances St., Madison, WI 53703, ☎ 608/256–5551 or 800/747–5551, FAX 608/256–2042) offers rail passes and low-cost airline tickets, mostly for flights that depart from Chicago.

In Canada, also contact **Travel Cuts** (✉ 187 College St., Toronto, Ontario M5T 1P7, ☎ 416/979–2406 or 800/667–2887).

The **Centro Turistico Studentesco** (CTS) is a student and youth travel agency with offices in major Italian cities, including Florence; CTS helps its clients find low-cost accommodations and bargain fares for travel in Italy and elsewhere and also serves as a meeting place for young people of all nations.

PUBLICATIONS

Check out the **Berkeley Guide to Italy** (available in bookstores; or contact Fodor's Travel Publications, ☎ 800/533–6478; $18.95 plus $4 shipping).

T

TELEPHONES

The country code for Italy is 39. For local access numbers abroad, contact **AT&T** USADirect (☎ 800/874–4000), **MCI** Call USA (☎ 800/444–4444), or **Sprint** Express (☎ 800/793–1153).

TOUR OPERATORS

Among the companies that sell tours and packages to Florence, Tuscany, and Umbria, the following are nationally known, have a proven reputation, and offer plenty of options.

GROUP TOURS

SUPER-DELUXE➤ **Abercrombie & Kent** (✉ 1520 Kensington Rd., Oak Brook, IL 60521-2141, ☎ 708/954–2944 or 800/323–7308, FAX 708/954–3324) and **Travcoa** (✉ Box 2630, 2350 S.E. Bristol St., Newport Beach, CA 92660, ☎ 714/476–2800 or 800/992–2003, FAX 714/476–2538).

DELUXE➤ **Globus** (✉ 5301 S. Federal Circle, Littleton, CO 80123-2980, ☎ 303/797–2800 or 800/221–0090, FAX 303/795–0962) and **Tauck Tours** (✉ Box 5027, 276 Post Rd. W, Westport, CT 06881, ☎ 203/226–6911 or 800/468–2825, FAX 203/221–6828). Specialists in Italy include **Central Holidays Tours** (✉ 206 Central Ave., Jersey

City, NJ 07307, ☎ 201/ 798–5777 or 800/935– 5000), and **Donna Franca Tours** (✉ 470 Commonwealth Ave., Boston, MA 02215, ☎ 617/375–9400 or 800/ 225–6290, dtours2156 @aol.com, http://www. astanet.com/get? dfrancatrs).

BUDGET➤ **Cosmos** (☞ Globus, *above*).

PACKAGES

Independent vacation packages are available from major airlines and tour operators. Among U.S. carriers, contact **American Airlines Fly AAway Vacations** (☎ 800/321–2121), **Delta Dream Vacations** (☎ 800/872–7786), and **United Vacations** (☎ 800/328–6877). Leading tour operators include **Central Holidays Tours** (☞ Group Tours, *above*), **DER Tours** (✉ 11933 Wilshire Blvd., Los Angeles, CA 90025, ☎ 310/479–4140 or 800/937–1235), **4th Dimension Tours** (✉ 7101 S.W. 99th Ave., #105, Miami, FL 33173, ☎ 305/279– 0014 or 800/877–1525, FAX 305/273–9777, http://www.4thdimen-sion.com), and **Jet Vacations** (✉ 1775 Broadway, New York, NY 10019, ☎ 212/ 474–8740 or 800/538– 2762). **Funjet Vacations,** based in Milwaukee, Wisconsin, and **Gogo Tours,** based in Ramsey, New Jersey, sell packages to central Italy only through travel agents.

FROM THE U.K.

Carefree Italy (✉ 44 Central Parade, New Addington, Surrey CR0 0JD, ☎ 01689/841– 900) has apartments,

castles, and farmhouses. **Page and Moy Holidays** (✉ 136-140 London Rd, Leicester, LE2 1EN, ☎ 0116/250–7676) has tours of historical sights. Also contact **Italian Escapades** (✉ 227 Shepherds Bush Rd., London W6 7AS, ☎ 0181/748–2661).

THEME TRIPS

Travel Contacts (✉ Box 173, Camberley, England GU15 1YE, ☎ 011/44/1/27667–7217, FAX 011/44/1/2766– 3477), which represents 150 tour operators, can satisfy just about any special interest in Italy.

ART AND ARCHITECTURE➤ **Endless Beginnings Tours** (✉ 9825 Dowdy Dr., #105, San Diego, CA 92126, ☎ 619/566–4166 or 800/822–7855, FAX 619/ 549–9655) explores the art, culture, and natural environment of Tuscany and Umbria.

BALLOONING➤ Contact **Buddy Bombard European Balloon Adventures** (✉ 855 Donald Ross Rd., Juno Beach, FL 33408, ☎ 407/775– 0039 or 800/862–8537, FAX 407/775–7008) for balloon tours during Siena's colorful Palio festival.

BICYCLING➤ **Ciclismo Classico** (✉ 13 Mara-thon St., Arlington, MA 02174, ☎ 617/646– 3377 or 800/866–7314, FAX 617/641–1512, info@ciclismoclassico. com) specializes in bike tours of Italy. Also try **Backroads** (✉ 1516 5th St., Berkeley, CA 94710-1740, ☎ 510/ 577–1555 or 800/462– 2848, FAX 510/527– 1444, goactive@ Backroads.com), **Bike**

Riders (✉ Box 254, Boston, MA 02113, ☎ 617/723–2354 or 800/ 473–7040), FAX 617/ 723–2355, bikeride@ tiac.net, http://www. tiac.net/users/bikeride), **Butterfield & Robin-son** (✉ 70 Bond St., Toronto, Ontario, Canada M5B 1X3, ☎ 416/864–1354 or 800/678–1147, FAX 416/864–0541, info@butterfield.com), **Progressive Travels** (✉ 224 W. Galer Ave., #C, Seattle, WA 98119, ☎ 206/285–1987 or 800/245–2229, FAX 206/ 285–1988), **Rocky Mountain Worldwide Cycle Tours** (✉ Box 1978, Canmore, Alberta, Canada TOL OMO, ☎ 403/678– 6770 or 800/661–2453, FAX 403/678–4451, rmct@cia.com, http:// www.worldweb.com/ rmct), and **Uniquely Europe** (✉ 2819 1st Ave., #280, Seattle, WA 98121-1113, ☎ 206/ 441–8682 or 800/426– 3615, FAX 206/441– 8862).

FOOD AND WINE➤ **Cuisine International** (✉ Box 25228, Dallas, TX 75225, ☎ 214/ 373–1161, FAX 214/ 373–1162) has week-long Italian cooking programs hosted by expert chefs in Tuscany and Umbria.

GOLF➤ **ITC Golf Tours** (✉ 4134 Atlantic Ave., #205, Long Beach, CA 90807, ☎ 310/595– 6905 or 800/257–4981) arranges customized itineraries in Tuscany.

HISTORY➤ History buffs should look into **Herodot Travel** (✉ 775 E. Blithedale, Box 234, Mill Valley, CA 94941, ☎ FAX 415/381–4031).

HOMES AND GARDENS➤ **Coopersmith's England** (✉ 6441 Valley View Rd., Oakland, CA 94611, ☎ 510/339–2499) and **Endless Beginnings Tours** (☞ Art and Architecture, *above*) visit gardens and villas around Tuscany.

HORSEBACK RIDING➤ **FITS Equestrian** (✉ 685 Lateen Rd., Solvang, CA 93463, ☎ 805/688–9494 or 800/666–3487, FAX 805/688–2943) has tours for every level of rider.

LEARNING➤ **Earthwatch** (✉ Box 403, 680 Mount Auburn St., Watertown, MA 02272, ☎ 617/926–8200 or 800/776–0188, FAX 617/926–8532, info@earthwatch.org, http://www.earthwatch.org) recruits volunteers to serve in its EarthCorps as short-term assistants to scientists on research expeditions. **Smithsonian Study Tours and Seminars** (✉ 1100 Jefferson Dr. SW, Room 3045, MRC 702, Washington, DC 20560, ☎ 202/357–4700, FAX 202/633–9250) focuses on art and culture.

SPAS➤ **Spa-Finders** (✉ 91 5th Ave., #301, New York, NY 10003-3039, ☎ 212/924–6800 or 800/255–7727) represents spas in Tuscany.

VILLA RENTALS➤ **Rentals in Italy** (✉ 1742 Calle Corva, Camarillo, CA 93010-8428, ☎ 805/987–5278 or 800/726–6702, FAX 805/482–7976) represents Cuendet, the largest villa-rental company in Italy. Cottages and villas can also be rented through **Eurovillas** (✉ 1398 55th St., Emery-

ville, CA 94608, ☎ FAX 707/648–0266) and **Villas International** (✉ 605 Market St., San Francisco, CA 94105, ☎ 415/281–0910 or 800/221–2260, FAX 415/281–0919).

WALKING/HIKING➤ For long strolls in the Tuscan countryside, try **Abercrombie & Kent** (☞ Group Tours, *above*), **Above the Clouds Trekking** (✉ Box 398, Worcester, MA 01602-0398, ☎ 508/799–4499 or 800/233–4499, FAX 508/797–4779), **Adventure Center** (✉ 1311 63rd St., #200, Emeryville, CA 94608, ☎ 510/654–1879 or 800/227–8747, FAX 510/654–4200), **Backroads** and **Butterfield & Robinson** (☞ Bicycling, *above*), **Country Walkers** (✉ Box 180, Waterbury, VT 05676-0180, ☎ 802/244–1387 or 800/464–9255, FAX 802/244–5661), **Himalayan Travel** (✉ 112 Prospect St., Stamford, CT 06901, ☎ 203/359–3711 or 800/225–2380 or FAX 203/359–3669), **Progressive Travels** (☞ Bicycling, *above*), **Mountain Travel-Sobek** (✉ 6420 Fairmount Ave., El Cerrito, CA 94530, ☎ 510/527–8100 or 800/227–2384, FAX 510/525–7710, Info@mtsobek.com, http://www.mtsobek.com), and **Wilderness Travel** (✉ 801 Allston Way, Berkeley, CA 94710, ☎ 510/548–0420 or 800/368–2794, FAX 510/548–0347, info@wildernesstravel.com).

ORGANIZATIONS

The **National Tour Association** (✉ NTA, 546 E. Main St., Lex-

ington, KY 40508, ☎ 606/226–4444 or 800/755–8687) and the **United States Tour Operators Association** (✉ USTOA, 211 E. 51st St., Suite 12B, New York, NY 10022, ☎ 212/750–7371) can provide lists of members and information on booking tours.

PUBLICATIONS

Contact the USTOA (☞ Organizations, *above*) for its **"Smart Traveler's Planning Kit."** Pamphlets in the kit include the "Worldwide Tour and Vacation Package Finder," "How to Select a Tour or Vacation Package," and information on the organization's consumer protection plan. Also get copy of the Better Business Bureau's **"Tips on Travel Packages"** (✉ Publication 24-195, 4200 Wilson Blvd., Arlington, VA 22203; $2).

TRAIN TRAVEL

Eurail and EuroPasses are available through travel agents and **Rail Europe** (✉ 226-230 Westchester Ave., White Plains, NY 10604, ☎ 914/682–5172 or 800/438–7245; ✉ 2087 Dundas E., Suite 105, Mississauga, Ontario L4X 1M2, ☎ 416/602–4195), **DER Tours** (✉ Box 1606, Des Plaines, IL 60017, ☎ 800/782–2424, FAX 800/282–7474), or **CIT Tours Corp.** (✉ 342 Madison Ave., Suite 207, New York, NY 10173, ☎ 212/697–2100 or 800/248–8687 or 800/248–7245 in western U.S.). Italian rail passes can be purchased through DER Tours or CIT Tours as well.

TRAVEL GEAR

For travel apparel, appliances, personal-care items, and other travel necessities, get a free catalog from **Magellan's** (☎ 800/962–4943, FAX 805/568–5406), **Orvis Travel** (☎ 800/541–3541, FAX 540/343–7053), or **TravelSmith** (☎ 800/950–1600, FAX 415/455–0554).

ELECTRICAL CONVERTERS

Send a self-addressed, stamped envelope to the **Franzus Company** (✉ Customer Service, Dept. B50, Murtha Industrial Park, Box 142, Beacon Falls, CT 06403, ☎ 203/723–6664) for a copy of the free brochure **"Foreign Electricity Is No Deep, Dark Secret."**

TRAVEL AGENCIES

For names of reputable agencies in your area, contact the **American Society of Travel Agents** (✉ ASTA, 1101 King St., Suite 200, Alexandria, VA 22314, ☎ 703/739–2782), the **Association of Canadian Travel Agents** (✉ Suite 201, 1729 Bank St., Ottawa, Ontario K1V 7Z5, ☎ 613/521–0474, FAX 613/521–0805) or the **Association of British Travel Agents** (✉ 55-57 Newman St., London W1P 4AH, ☎ 0171/637–2444, FAX 0171/637–0713).

U

U.S. GOVERNMENT TRAVEL BRIEFINGS

The U.S. Department of State's American Citizens Services office (✉ Room 4811, Washington, DC 20520; enclose SASE) issues **Consular Information Sheets** on all foreign countries. These cover issues such as crime, security, political climate, and health risks as well as listing embassy locations, entry requirements, currency regulations, and providing other useful information. For the latest information, stop in at any U.S. passport office, consulate, or embassy; call the interactive hot line (☎ 202/647–5225, FAX 202/647–3000); or, with your PC's modem, tap into the department's computer bulletin board (☎ 202/647–9225).

V

VISITOR INFORMATION

Contact the **Italian Government Travel Office** in the United States (✉ 630 5th Ave., Suite 1565, New York, NY 10111, ☎ 212/245–4822, FAX 212/586–9249; ✉ 500 N. Michigan Ave., Chicago, IL 60611, ☎ 312/644–0990, FAX 312/644–3019; ✉ 12400 Wilshire Blvd., Suite 550, Los Angeles, CA 90025, ☎ 310/820–0098, FAX 310/820–6357) or in Canada (✉ 1 Pl. Ville Marie, Montréal, Québec H3B 3M9, ☎ 514/866–7667).

W

WEATHER

For current conditions and forecasts, plus the local time and helpful travel tips, call the **Weather Channel Connection** (☎ 900/932–8437; 95¢ per minute) from a Touch-Tone phone.

The *International Traveler's Weather Guide* (✉ Weather Press, Box 660606, Sacramento, CA 95866, ☎ 916/974–0201 or 800/972–0201; $10.95 includes shipping), written by two meteorologists, provides month-by-month information on temperature, humidity, and precipitation in more than 175 cities worldwide.

SMART TRAVEL TIPS A TO Z

Basic Information on Traveling in Florence, Tuscany, and Umbria and Savvy Tips to Make Your Trip a Breeze

A

AIR TRAVEL

If time is an issue, **always look for nonstop flights,** which require no change of plane. If possible, **avoid connecting flights,** which stop at least once and can involve a change of plane, even though the flight number remains the same; if the first leg is late, the second waits.

For better service, **fly smaller or regional carriers,** which often have higher passenger satisfaction ratings. Sometimes they have such in-flight amenities as leather seats or greater legroom and they often have better food.

CUTTING COSTS

The Sunday travel section of most newspapers is a good place to look for deals.

MAJOR AIRLINES➣ The least-expensive airfares from the major airlines are priced for round-trip travel and are subject to restrictions. Usually, you must **book in advance and buy the ticket within 24 hours** to get cheaper fares, and you may have to **stay over a Saturday night.** The lowest fare is subject to availability, and only a small percentage of the plane's total seats is sold at that price. It's smart to **call a number of airlines, and when you are quoted a**

good price, book it on the spot—the same fare may not be available on the same flight the next day. Airlines generally allow you to change your return date for a $25 to $50 fee. If you don't use your ticket, you can apply the cost toward the purchase of a new ticket, again for a small charge. However, most low-fare tickets are nonrefundable. To get the lowest airfare, **check different routings.** If your destination has more than one gateway, **compare prices to different airports.**

FROM THE U.K.➣ To save money on flights, **look into an APEX or Super-Pex ticket.** APEX tickets must be booked in advance and have certain restrictions. Super-PEX tickets can be purchased right at the airport.

CONSOLIDATORS➣ Consolidators buy tickets for scheduled flights at reduced rates from the airlines, then sell them at prices below the lowest available from the airlines directly—usually without advance restrictions. Sometimes you can even get your money back if you need to return the ticket. Carefully read the fine print detailing penalties for changes and cancellations. If you doubt the reliability of a consolidator, **confirm your reservation with the airline.**

ALOFT

AIRLINE FOOD➣ If you hate airline food, **ask for special meals when booking.** These can be vegetarian, low-cholesterol, or kosher, for example; commonly prepared to order in smaller quantities than standard fare, they can be tastier.

JET LAG➣ To avoid this syndrome, which occurs when travel disrupts your body's natural cycles, try to maintain a normal routine. At night, **get some sleep.** By day, move about the cabin to **stretch your legs, eat light meals, and drink water—not alcohol.**

SMOKING➣ Smoking is not allowed on flights of six hours or less within the continental United States. Smoking is also prohibited on flights within Canada. For U.S. flights longer than six hours or international flights, **contact your carrier regarding their smoking policy.** Some carriers have prohibited smoking throughout their system; others allow smoking only on certain routes or even certain departures of that route.

B

BUSINESS HOURS

Banks are open weekdays 8:30–1:30 and 2:45–3:45.

Most **churches** are open from early morning until noon or 12:30, when they close for two hours or more; they open again in the afternoon, closing about 7 PM or later. Major cathedrals and basilicas are open all day. Note that sightseeing in churches during religious rites is usually discouraged. Be sure to have a fistful of 100-lire coins handy for the *luce* (light) machines that illuminate the works of art in the perpetual dusk of ecclesiastical interiors. A pair of binoculars will help you get a good look at painted ceilings and domes.

Museum hours vary and may change with the seasons. Many important national museums are closed one day a week, often on Monday. Always check locally.

Most **shops** are open 9:30–1 and 3:30 or 4–7 or 7:30. In all but resorts and small towns, shops close on Sunday and one half-day during the week. Some tourist-oriented shops are open all day, also on Sunday, as are some department stores and supermarkets.

Post offices are open 8–2; central and main district post offices stay open until 8 or 9 PM for some operations. The main post office in major cities is open on Sunday 8:30–7.

Barbers and hairdressers, with some exceptions, are closed Sunday and Monday.

NATIONAL HOLIDAYS

January 1 (New Year's Day); January 6 (Epiphany); March 30, 31,

(Easter Sunday and Monday); April 25 (Liberation Day); May 1 (Labor Day or May Day); August 15 (Assumption of Mary, also known as Ferragosto); November 1 (All Saints' Day); December 8 (Immaculate Conception); December 25, 26 (Christmas Day and Boxing Day).

The feast days of patron saints are also holidays, observed locally. Many businesses and shops may be closed in Florence, Genoa, and Turin on June 24 (St. John the Baptist).

C

CAMERAS, CAMCORDERS, & COMPUTERS

IN TRANSIT

Always **keep your film, tape, or disks out of the sun;** never put these on the dashboard of a car. Carry an extra supply of batteries, and **be prepared to turn on your camera, camcorder, or laptop computer for security personnel** to prove that it's real.

X-RAYS

Always **ask for hand inspection at security.** Such requests are virtually always honored at U.S. airports, and are usually accommodated abroad. Photographic film becomes clouded after successive exposure to airport x-ray machines. Videotape and computer disks are not harmed by X-rays, but **keep your tapes and disks away from metal detectors.**

CUSTOMS

Before departing, **register your foreign-made**

camera or laptop with U.S. Customs. If your equipment is U.S.-made, call the consulate of the country you'll be visiting to find out whether it should be registered with local customs upon arrival.

CAR RENTAL

CUTTING COSTS

To get the best deal, **book through a travel agent who is willing to shop around.** Ask your agent to **look for fly-drive packages,** which also save you money, and **ask if local taxes are included** in the rental or fly-drive price. These can be as high as 20% in some destinations. Don't forget to find out about required deposits, cancellation penalties, drop-off charges, and the cost of any required insurance coverage.

Also **ask your travel agent about a company's customer-service record.** How has it responded to late plane arrivals and vehicle mishaps? Are there often lines at the rental counter, and—if you're traveling during a holiday period—does a confirmed reservation guarantee you a car?

Always **find out what equipment is standard** at your destination before specifying what you want; automatic transmission and air-conditioning are usually optional—and very expensive.

Be sure to **look into wholesalers**—companies that do not own their own fleets but rent in bulk from those that do and often offer better rates than traditional car-rental operations. Prices are best during off-peak periods; rentals booked through wholesalers must be paid for before you leave the United States.

INSURANCE

When driving a rented car, you are generally responsible for any damage to or loss of the rental vehicle. Before you rent, **see what coverage you already have** under the terms of your personal auto insurance policy and credit cards.

If you do not have auto insurance or an umbrella insurance policy that covers damage to third parties, purchasing CDW or LDW is highly recommended.

Collision policies that car-rental companies sell for European rentals typically do not cover stolen vehicles. Before you buy additional coverage for theft, find out if your credit card or personal auto insurance will cover the loss. All car-rental companies operating in Italy mandate the purchase of theft-protection policies.

LICENSE REQUIREMENTS

In Italy your own driver's license is acceptable. An International Driver's Permit is a good idea; it's available from the American or Canadian automobile associations, or, in the United Kingdom, from the AA or RAC.

SURCHARGES

Before you pick up a car in one city and leave it in another, **ask about drop-off charges or one-**

way service fees, which can be substantial. Note, too, that some rental agencies charge extra if you return the car before the time specified on your contract. To avoid a hefty refueling fee, **fill the tank just before you turn in the car**—but be aware that gas stations near the rental outlet may overcharge.

CHILDREN & TRAVEL

Although Italians love children and are generally very tolerant and patient with them, they provide few amenities for them. In restaurants and trattorias you may find a high chair or a cushion for the child to sit on, but rarely do they offer a children's menu. Order a *mezza porzione* (half-portion) of any dish, or ask the waiter for a *porzione da bambino* (child's portion).

Discounts do exist. Always ask about a *sconto-bambino* (child's discount) before purchasing tickets. Children under six or under a certain height ride free on municipal buses and trams. Children under 18 are admitted free to state-run museums and galleries, and there are similar privileges in many municipal or private museums.

When traveling with children, **plan ahead** and **involve your youngsters** as you outline your trip. When packing, **include a supply of things to keep them busy** en route (☞ Children & Travel *in* Important Contacts A to Z). On sightseeing days, try to **schedule**

activities of special interest to your children, like a trip to a zoo or a playground. If you **plan your itinerary around seasonal festivals,** you'll never lack for things to do. In addition, **check local newspapers for special events** mounted by public libraries, museums, and parks.

BABY-SITTING

For recommended local sitters, **check with your hotel desk.**

DRIVING

If you are renting a car, don't forget to **arrange for a car seat when you reserve.** Sometimes they're free.

FLYING

As a general rule, infants under two not occupying a seat fly at greatly reduced fares and occasionally for free. If your children are two or older **ask about special children's fares.** Age limits for these fares vary among carriers. Rules also vary regarding unaccompanied minors, so again, check with your airline.

BAGGAGE➣ In general, the adult baggage allowance applies to children paying half or more of the adult fare. If you are traveling with an infant, **ask about carry-on allowances** before departure. In general, for infants charged 10% of the adult fare you are allowed one carry-on bag and a collapsible stroller, which may have to be checked; you may be limited to less if the flight is full.

SAFETY SEATS➣ According to the FAA, it's a

good idea to **use safety seats aloft** for children weighing less than 40 pounds. Airline policies vary. U.S. carriers allow FAA-approved models but usually require that you buy a ticket, even if your child would otherwise ride free, since the seats must be strapped into regular seats. However, some U.S. and foreign-flag airlines may require you to hold your baby during takeoff and landing—defeating the seat's purpose. Other foreign carriers may not allow infant seats at all, or may charge a child rather than an infant fare for their use.

FACILITIES➤ When making your reservation, **request children's meals or freestanding bassinets** if you need them; the latter are available only to those seated at the bulkhead, where there's enough legroom. If you don't need a bassinet, **think twice before requesting bulkhead seats**—the only storage space for in-flight necessities is in inconveniently distant overhead bins.

GAMES

Milton Bradley and Parker Brothers have travel versions of some of their most popular games, including Yahtzee, Trouble, Sorry, and Monopoly. Prices run $5 to $8. Look for them in the travel section of your local toy store.

LODGING

Most hotels allow children under a certain age to stay in their parents' room at no extra charge; others charge them as extra

adults. Be sure to **ask about the cutoff age.**

CUSTOMS & DUTIES

To speed your clearance through customs, **keep receipts for all your purchases abroad** and **be ready to show the inspector what you've bought.** If you feel that you've been incorrectly or unfairly charged a duty, you can **appeal assessments in dispute.** First ask to see a supervisor. If you are still unsatisfied, **write to the port director** of your point of entry, sending your customs receipt and any other appropriate documentation. The address will be listed on your receipt. If you still don't get satisfaction, you can take your case to customs headquarters in Washington.

IN ITALY

Of goods obtained anywhere outside the EU or goods purchased in a duty-free shop within an EU country, the allowances are: (1) 200 cigarettes or 100 cigarillos or 50 cigars or 250 grams of tobacco; (2) 2 liters of still table wine or 1 liter of spirits over 22% volume or 2 liters of spirits under 22% volume or 2 liters of fortified and sparkling wines; and (3) 50 milliliters of perfume and 250 milliliters of toilet water.

Of goods obtained (duty and tax paid) within another EU country, the allowances are: (1) 800 cigarettes or 400 cigarillos or 400 cigars or 1 kilogram of tobacco; (2) 90 liters of still table wine plus (3) 10 liters of spirits over

22% volume plus 20 liters of spirits under 22% volume plus 60 liters of sparkling wines plus 110 liters of beer.

IN THE U.S.

You may bring home $400 worth of foreign goods duty-free if you've been out of the country for at least 48 hours and haven't already used the $400 allowance, or any part of it, in the past 30 days.

Travelers 21 or older may bring back 1 liter of alcohol duty-free, provided the beverage laws of the state through which they reenter the United States allow it. In addition, regardless of their age, they are allowed 100 non-Cuban cigars and 200 cigarettes. Antiques, which the U.S. Customs Service defines as objects more than 100 years old, are duty-free. Original works of art done entirely by hand are also duty-free. These include, but are not limited to, paintings, drawings, and sculptures.

Duty-free, travelers may mail packages valued at up to $200 to themselves and up to $100 to others, with a limit of one parcel per addressee per day (and no alcohol or tobacco products or perfume valued at more than $5); on the outside, the package must be labeled as being either for personal use or an unsolicited gift, and a list of its contents and their retail value must be attached. Mailed items do not affect your duty-free allowance on your return.

IN CANADA

If you've been out of Canada for at least seven days, you may bring in C$500 worth of goods duty-free. If you've been away for fewer than seven days but for more than 48 hours, the duty-free allowance drops to C$200; if your trip lasts between 24 and 48 hours, the allowance is C$50. You cannot pool allowances with family members. Goods claimed under the C$500 exemption may follow you by mail; those claimed under the lesser exemptions must accompany you.

Alcohol and tobacco products may be included in the seven-day and 48-hour exemptions but not in the 24-hour exemption. If you meet the age requirements of the province or territory through which you reenter Canada, you may bring in, duty-free, 1.14 liters (40 imperial ounces) of wine or liquor *or* 24 12-ounce cans or bottles of beer or ale. If you are 16 or older, you may bring in, duty-free, 200 cigarettes, 50 cigars or cigarillos, and 400 tobacco sticks or 400 grams of manufactured tobacco. Alcohol and tobacco must accompany you on your return.

An unlimited number of gifts with a value of up to C$60 each may be mailed to Canada duty-free. These do not affect your duty-free allowance on your return. Label the package "Unsolicited Gift— Value Under $60." Alcohol and tobacco are excluded.

IN THE U.K.

If your journey was wholly within European Union (EU) countries, you no longer need to pass through customs when you return to the United Kingdom. If you plan to bring back large quantities of alcohol or tobacco, check in advance on EU limits.

D

DISABILITIES & ACCESSIBILITY

Italy has only recently begun to provide facilities such as ramps, telephones, and rest rooms for people with disabilities; such things are still the exception, not the rule. Travelers' wheelchairs must be transported free of charge, according to Italian law, but the logistics of getting a wheelchair on and off trains and buses can make this requirement irrelevant. Seats are reserved for people with disabilities on public transportation, but few buses have lifts for wheelchairs. High, narrow steps for boarding trains create additional problems. In many monuments and museums, even in some hotels and restaurants, architectural barriers make it difficult, if not impossible, for those with disabilities to gain access. In Florence, however, the Uffizi is accessible by wheelchair.

Bringing a Seeing Eye dog into Italy requires an import license, a current certificate detailing the dog's inoculations, and a letter from your veterinarian certifying the dog's health.

Contact the nearest Italian consulate for particulars.

When discussing accessibility with an operator or reservationist, ask hard questions. Are there any stairs, inside *or* out? Are there grab bars next to the toilet *and* in the shower/tub? How wide is the doorway to the room? To the bathroom? For the most extensive facilities, meeting the latest legal specifications, **opt for newer accommodations,** which more often have been designed with access in mind. Older properties or ships must usually be retrofitted and may offer more limited facilities as a result. Be sure to **discuss your needs before booking.**

DISCOUNTS & DEALS

You shouldn't have to pay for a discount. In fact, you may already be eligible for all kinds of savings. Here are some time-honored strategies for getting the best deal.

LOOK IN YOUR WALLET

When you **use your credit card to make travel purchases,** you may get free travel-accident insurance, collision damage insurance, medical or legal assistance, depending on the card and bank that issued it. American Express, Visa, and MasterCard provide one or more of these services, so **get a copy of your card's travel benefits.** If you are a member of the AAA or an oil-company-sponsored road-assistance plan, always **ask hotel or car-rental reservationists for auto-club discounts.** Some clubs offer additional discounts on tours, cruises, or admission to attractions. And don't forget that auto-club membership entitles you to free maps and trip-planning services.

SENIORS CITIZENS & STUDENTS

As a senior-citizen traveler, you may be eligible for special rates, but you should mention your senior-citizen status up front. If you're a student or under 26 you can also get discounts, especially if you have an official ID card (☞ Senior-Citizen Discounts *and* Students on the Road, *below*).

DIAL FOR DOLLARS

To save money, **look into "1-800" discount reservations services,** which often have lower rates. These services use their buying power to get a better price on hotels, airline tickets, and sometimes even car rentals. When booking a room, always **call the hotel's local toll-free number** (if one is available) rather than the central reservations number—you'll often get a better price. Ask the reservationist about special packages or corporate rates, which are usually available even if you're not traveling on business.

JOIN A CLUB?

Discount clubs can be a legitimate source of savings, but you must use the participating hotels and visit the participating attractions in order to realize any benefits. Remember, too, that you have to pay a fee to join, so **determine if you'll save enough to warrant your membership fee.** Before booking with a club, **make sure the hotel or other supplier isn't offering a better deal.**

GET A GUARANTEE

When shopping for the best deal on hotels and car rentals, **look for guaranteed exchange rates,** which protect you against a falling dollar. With your rate locked in, you won't pay more even if the price goes up in the local currency.

DRIVING

FUEL

Only a few gas stations are open on Sunday, and most close for a couple of hours at lunchtime and at 7 PM for the night. Self-service pumps may be few and far between outside major cities. Gas stations on autostradas are open 24 hours.

PARKING

Parking space is at a premium in Florence. Parking in an area signposted ZONA DISCO is allowed for limited periods (30 minutes to 2 hours or more—the limit is posted); if you don't have the cardboard disk to show what time you parked, you can use a piece of paper. It's advisable to leave your car only in guarded parking areas. Unofficial parking attendants can help you find a space but offer no guarantees. In major cities your car may be towed away if illegally parked.

RULES OF THE ROAD

Driving is on the right, as in the United States. Regulations are largely as in Britain and the United States, except that the police have the power to levy on-the-spot fines. In most Italian towns the use of the horn is forbidden in certain, if not all, areas; a large sign, ZONA DI SILENZIO, indicates where. Speed limits are 130 kph (80 mph) on autostradas and 110 kph (70 mph) on state and provincial roads, unless otherwise marked. Fines for driving after drinking are heavy, with the additional possibility of six months' imprisonment, but testing is not routine.

H

HEALTH

The Centers for Disease Control and Prevention (CDC) in Atlanta caution that most of Southern Europe is in the "intermediate" range for risk of contracting traveler's diarrhea. Part of this risk may be attributed to an increased consumption of olive oil and wine, which can have a laxative effect on stomachs used to a different diet. To avoid this, **watch what you eat.** Stay away from ice, uncooked food, and unpasteurized milk and milk products, and **drink only bottled water or water that has been boiled** for at least 20 minutes. Mild cases may respond to Imodium (known generically as loperamide) or Pepto-Bismol (not as strong), both of which can be purchased over the counter. Drink plenty of purified water or tea—chamomile is a good folk remedy for diarrhea. In severe cases, rehydrate yourself with a salt-sugar solution (½ teaspoon salt and 4 tablespoons sugar per quart of water).

The CDC also advises all international travelers to swim only in chlorinated swimming pools, unless they are absolutely certain the local beaches and freshwater lakes are not contaminated.

I
INSURANCE

Travel insurance can protect your monetary investment, replace your luggage and its contents, or provide for medical coverage should you fall ill during your trip. Most tour operators, travel agents, and insurance agents sell specialized health-and-accident, flight, trip-cancellation, and luggage insurance as well as comprehensive policies with some or all of these coverages. Comprehensive policies may also reimburse you for delays due to weather—an important consideration if you're traveling during the winter months. Some health-insurance policies do not cover preexisting conditions, but waivers may be available in specific cases. Coverage is sold by the companies listed in Important Contacts A to Z; these companies act as the policy's administrators.

The actual insurance is usually underwritten by a well-known name, such as The Travelers or Continental Insurance.

Before you make any purchase, **review your existing health and homeowner's policies** to find out whether they cover expenses incurred while traveling.

BAGGAGE

Airline liability for baggage is limited to $1,250 per person on domestic flights. On international flights, it amounts to $9.07 per pound or $20 per kilogram for checked baggage (roughly $640 per 70-pound bag) and $400 per passenger for unchecked baggage. Insurance for losses exceeding the terms of your airline ticket can be bought directly from the airline at check-in for about $10 per $1,000 of coverage; note that it excludes a rather extensive list of items, shown on your airline ticket.

COMPREHENSIVE

Comprehensive insurance policies include all the coverages described above plus some that may not be available in more specific policies. If you have purchased an expensive vacation, especially one that involves travel abroad, comprehensive insurance is a must; **look for policies that include trip delay insurance,** which will protect you in the event that weather problems cause you to miss your flight, tour, or cruise. A few insurers will also sell you a waiver for preexisting medical conditions.

Some of the companies that offer both these features are Access America, Carefree Travel, Travel Insured International, and TravelGuard (☞ Insurance *in* Important Contacts A to Z).

FLIGHT

You should **think twice before buying flight insurance.** Often purchased as a last-minute impulse at the airport, it pays a lump sum when a plane crashes, either to a beneficiary if the insured dies or sometimes to a surviving passenger who loses his or her eyesight or a limb. Supplementing the airlines' coverage described in the limits-of-liability paragraphs on your ticket, it's expensive and basically unnecessary. Charging an airline ticket to a major credit card often automatically provides you with coverage that may also extend to travel by bus, train, and ship.

HEALTH

Medicare generally does not cover health care costs outside the United States; nor do many privately issued policies. If your own health insurance policy does not cover you outside the United States, **consider buying supplemental medical coverage.** It can reimburse you for $1,000–$150,000 worth of medical and/or dental expenses incurred as a result of an accident or illness during a trip. These policies also may include a personal-accident or death-and-dismemberment provision, which pays a lump sum ranging from $15,000 to $500,000 to your beneficiaries if you die or to you if you lose one or more limbs or your eyesight, and a medical-assistance provision, which may either reimburse you for the cost of referrals, evacuation, or repatriation and other services, or automatically enroll you as a member of a particular medical-assistance company. (☞ Health Issues *in* Important Contacts A to Z.)

U.K. TRAVELERS

You can buy an annual travel insurance policy valid for most vacations during the year in which it's purchased. If you are pregnant or have a preexisting medical condition make sure you're covered before buying such a policy.

TRIP

Without insurance, you will lose all or most of your money if you cancel your trip regardless of the reason. Especially if your airline ticket, cruise, or package tour is nonrefundable and cannot be changed, it's essential that you **buy trip-cancellation-and-interruption insurance.** When considering how much coverage you need, look for a policy that will cover the cost of your trip plus the nondiscounted price of a one-way airline ticket should you need to return home early. Read the fine print carefully, especially sections that define "family member" and "preexisting medical conditions." Also **consider default or bankruptcy insurance,** which protects you against a supplier's failure to deliver. Be aware, however, that if you buy such a policy from a travel agency, tour operator, airline, or cruise line, it may not cover default by the firm in question.

L

LANGUAGE

In cities like Florence, language is no problem. You can always find someone who speaks at least a little English, albeit with a heavy accent; remember that the Italian language is pronounced exactly as it is written (many Italians try to speak English as it is written, with disconcerting results). You may run into a language barrier in the countryside, but a phrase book and close attention to the Italians' astonishing use of pantomime and expressive gestures will go a long way.

Try to master a few phrases for daily use, and familiarize yourself with the terms you'll need to decipher signs and museum labels. To get the most out of museums, you'll need English-language guidebooks to exhibits; look for them in bookstores and on newsstands, as those sold at the museums are not necessarily the best.

LODGING

Italy offers a good choice of accommodations, especially in the main tourist capitals like Florence. It is becoming more difficult to find satisfactory accommodations in the lower categories in Florence, however, as more and more hotels are being refurbished and upgraded.

APARTMENT & VILLA RENTAL

If you want a home base that's roomy enough for a family and comes with cooking facilities, **consider taking a furnished rental.** This can also save you money, but not always—some rentals are luxury properties (economical only when your party is large). Home-exchange directories list rentals—often second homes owned by prospective house swappers—and some services search for a house or apartment for you (even a castle if that's your fancy) and handle the paperwork. Some send an illustrated catalog; others send photographs only of specific properties, sometimes at a charge; up-front registration fees may apply.

HOME EXCHANGE

If you would like to find a house, an apartment, or some other type of vacation property to exchange for your own while on holiday, **become a member of a home-exchange organization,** which will send you its updated listings of available exchanges for a year, and will include your own listing in at least one of them. Arrangements for the actual exchange are made by the two parties involved, not by the organization.

HOTELS

Italian hotels are classified from five-star

(deluxe) to one-star (very basic hotels and small inns). Stars are assigned according to standards set by regional boards (there are 20 in Italy), but rates are set by each hotel. During slack periods, or when a hotel is not full, it is often possible to negotiate a discounted rate. In the major cities, room rates are on a par with other European capitals: Deluxe and four-star rates can be downright extravagant. In those categories, **ask for one of the better rooms,** since less desirable rooms—and there usually are some—don't give you what you're paying for. Except in deluxe and some four-star hotels, rooms may be very small compared to U.S. standards.

In all hotels there is a rate card inside the door of your room, or inside the closet door; it tells you exactly what you will pay for that particular room (rates in the same hotel may vary according to the location and type of room). On this card, breakfast and any other optionals must be listed separately. Any discrepancy between the basic room rate and that charged on your bill is cause for complaint to the manager and to the local tourist office.

Although by law breakfast is supposed to be optional, most hotels quote room rates including breakfast. When you book a room, specifically **ask whether the rate includes breakfast** (*colazione*). You are under no obligation to take breakfast at your hotel, but in practice most hotels expect you to do so. It is encouraging to note that many of the hotels we recommend are offering generous buffet breakfasts instead of simple, even skimpy "continental breakfasts." Remember, if the latter is the case, you can **eat for less at the nearest coffee bar.**

Hotels that we list as ($$) and ($)—moderate to inexpensively priced accommodations—may charge extra for optional air-conditioning. In older hotels the quality of the rooms may be very uneven; if you don't like the room you're given, request another. This applies to noise, too. Front rooms may be larger and have a view, but they also may have a lot of street noise. **If you're a light sleeper, request a quiet room when making reservations.** Specify whether you care about having either a bath or shower, since not all rooms have both.

Always inquire about special rates. You can save considerably on hotel rooms in Florence during the off-seasons.

M

MAIL

Airmail letters (lightweight stationery) to the United States and Canada cost 1,250 lire for the first 19 grams and an additional 400 lire for every additional unit of 20 grams. Airmail postcards cost 1,000 lire if the message is limited to a few words and a signature; otherwise, you pay the letter rate. Airmail letters to the United Kingdom cost 750 lire; postcards, 600 lire. You can buy stamps at tobacconists.

RECEIVING MAIL

Mail service is generally slow; allow up to 10 days for mail from Britain, 15 days from North America. Correspondence can be addressed to you care of the Italian post office. Letters should be addressed to your name, "c/o Ufficio Postale Centrale," followed by "Fermo Posta" on the next line, and the name of the city (preceded by its postal code) on the next. You can collect it at the central post office by showing your passport or photo-bearing ID and paying a small fee. American Express also has a general-delivery service. There's no charge for cardholders, holders of American Express Traveler's checks, or anyone who booked a vacation with American Express.

MEDICAL ASSISTANCE

No one plans to get sick while traveling, but it happens, so **consider signing up with a medical assistance company.** These outfits provide referrals, emergency evacuation or repatriation, 24-hour telephone hot lines for medical consultation, cash for emergencies, and other personal and legal assistance. They also dispatch medical personnel and arrange for the relay of medical records. Coverage varies by plan, so **read the fine print carefully.**

MONEY

The unit of currency in Italy is the lira. There

are bills of 100,000, 50,000, 10,000, 5,000, 2,000, and 1,000 lire. Coins are 500, 200, 100 and 50 lire. At press time, the exchange rate was about 1,595 lire to the U.S. dollar, 1,157 lire to the Canadian dollar, and 2,402 lire to the pound sterling.

ATMS

CASH ADVANCES➤ Before leaving home, **make sure that your credit cards have been programmed for ATM use** in Italy. Note that Discover is accepted mostly in the United States. Local bank cards often do not work overseas either; **ask your bank about a Visa debit card,** which works like a bank card but can be used at any ATM displaying a Visa logo.

TRANSACTION FEES➤ Although fees charged for ATM transactions may be higher abroad than at home, Cirrus and Plus exchange rates are excellent, because they are based on wholesale rates offered only by major banks.

COSTS

Florence's prices are in line with those in the rest of Europe, with costs comparable to those in other major capitals, such as Paris and London. The days when the country's high-quality attractions came with a comparatively low Mediterranean price tag are long gone. With the cost of labor and social benefits rising and an economy weighed down by the public debt, Italy is therefore not a bargain, but there is an effort to hold the line

on hotel and restaurant prices that had become inordinately expensive by U.S. standards. Depending on season and occupancy, you may be able to obtain unadvertised lower rates in hotels; always inquire. Everywhere in Italy, if you want the luxury of four- and five-star hotels, be prepared to pay top rates.

When you make hotel reservations, ask explicitly whether breakfast is included in the rate. By law, breakfast is optional, but some hotels pressure guests to eat breakfast on the premises—and then charge a whopping amount for it. Find out what breakfast will cost at the time you book, or at least when you check in, and if it seems high, avoid misunderstanding by clearly stating that you want a room without breakfast.

Admission to the Uffizi Gallery is 12,000 lire. A movie ticket is 12,000 lire; going to a disco will set you back about 35,000 lire. A daily English-language newspaper is 2,400 lire.

A taxi ride (1 mile) costs about 10,000 lire. An inexpensive hotel room for two, including breakfast, in Florence is about 190,000 lire; an inexpensive Florence dinner is 35,000 lire, and a ½ liter carafe of house wine, 4,000 lire. A simple pasta item on the menu runs about 12,000 lire, a cup of coffee 1,200–1,400 lire, and a Rosticerria lunch, about 14,000 lire. A McDonald's Big Mac is 4,800 lire, a Coke (standing) at a café is

2,200 lire, and a pint of beer in a pub is 7,000 lire.

EXCHANGING CURRENCY

For the most favorable rates, **change money at banks.** You won't do as well at exchange booths in airports or rail and bus stations, in hotels, in restaurants, or in stores, although you may find their hours more convenient. To avoid lines at airport exchange booths, **get a small amount of the local currency before you leave home.**

TAXES

HOTEL➤ The service charge and the 9% IVA, or VAT tax, are included in the rate except in five-star deluxe hotels, where the IVA (13% on luxury hotels) may be a separate item added to the bill at departure.

RESTAURANT➤ A service charge of approximately 15% is added to all restaurant bills; in some cases the menu may state that the service charge is already included in the menu prices.

VAT➤ Value-added tax (IVA) is 12% on clothing, 19% on luxuries. On most consumer goods, it is already included in the amount shown on the price tag, whereas on services, it may not be.

To get an IVA refund when you are leaving Italy, take the goods and the invoice to the customs office at the airport or other point of departure and have the invoice stamped. (If you return to the United

States or Canada directly from Italy, go through the procedure at Italian customs; if your return is, say, via Britain, take the Italian goods and invoice to British customs.) Under Italy's IVA-refund system, a non-EU resident can obtain a refund of tax paid after spending a total of 300,000 lire in one store (before tax—and note that price tags and prices quoted, unless otherwise stated, include IVA). Shop with your passport and ask the store for an invoice itemizing the article(s), price(s), and the amount of tax. Once back home—and within 90 days of the date of purchase—mail the stamped invoice to the store, which will forward the IVA rebate to you. A growing number of stores in Italy (and Europe) are members of the Tax-Free Shopping System, which expedites things by providing an invoice that is actually a Tax-Free Cheque in the amount of the refund. Once stamped, it can be cashed at the Tax-Free Cash refund window at major airports and border crossings.

TRAVELER'S CHECKS

Whether or not to buy traveler's checks depends on where you are headed; **take cash to rural areas and small towns, traveler's checks to cities.** The most widely recognized checks are issued by American Express, Citicorp, Thomas Cook, and Visa. These are sold by major commercial banks for 1%–3% of the checks'

face value—it pays to **shop around.** Both American Express and Thomas Cook issue checks that can be countersigned and used by either you or your traveling companion. So you won't be left with excess foreign currency, **buy a few checks in small denominations** to cash toward the end of your trip. Before leaving home, **contact your issuer for information on where to cash your checks** without a incurring a transaction fee. Record the numbers of all your checks, and keep this listing in a separate place, crossing off the numbers of checks you have cashed.

WIRING MONEY

For a fee of 3%–10%, depending on the amount of the transaction, you can have money sent to you from home through Money-Gram^{SM} or Western Union (☞ Money Matters *in* Important Contacts A to Z). The transferred funds and the service fee can be charged to a Master-Card or Visa account.

P
PACKING FOR FLORENCE, TUSCANY, AND UMBRIA

The weather is considerably milder in Italy than in the north and central United States or Great Britain. In summer, stick with clothing that's as light as possible, although a sweater may be necessary in the cool of the evening, especially in the mountains and even during the hot months. Brief

summer afternoon thunderstorms are common, so carry an umbrella. During the winter, bring a medium-weight coat and a raincoat; northern Italy calls for heavier clothes, gloves, hats, and boots. Central heating may not be up to your standards, and interiors can be cold and damp; take wools or flannel rather than sheer fabrics. Bring sturdy shoes for winter, and comfortable walking shoes in any season.

Italians dress well and are not sloppy. They do not usually wear shorts in the city, unless longish Bermudas happen to be in fashion. Men aren't required to wear ties or jackets anywhere, except in some of the grander hotel dining rooms and top-level restaurants, but are expected to look reasonably sharp. Formal wear is the exception rather than the rule at the opera nowadays, though people in expensive seats usually do get dressed up.

Dress codes are strict for visits to churches: women must cover bare shoulders and arms—a shawl will do—but no longer need to cover their heads. Shorts are taboo for both men and women.

Take your own soap if you stay in budget hotels, as many do not provide it or else give guests only one tiny bar per room. Bring an extra pair of eyeglasses or contact lenses in your carry-on luggage, and if you have a health problem, **pack enough medication** to last the

THE GOLD GUIDE / SMART TRAVEL TIPS

trip or have your doctor write you a prescription using the drug's generic name, because brand names vary from country to country (you'll then need a duplicate prescription from a local doctor). It's important that you **don't put prescription drugs or valuables in luggage to be checked,** for it could go astray. To avoid problems with customs officials, carry medications in the original packaging. Also, don't forget the addresses of offices that handle refunds of lost traveler's checks.

ELECTRICITY

To use your U.S.-purchased electric-powered equipment, **bring a converter and an adapter.** The electrical current in Italy is 220 volts, 50 cycles alternating current (AC); wall outlets take plugs with two round prongs.

If your appliances are dual-voltage, you'll need only an adapter. Hotels sometimes have 110-volt outlets for low-wattage appliances near the sink, marked FOR SHAVERS ONLY; don't use them for high-wattage appliances like blow-dryers. If your laptop computer is older, carry a converter; new laptops operate equally well on 110 and 220 volts, so you need only an adapter.

LUGGAGE

Airline baggage allowances depend on the airline, the route, and the class of your ticket; ask in advance. In general, on domestic flights and on international flights between the United States and foreign destinations, you are entitled to check two bags. A third piece may be brought on board, but it must fit easily under the seat in front of you or in the overhead compartment. In the United States, the FAA gives airlines broad latitude regarding carry-on allowances, and they tend to tailor them to different aircraft and operational conditions. Charges for excess, oversize, or overweight pieces vary.

If you are flying between two foreign destinations, note that baggage allowances may be determined not by piece but by weight—generally 88 pounds (40 kilograms) in first class, 66 pounds (30 kilograms) in business class, and 44 pounds (20 kilograms) in economy. If your flight between two cities abroad *connects* with your transatlantic or transpacific flight, the piece method still applies.

SAFEGUARDING YOUR LUGGAGE➤ Before leaving home, **itemize your bags' contents** and their worth, and label them with your name, address, and phone number. (If you use your home address, cover it so that potential thieves can't see it readily.) Inside each bag, **pack a copy of your itinerary.** At check-in, **make sure that each bag is correctly tagged** with the destination airport's three-letter code. If your bags arrive damaged—or fail to arrive at all—file a written report with the airline before leaving the airport.

PASSPORTS & VISAS

If you don't already have one, **get a passport.** It is advisable that you **leave one photocopy of your passport's data page** with someone at home and keep another with you, separated from your passport, while traveling. If you lose your passport, promptly call the nearest embassy or consulate and the local police; having the data page information can speed replacement.

IN THE U.S.

All U.S. citizens, even infants, need only a valid passport to enter Italy for stays of up to 90 days. Application forms for both first-time and renewal passports are available at any of the 13 U.S. Passport Agency offices and at some post offices and courthouses. Passports are usually mailed within four weeks; allow five weeks or more in spring and summer.

CANADIANS

You need only a valid passport to enter Italy for stays of up to 90 days. Passport application forms are available at 28 regional passport offices, as well as post offices and travel agencies. Whether for a first or a renewal passport, you must apply in person. Children under 16 may be included on a parent's passport but must have their own to travel alone. Passports are valid for five years and are usually mailed within two to three weeks of application.

U.K. CITIZENS

Citizens of the United Kingdom need only a valid passport to enter Italy for stays of up to 90 days. Applications for new and renewal passports are available from main post offices and at the passport offices in Belfast, Glasgow, Liverpool, London, Newport, and Peterborough. You may apply in person at all passport offices, or by mail to all except the London office. Children under 16 may travel on an accompanying parent's passport. All passports are valid for 10 years. Allow a month for processing.

S
SAFETY

The best way to protect yourself against purse snatchers and pickpockets is to wear a money belt. If you carry a bag or camera, make sure it has straps that you can sling across your body bandolier-style. Beware of pickpockets in big-city buses and subways and when making your way through the corridors of crowded trains.

SENIOR CITIZENS

Older travelers planning to visit Italy during the hottest months should be aware that few public buildings, restaurants, and shops are air-conditioned. Public rest rooms are few and far between, other than those in coffee bars, restaurants, museums, and hotels. Older travelers may find it difficult to board trains and some buses and trams

with very high steps and narrow treads.

DISCOUNTS

To qualify for age-related discounts, **mention your senior-citizen status up front** when booking hotel reservations, not when checking out, and before you're seated in restaurants, not when paying the bill. Note that discounts may be limited to certain menus, days, or hours. When renting a car, **ask about promotional car-rental discounts**—they can net even lower costs than your senior-citizen discount.

EU citizens over 60 are entitled to free admission to state museums, as well as to many other museums—always ask at the ticket office. Older travelers may be eligible for special fares on Alitalia.

SHOPPING

The notice PREZZI FISSI (fixed prices) means just that; in shops displaying this sign it's a waste of time to bargain unless you're buying a sizable quantity of goods or a particularly costly object. Always bargain, however, at outdoor markets (except food markets) and when buying from street vendors. For a comprehensive introduction to the joys of shopping, Italian-style, *see* Pleasures & Pastimes *in* Chapter 1.

STUDENTS ON THE ROAD

To save money, **look into deals available through student-oriented travel agencies.** To

qualify, you'll need to have a bona fide student ID card. Members of international student groups are also eligible (☞ Students *in* Important Contacts A to Z). Many museums offer discount admission to students; always inquire at the ticket office.

T
TELEPHONES

The long-distance services of AT&T, MCI, and Sprint make calling home relatively convenient, but in many hotels you may find it impossible to dial the access number. The hotel operator may also refuse to make the connection. Instead, the hotel will charge you a premium rate—as much as 400% more than a calling card—for calls placed from your hotel room. To avoid such price gouging, travel with more than one company's long-distance calling card—a hotel may block Sprint but not MCI. If the hotel operator claims that you cannot use any phone card, ask to be connected to an international operator, who will help you to access your phone card. You can also dial the international operator yourself. If none of this works, try calling your phone company collect in the United States. If collect calls are also blocked, call from a pay phone in the hotel lobby. Before you go, **find out the local access codes** for your destinations.

You can also make long-distance calls from Telefoni offices, where operators will assign you a booth, help you place your call, and collect payment when you have finished, at no extra charge. There are Telefoni offices (designated TELECOM) in all cities and towns, usually in major train stations and in the center business districts. **You can make collect calls from any phone by dialing 172-1011, which will get you an English-speaking operator.** Rates to the United States are lowest around the clock on Sunday and 11 PM–8 AM, Italian time, on weekdays.

You can place a direct call to the United States by reversing the charges or using your phone credit card number. When calling from pay telephones, insert a 200-lire coin which will be returned upon completion of your call. You automatically reach an operator in the country of destination and thereby avoid all language difficulties.

OPERATORS AND INFORMATION

For general information in English, dial 176. To place calls from one European country to another via operator-assisted service, dial 15. **To place intercontinental telephone calls** via operator-assisted service (or for intercontinental information), dial 170 or long-distance access numbers (☞ Telephone Matters *in* Important Contacts, *above*).

PAY PHONES

Pay phones take either a 200-lire coin, two 100-lire coins, a 500-lire coin, or a *carta telefonica* (prepaid calling card). Scheda phones are becoming common everywhere. You buy the card (values vary— 5,000 lire, 10,000 lire, etc.) at Telefoni offices, post offices, and tobacconists. Tear off the corner of the card, and insert it in the slot. When you dial, its value appears in the window. After you hang up, the card is returned so you can use it until its value runs out.

TIPPING

Tipping practices vary, depending on where you are. The following guidelines apply in major cities, but Italians tip smaller amounts in smaller cities and towns.

In restaurants a service charge of about 15% usually appears as a separate item on your check. A few restaurants state on the menu that cover and service charge are included. Either way, it's customary to leave an additional 5%–10% tip for the waiter, depending on the service. Tip checkroom attendants 500 lire per person, rest room attendants 200 lire; in both cases tip more in expensive hotels and restaurants. Tip 100 lire for whatever you drink standing up at a coffee bar, 500 lire or more for table service in a smart café, and less in neighborhood cafés. At a hotel bar tip 1,000 lire and up for a round or two of cocktails.

Taxi drivers are usually happy with 5%–10% of the meter amount. Railway and airport porters charge a fixed rate per bag. Tip an additional 500 lire per person, but more if the porter is very helpful. Theater ushers expect 500 lire per person, but more for very expensive seats. Give a barber 2,000–3,000 lire and a hairdresser's assistant 3,000–8,000 lire for a shampoo or cut, depending on the type of establishment.

On sightseeing tours, tip guides about 2,000 lire per person for a half-day group tour, more if they are very good. In museums and other places of interest where admission is free, a contribution is expected; give anything from 500 to 1,000 lire for one or two persons, more if the guardian has been especially helpful. Service station attendants are tipped only for special services.

In hotels, give the *portiere* (concierge) about 15% of his bill for services, or 5,000– 10,000 lire if he has been generally helpful. For two people in a double room, leave the chambermaid about 1,000 lire per day, or about 4,000–5,000 a week, in a moderately priced hotel; tip a minimum of 1,000 lire for valet or room service. Increase these amounts by one-half in an expensive hotel, and double them in a very expensive hotel. In very expensive hotels, tip doormen 1,000 lire for calling a cab and 2,000 lire for carrying bags to the check-in desk, bellhops 3,000–5,000 lire for carrying your bags to the room and 3,000–5,000 lire for room service. One-third to one-half of these amounts is acceptable in moderately priced hotels.

TOUR OPERATORS

A package or tour to Florence, Tuscany, or Umbria can make your vacation less expensive and more hassle-free. Firms that sell tours and packages reserve airline seats, hotel rooms, and rental cars in bulk and pass some of the savings on to you. In addition, the best operators have local representatives available to help you at your destination.

A GOOD DEAL?

The more your package or tour includes, the better you can predict the ultimate cost of your vacation. Make sure you know exactly what is covered, and **beware of hidden costs.** Are taxes, tips, and service charges included? Transfers and baggage handling? Entertainment and excursions? These can add up.

Most packages and tours are rated deluxe, first-class superior, first class, tourist, or budget. The key difference is usually accommodations. If the package or tour you are considering is priced lower than in your wildest dreams, **be skeptical.** Also, **make sure your travel agent knows the accommodations** and other services. Ask about the hotel's location, room size, beds, and whether it has a pool, room service, or programs for children, if you care about these. Has your agent been there in person or sent others you can contact?

BUYER BEWARE

Each year a number of consumers are stranded

or lose their money when operators—even very large ones with excellent reputations—go out of business. To avoid becoming one of them, take the time to **check out the operator**—find out how long the company has been in business and ask several agents about its reputation. Next, **don't book unless the firm has a consumer-protection program.** Members of the USTOA and the NTA are required to set aside funds for the sole purpose of covering your payments and travel arrangements in case of default. Non-member operators may instead carry insurance; look for the details in the operator's brochure—and for the name of an underwriter with a solid reputation. Note: When it comes to tour operators, **don't trust escrow accounts.** Although there are laws governing those of charter-flight operators, no governmental body prevents tour operators from raiding the till.

Next, **contact your local Better Business Bureau and the attorney general's offices** in both your own state and the operator's; have any complaints been filed? Finally, **pay with a major credit card.** Then you can cancel payment, provided that you can document your complaint. Always **consider trip-cancellation insurance** (☞ Insurance, *above*).

BIG VS. SMALL➤ Operators that handle several hundred thousand travelers per year can use their purchasing power to give you a

good price. Their high volume may also indicate financial stability. But some small companies provide more personalized service; because they tend to specialize, they may also be more knowledgeable about a given area.

USING AN AGENT

Travel agents are excellent resources. In fact, large operators accept bookings made only through travel agents. But it's good to **collect brochures from several agencies** because some agents' suggestions may be skewed by promotional relationships with tour and package firms that reward them for volume sales. If you have a special interest, **find an agent with expertise in that area;** ASTA can provide leads in the United States. (Don't rely solely on your agent, though; agents may be unaware of small-niche operators, and some special-interest travel companies only sell direct.)

SINGLE TRAVELERS

Prices are usually quoted per person, based on two sharing a room. If traveling solo, you may be required to pay the full double-occupancy rate. Some operators eliminate this surcharge if you agree to be matched up with a roommate of the same sex, even if one is not found by departure time.

TRAIN TRAVEL

To save money, **look into rail passes** (☞ Train Travel *in* Important Contacts A to Z).

But be aware that if you don't plan to cover many miles, you may come out ahead by buying individual tickets.

All Italian trains have first and second classes. On local trains the higher first-class fare gets you little more than a clean doily on the headrest of your seat, but on long-distance trains you get wider seats and more legroom and better ventilation and lighting. At peak travel times, first-class train travel is worth the difference. Remember to always make seat reservations in advance, for either class.

The fastest trains on the Ferrovie dello Stato (FS), the Italian State Railways, are the Pendolino Eurostar (ETR 460 trains), operating on several main lines, including Rome–Milan, via Florence and Bologna; seat reservations and supplement are included in the fare; next fastest trains are the Intercity (IC) trains, for which you pay a supplement and for which seat reservations may be required and are always advisable. *Interregionale* trains usually make more stops and are a little slower. *Regionale* and *locale* trains are the slowest; many serve commuters.

To avoid long lines at station windows, **buy tickets and make seat reservations up to two months in advance** at travel agencies displaying the FS emblem. Agencies cannot make same-day seat reservations, but can sell tickets for the same day. If you have to reserve at the last minute, reservation offices at the station accept reservations up to three hours before departure. You may be able to get a seat assignment just before boarding the train; look for the conductor on the platform. Trains can be very crowded on weekends and during holiday and vacation seasons; reserve seats in advance or, if the train originates where you get on, get to the station early to find a seat. A card just outside the compartment or over the seat indicates whether it has been reserved. Carry compact bags for easy overhead storage. All tickets must be date-stamped in the small yellow or red machines near the tracks before you board. Once stamped, your ticket is valid for six hours if your destination is within 200 kilometers, for 24 hours for destinations beyond that. You can get on and off at will for the duration of the ticket's validity. If you don't stamp your ticket in the machine, you must actively seek out a conductor to validate the ticket on the train, paying 10,000 lire extra for the service. If you merely wait in your seat for him to collect your ticket, you must pay a 30,000 lire fine in addition. You also pay a hefty penalty if you purchase your ticket on board the train. You can buy train tickets for destinations within a 100-kilometer (62-mile) range at tobacconists and at ticket machines in stations.

There is refreshment service on all long-distance trains, with mobile carts and a cafeteria or dining car. Tap water on trains is not drinkable.

If Italy is your only destination in Europe, **consider purchasing an Italian Railpass,** which allows unlimited travel on the entire Italian Rail network. Prices begin at $132 for four days of travel in second class within a one-month period and $194 in first class. Passes which are good for longer periods of time are also available, as are flexipasses, which allow a limited amount of train travel within a certain period.

Once in Italy, **inquire about the Carta Verde if you're under 26** (40,000 lire for one year), which entitles the holder to a 20% discount on all first- and second-class tickets. Those under 26 should also inquire about discount travel fares under the Billet International Jeune (BIJ) scheme. The special one-trip tickets are sold by EuroTrain International at its offices in various European cities and by travel agents, mainline rail stations, and youth travel specialists.

You can **purchase the Carta d'Argento if you're over 60** (40,000 lire for one year), good for a 30% discount on all first- and second-class tickets, except for travel June 26–

August 14 and December 18–28.

Italy is one of 17 countries in which you can **use EurailPasses,** which provide unlimited first-class rail travel, in all of the participating countries, for the duration of the pass. If you plan to rack up the miles, get a standard pass. These are available for 15 days ($522), 21 days ($678), one month ($838), two months ($1,148), and 3 months ($1,468). If your plans call for only limited train travel, **look into a Europass,** which costs less money than a EurailPass. Unlike EurailPasses, however, you get a limited number of travel days, in a limited number of countries, during a specified time period. For example, a two month pass ($316) allows between five and fifteen days of rail travel, but costs $200 less than the least expensive EurailPass. Keep in mind, however, that the Europass is good only in France, Germany, Italy, Spain, and Switzerland, and the number of countries you can visit is further limited by the type of pass you buy. For example, the basic two-month pass allows you to visit only three of the five participating countries.

In addition to standard EurailPasses, **ask about special rail-pass plans.** Among these are the Eurail Youthpass (for those under age 26), the Eurail Saverpass (which gives a discount for two or more people traveling together), a Eurail Flexipass (which allows

a certain number of travel days within a set period), and the Euraildrive Pass and the Europass Drive (which combine travel by train and rental car).

Whichever pass you choose, remember that you must **purchase your EurailPass or Europass before you leave** for Europe.

Many travelers assume that rail passes guarantee them seats on the trains they wish to ride. Not so. You need to **book seats ahead even if you are using a rail pass**; seat reservations are required on some European trains, particularly high-speed trains, and are a good idea on trains that may be crowded—particularly in summer on popular routes. You will also need a reservation if you purchase sleeping accommodations.

For those planning to travel through Italy by rail, a unique guide is *Italy by Train* by Tim Jepson (Fodor's Travel Publications, ☎ 800/533–6478, or from bookstores; $16).

TRAVEL GEAR

Travel catalogs specialize in useful items that can **save space when packing** and make life on the road more convenient. Compact alarm clocks, travel irons, travel wallets, and personal-care kits are among the most common items you'll find. They also carry dual-voltage appliances, currency converters and foreign-language phrase books. Some catalogs even carry miniature

coffeemakers and water purifiers.

U.S. GOVERNMENT

The U.S. government can be an excellent source of travel information. Some of this is free and some is available for a nominal charge. When planning your trip, **find out what government materials are available.** For just a couple of dollars, you can get a variety of publications from the Consumer Information Center in Pueblo, Colorado. Free consumer information also is available from individual government agencies, such as the Department of Transportation or the U.S. Customs Service. For specific titles, see the appropriate publications entry in Important Contacts A to Z, *above.*

W WHEN TO GO

The main tourist season runs from April to mid-October. It follows that for serious sightseers the best months are from fall to early spring. The so-called low season may be cooler and inevitably rainier, but it has its rewards: less time waiting on lines and closer-up, unhurried views of what you want to see. Weatherwise, the best months for sightseeing are April, May, June, September, and October, generally pleasant and not too hot. The hottest months are July and August, when brief afternoon thunderstorms are common in inland areas. Winters are relatively mild in most places on the main tourist circuit but always include some rainy spells.

Foreign tourists crowd the major art cities like Florence at Easter, when Italians flock to resorts and to the country. From March through May, bus loads of eager schoolchildren on excursions take cities of artistic and historical interest by storm.

If you can avoid it, don't travel at all in Italy in August, when much of the population is on the move, especially around Ferragosto, the August 15 national holiday, when cities are deserted and many restaurants and shops are closed. (Of course, with residents away on vacation, this makes crowds less of a bother for tourists.)

CLIMATE

The following are average daily maximum and minimum temperatures for Florence.

Jan.	48F	9C	**May**	73F	23C	**Sept.**	79F	26C
	36	2		54	12		59	15
Feb.	52F	11C	**June**	81F	27C	**Oct.**	68F	20C
	37	3		59	15		52	11
Mar.	57F	14C	**July**	86F	30C	**Nov.**	57F	14C
	41	5		64	18		45	7
Apr.	66F	19C	**Aug.**	86F	30C	**Dec.**	52F	11C
	46	8		63	17		39	10

1 Destination: Florence, Tuscany, and Umbria

INTRODUCTION

J UST AS TUSCANY AND UMBRIA straddle the boot, so their contribution to the Italian jigsaw is massive and inescapable. Their influence pervades Italian culture and percolates far beyond, to the extent that their impact has been felt throughout European and even world history. Tuscany—and to a lesser extent Umbria—saw the birth of humanism, that classically leaning, secular-tending current that effloresced in the Renaissance and to which the West owes its cultural complexion. In the graphic arts, architecture, astronomy, sculpture, engineering, art history, poetry, political theory, biography . . . in every field of human endeavor the people of these regions have loomed large. The Italian language itself is Tuscan, due largely to Dante's use of his local dialect to compose his *Divine Comedy*. When Italy became a modern state in 1865, Florence was the natural choice for the national capital until Rome's entry six years later.

It is hard to think of any other area that has seen such a dense concentration of human achievement as Tuscany and Umbria, but it is equally difficult to find anywhere so riven by conflict and factions. The strange thing is how neatly the periods of maximum creativity and bellicosity coincided. Was the restless, innovative impulse a consequence of the social turmoil, or the principal cause of it? It is surely no accident that Tuscany and Umbria in general and Florence in particular contain the most quarrelsome elements ever thrown together, as a cursory flip through some of the names in the local annals can testify: the Florentine Niccolò Machiavelli, who became a very synonym for the Devil (Old Nick); Savonarola, whose energetic career pitched church and state into headlong confrontation, igniting the famous "Bonfire of Vanities" in Florence's main square, site of the Dominican friar's own incineration not long afterwards; the town of Pistoia, from which the word "pistol" is derived; Perugia, populated, according to the historian Sigismondo, by "the most warlike

people in Italy, who always preferred Mars to the Muse" . . . the very street-names of Florence and Siena recall the clash of medieval factions. Outside the towns, there is hardly a hill, stream, or mountain pass whose name does not evoke some siege, battle, or act of treachery. The historic rivalry of Guelph and Ghibelline never reached such intense acrimony as in these seemingly tranquil hills, and nowhere was allegiance worn so lightly, with communes and families swapping sides whenever their rivals changed theirs.

The sense of opposition is alive in Tuscany and Umbria today just as strongly as it ever was. Visitors can witness it on every two-toned marble church front. Blacks and whites imperial, feudal and commercial, Renaissance and Gothic—the antagonism is embedded in art history, revived in every discussion of the background of every great work. It is a fixed feature of the local scene: the Sienese are still suspicious of the Florentines, the Florentines disdainful of the Sienese, while Siena itself seems to live in a permanent state of warfare within its own city walls, as any spectator of the Palio and the months of preparation that precede it can testify. Outsiders contribute to the debate: for Mary McCarthy, Florence was manly, Siena feminine, and tourists take sides whenever they lay down their reasons for preferring Florence to Siena or vice versa, as if there had to be a dualistic appreciation of the two.

Walking through the city streets of present-day Florence, you can't fail to be struck by the contrast between the austere and unwelcoming external appearance of the palaces and the sumptuous comforts within, or by the 1990s elegance and modernity of the Florentines in the midst of the thoroughly medieval churches and piazzas. Florence is a modern industrial city, and the Florentines themselves perennial modernists, their eyes fixed firmly in front. This helps to explain both their past inventiveness and the ambivalent attitude they hold toward that same past, composed of roughly equal parts of ennui and fierce pride. To its inhabitants, that the city of Florence stands on a par with Athens and Rome is self-evident: To them tourism, which feeds on the past, is reactionary, decadent, and often intrusive, making a burden of the historical heritage. It is tolerated as a business, in a city that has a high regard for business . . . but it is only one of many. In Italy, Florentines are reckoned the most impenetrable, cautious, and circumspect of Italians, a reputation they have held since the days of the Medicis. Nevertheless, Italians have coined a word—*fiorentinità*—to refer to the good taste and fine workmanship that are flaunted here, in a city renowned for its leather goods, handbags, shoes, jewelry, and a host of famous brandnames. Pucci, Gucci, Ferragamo, Cellerini are just four of the high-profile craft-turned-fashion designers that exude *fiorentinità*. Neither are the region's cuisine and fine wines to be taken lightly. Talk to any Florentines about these present-day aspects of their civilization, and they will perk up and debate enthusiastically; mention their past glories and they will stifle a yawn.

Other Tuscan cities possess the same compelling mix of elements: What Tuscany's older centers share is an immaculate medieval setting, modern life taking place within the shell of the past; what divides them is a complex mental set. Needless to say, all of them were rivals at one time or another, and each prevailed in distinct spheres. Pisa, for example, was one of Italy's four great maritime republics, its architectural style visible wherever its ships touched port. Once the most powerful force in the Tyrrhenian, it lost its hegemony on the sea to its trading rival, Genoa, and, land, to Florence. Pisa owed its prestige to a university that bequeathed a scholarly, scientific, and legal tradition to the town, and to its location on the River Arno, though this position much later was responsible for its being one of the most devastated cities in World War II. Skillful rebuilding has ensured a relatively harmonious appearance, however, and the city would still hold plenty of interest if the Leaning Tower had never been built.

Livorno, on the other hand, the main Tuscan port of today, is the Pisa that never was. By Tuscan standards it is a recent affair, developed as a sea outlet for Florence after Pisa's port had silted up. Livorno reveals a highly un-Tuscan cosmopolitan character, a result of 16th-century growth that brought immigration. Livorno's most famous son, the sculptor Amedeo Modigliani, for example, was brought up speaking French, Italian, English, and Hebrew, though in other ways this hard-drinking Bohemian did not typify the soberly respectable citizens for whom Livorno is best known. Also heavily bombed in the war, the port was not restored as tastefully as Pisa, though it can at least boast a vigorous culinary tradition, with its range of fresh seafood.

SOUTH FROM LIVORNO stretches a riviera of varying degrees of summer saturation, including numerous select spots where sun- and sea-bathing can be enjoyed in relative peace. The island of Elba—scene of Napoléon's nine-month incarceration—is today more likely to be somewhere to escape to rather than from, and together with the islands of Giglio and Capraia offers everything from absurd overdevelopment to true isolation.

Lucca, the principal enemy of Pisa during the Middle Ages, has been called "the most enchanting walled town in the world." The city's formidable girdle of walls has resisted the intrusions of modern life better than any other Tuscan center and contains within a wealth of palaces and churches wildly out of proportion to the size of what is, after all, a small provincial town. Much of Lucca's present-day success is based on, of all things, the manufacture of lingerie.

A much weightier substance—gold—forms, together with antique furniture, the basis of the wealth of the less imposing town of Arezzo. Such worldly items again form a counterpoint to the fact that this town has produced more than its fair share of pioneers in literature (Petrarch, Pietro Aretino), art (Vasari), and music (Guido d'Arezzo, also called Guido Monaco, inventor of notation and the musical scale).

Arezzo shares a university with Siena, another Tuscan town preserved in the aspic of its medieval past. It is said that there are three subjects you should avoid if you're in a hurry while in Siena: wild pigs (a prized quarry for hunters), the Palio (an object of fanatical zeal), and the battle of Montanerti (Siena's moment of military glory—a perennial obsession). To the rest of Italy, Siena is best known for its banks and its mystics—a characteristically incompatible duo—though foreign visitors are more enchanted by the city's artworks, its easy pace of life, and the pleasing hue of its rose-colored buildings.

Prato and Pistoia, a short roll up the *autostrada* (toll highway) from Florence, have traditionally fallen within the sphere of that city's influence. Prato combines some choice examples of Renaissance art and architecture with a strong industrial identity, mainly based on its wool exports; Pistoia, on the other hand, was renowned for its ironwork, and its citizens for their murderous propensities.

ACROSS THE REGIONAL boundary in Umbria, the hilltop town of Perugia is dominated by the cold gothic stone of its major monuments, its secretive alleys and steps, yet its animating spirit is among the most progressive and trend-setting in Italy. Within its medieval walls the town hosts one of Europe's prime jazz festivals, a modern tradition that has taken its lead from the international Two Worlds festival at nearby Spoleto. As in Tuscany, modernity lives alongside medievalism in Umbria, a case not so much of collision as coexistence. In the same spirit, the imposing monuments of its towns were built by a new wealthy mercantile class in the teeth of almost uninterrupted warfare throughout the Middle Ages. Spoleto, Gubbio, and Orvieto owed their influence not so much to their continual brawling as to their interchange of goods and ideas. A university was founded in Perugia as early as 1308, and it was the small Umbrian town of Foligno that published the first edition of Dante's *Divine Comedy*. The belligerence of the age paralleled an intense spiritual activity, championed by such towering religious figures as St. Francis, St. Clare, St. Benedict, and the locally venerated St. Rita (as well as the more worldly St. Valentine)—a legacy nowhere so apparent as in the town of Assisi.

Although many of the urban centers of Tuscany and Umbria have cleanly defined boundaries beyond which the countryside abruptly begins, the towns harmonize with the surrounding landscape more closely than anywhere else in Italy. Even if devoid of museums or souvenir shops, the hinterland holds as much of the region's quintessential character as the cities of Tuscany and Umbria, and such unsung treasures as San Gimignano, Todi, and Bevagna are as revealing as anything seen in the galleries. This is your chance to immerse yourself in the region's less tangible pleasures, to rest your eyes on the gentle ochre stone of villages artfully situated above vine-strung, neatly terraced slopes. From the wine-producing hills of Chianti to the Carrara mountains where Michelangelo quarried to the soft contours of the Vale of Spoleto, the tidy cypress-speared landscape displays a weird inertia like some illustration from a fable. It has a geometric precision that underlines the strict rural economy practiced by the Tuscan and Umbrian peasants, for whom every tree has its purpose. The Tuscans in particular have long been considered the most skilled and intelligent of Italian farmers, having created for themselves a region that is largely self-sufficient, producing a little of everything, and excelling in certain areas, not least in wine-production, for which the Tuscans have nurtured one of the most dynamic wine regions of Italy.

Like the great examples of urban architecture, the country in Tuscany and Umbria presents, for the most part, an ordered, rational, controlled appearance. It is the crust of civilization concealing the greatest paradox of all in this heartland of reason and classical elegance. For buried underneath lies a much older, earthier civilization of which most visitors to the region are oblivious. In every respect the ancient Etruscan civilization that flourished here was opposed to the values of the Renaissance, its vital, animistic spirit murky, dark, and mysterious to us, mainly known from subterranean tombs and wall-paintings. Almost erased from the face of the earth by the Romans, the Etruscan culture—its centers scattered throughout Tuscany and Umbria (Perugia, Orvieto, Chiusi, Roselle, Vetulonia, Volterra, Cortona, Arezzo, Fiesole were the main ones)—was central to the history of Tuscany and Umbria. Like the Hermes Trimegistus incongruously placed on the marble pavement of Siena's cathedral, the Etruscans are a mischievous element amid the harmony of Renaissance Tuscany and Umbria. Their precise influence is unclear, but it may well turn out to have been the contentious and destructive spirit ever-present in the golden age of these regions, harassing, hindering, entangling. Alternatively, it may have been the restless worm of invention, the defiant individuality that brought about the triumph of art in the face of adversity—which is, after all, the greatest achievement of Tuscany and Umbria.

—*Robert Andrews*

Born and educated in England, writer/journalist Robert Andrews inherited his interest in Italy from his Italian mother. He contributes to Harpers & Queen, Time Out, *and other magazines as well as to travel books.*

WHAT'S WHERE

Florence

Florence, the "Athens of Italy" and the key to the Renaissance, hugs the banks of the Arno River where it lies folded in the emerald green hills of north-central Tuscany. Elegant and somewhat aloof, as if set apart by its past greatness, this historic center of European civilization still shares with Rome the honor of first place among Italian cities for the abundance and importance of its artistic works. Every street, square, and *vicolo* (alley) functions as a display window of Romanesque, Gothic, or Renaissance architecture in churches, palaces, and towers. Gaze at Michelangelo's towering *David*. Explore the Uffizi—shrine of the Renaissance—where you'll find Botticelli's and Raphael's most reverential Madonnas. Marvel at the magnificent chapels and homes (particularly the Palazzo Medici-Riccardi) of the Medici family, whose art patronage rocketed Florence to the forefront of the Renaissance. Impressive piazzas and an incomparable 15th-century skyline make outdoor sightseeing in Florence particularly rewarding. World-class stores and restaurants make shopping and dining memorable as well: perhaps you'll discover a gold necklace fashioned from a 19th-century watch,

enjoy the famous *bistecca alla fiorentina* (Florentine steak), or take a twilight stroll along the Arno. Such experiences can make up the stock of some of your most precious memories.

Tuscany

Without a doubt, Nature outdid herself in Tuscany. Punctuated by thickly wooded hills, snowcapped peaks, sun-warmed vineyards, olive groves, and dramatic hill towns, Tuscany's milk-and-honey vistas have changed little since Renaissance artists first beheld them. Not surprisingly, you'll find some of Italy's greatest art treasures here, including the 13th-century Leaning Tower of Pisa and Piero della Francesca's *Legend of the True Cross* frescoes in Arezzo. The time traveler will love Siena, "the Pompeii of the Middle Ages" (as it was called by the philosopher Taine). One of the best-preserved medieval towns, it is known both for its Gothic school of art and for the eponymous hue that tints its buildings. Every July and August, the city explodes in a frenzy of excitement at the historic Corsa del Palio (Parade of the Banner)—an all-day festival that culminates in the dizzying horse race at Piazza del Campo.

Escape to a celebrated Tuscan hill town—perched dramatically above a fertile valley—such as San Gimignano (with its Manhattan-like skyline of medieval towers) and experience the Who–turned-back-the-clock? sensation of Mark Twain's Connecticut Yankee when he arrived in King Arthur's court. With a glass of Vernaccia di San Gimignano in hand, you'll feel like lingering long.

Umbria and the Marches

Legends linger here in the evergreen land of the saints, the birthplace of St. Francis and St. Claire (Assisi), St. Benedict (Norcia), and St. Rita (Cascia). The strange, bluish haze that tints the landscape has inspired writers to characterize the region as mystical and ethereal. Here, medieval enclaves wear their ancient histories lightly, and majestic valleys refuse to pose for tourists' cameras. Umbria's rich artistic inheritance includes the frescoes of Giotto and Pietro Lorenzetti in Assisi's Basilica of St. Francis, the brooding Palazzo dei Consoli in Gubbio, and the Gothic glory of Orvieto's cathedral. For a "deep, delicious bath of medievalism," as Henry

James wrote, a visit to Assisi is an imperative; the spirit of St. Francis gently permeates the hillside town. For more urbane pleasures, head for Spoleto's celebrated Festival of Two Worlds or Perugia's popular jazz concerts. Eastward, in the off-the-beaten-track region of the Marches, is Urbino, where the Renaissance first came to full flower. It is full of treasures by such illustrious artists as Bramante, Raphael, and Piero della Francesca. A visit to its Ducal Palace reveals more about the wealth and artistic energy of the Renaissance than a shelf of history books.

PLEASURES AND PASTIMES

The Art of Enjoying Art

Travel veterans will tell you that the endless series of masterpieces in Italy's churches, palaces, and museums can cause first-time visitors—eyes glazed over from a heavy downpour of images, dates, and names—to lean, Pisa-like, on their companions for support. After a surfeit of Botticellis, and Bronzinos, and the 14th Raphael, even the miracle of the High Renaissance may begin to pall. The secret, of course, is to act like a turtle—not a hare—and take your sweet time. Instead of trotting after briskly efficient tour guides, allow the splendors of the age to unfold—slowly. Get out and explore the actual settings—medieval chapels, Rococo palaces, and Romanesque town squares—for which these marvelous examples of Italy's art and sculpture were conceived centuries ago and where many of them may still be seen in situ.

Musems are only the most obvious places to view art; there are always the trompe l'oeil renderings of Assumptions that float across Baroque church ceilings and piazza scenes that might be Renaissance paintings brought to life. Instead of studying a Gothic statue in Florence's Bargello, spend an hour in the medieval cloisters of the nearby convent of San Marco; by all means, take in Michelangelo's *Slaves* in Florence's Accademia, but then meander down the 15th-century street, a short bus ride away, where he was born. You'll find that after three days traipsing through

museums, a walk through a quiet neighborhood will act as a much-needed restorative of perspective. You'll even discover more artistic treasures along the streets of Italy than in many a museum back home.

To truly enjoy art, it also helps to know some basic vocabulary. Of course, there may be many art treasures that will not quicken your pulse, but one morning you may see a Caravaggio so perfect, so beautiful, that your knees will buckle.

Il Dolce Far Niente

When Italians work, they work harder than anyone—and when they play, they do that harder than anyone, too. After all, the idea of vacation was probably invented by some hardworking Roman emperor and, ever since, the Italians have been finetuning what they call il dolce far niente—the sweet art of idleness. Today, even relaxing can feel like a chore, but thanks to Italy's opulent villas, picture-perfect coastal resorts, and dreamy hill towns, you can idle here more successfully than anywhere else. Tourists could learn from the natives who just breathe in the beauty and relax. But it takes more than trading in a silk tie for a T-shirt; you have to adjust to the deeper, subtler rhythms of leisure, Italian-style. Unclocked hours spent over a Campari in a sun-splashed café, days spent soaking up the sun on the Amalfi coast, an afternoon spent painting a watercolor on the shores of Lake Como: You may be pleasantly surprised to find that such pursuits prove more beneficial than forced marches through the obligatory sights. Remember—the luxury is often in the lingering.

Dining

In Italy, cookery is civilization. In the days of the Roman legions, pundits used to say *"Ubi Roma ibi allium"* (Where there are Romans, there is garlic). Ever since the days of the Caesars—when emperors quickly learned the wisdom of *"Stomaco pieno, anima consolata"* (Full stomach, satisfied soul)—Italian chefs have taken one of life's sensory pleasures and made it into an art, and today travelers can feast on an incredible array of culinary delights. Of course, Italian food has come a long way since the days when Horace, the great poet of ancient Rome, feasted on lamprey boiled in five-year-old wine, the liver of a goose fattened on figs, and apples picked by the light of the waning moon. But you can still enter restaurants in Bologna, enjoy a dish of tortellini, and be told, *"Anche Dante le ha mangiato cósi"* (Dante also ate them this way). In fact, the newest trend in Italian cooking is to serve up the old—the simple, rustic, time-honored forms of cucina *simpatica, rustica,* and *trattoria*—with a nouvelle flair.

Among Italian chefs, there is concern that membership in the European Union will affect the country's unique regional cooking. The use of processed ingredients and nonorganically grown vegetables is taking its toll. Happily, food critics rejoice that much of Italian cooking remains *puro* and *sincero*—true to the country's culinary traditions.

Dining is a marvelous part of the total Italian experience, a chance to enjoy authentic specialties and ingredients. Visitors have a choice of eating places, ranging from a *ristorante* (restaurant) to a trattoria, *tavola calda,* or *rosticceria.* A trattoria is usually a family-run place, simpler in decor, menu, and service than a ristorante, and slightly less expensive. Some rustic-looking spots call themselves *osterie* but are really restaurants. (A true *osteria* is a wineshop—a basic, down-to-earth tavern.) The countless fast-food places opening everywhere are variations of the older Italian institutions of the tavola calda or rosticceria, which offer a selection of hot and cold dishes to be taken out or eaten on the premises. At either a tavola calda or rosticceria some items are priced by the portion, others by weight. You usually select your food, find out how much it costs, and then pay the cashier, who gives you a stub that you hand to the man at the counter when you pick up the food.

None of the above eateries serves breakfast; in the morning you go to a coffee bar, which is where you can also find sandwiches, pastries, and other snacks that are perfect for later in the day. Tell the cashier what you want, pay for it, and then take the stub to the counter, where you order. Remember that table service is extra; don't sit at a table unless you want to be served. On the other hand, if you do sit down, you'll be allowed to linger as long as you like.

In eating places of all kinds, the menu is posted in the window or just inside the door so you can see what you're getting into (in a snack bar or tavola calda the price list is usually displayed near the cashier). In all but the simplest places there's a *coperto* (cover charge) and usually also a *servizio* (service charge) of 10%–15%, only part of which goes to the waiter. A *menù turistico* (tourist menu) includes taxes and service, but beverages are usually extra.

Generally, a typical meal in a restaurant or trattoria consists of at least two courses: a first course of pasta, risotto, or soup; and a second course of meat or fish. Side dishes such as vegetables and salads cost extra, as do desserts. There is no such thing as a side dish of pasta; pasta is a course in itself and Italians would never think of serving a salad with it; the salad comes later. Years ago, pasta dishes were inexpensive because restaurateurs made their profit on the total of the first and second courses. Now, tourists and even some diet-conscious Italians tend to order only one course—usually a pasta, perhaps followed by a salad or vegetables—so hosts have jacked up the price of first courses. Now, about antipasto: Many a misunderstanding arises over a lavish offering of antipasto, which literally means "before the meal." No matter how generous and varied the antipasto, the host expects those who have one to order at least one other course. Pizza is in a category by itself and is a one-dish meal, even for the Italians. But some replace the starter course of pasta with a small pizza.

Tap water is safe almost everywhere unless labeled *"non potabile."* Most people order bottled *acqua minerale* (mineral water), either *gassata* (carbonated), or *naturale,* or *non gassata* (without bubbles). In a restaurant you order it by the *litro* (liter) or *mezzo litro* (half-liter); often the waiter will bring it without being asked, so if you don't like it, or want to keep your check down, make a point of ordering *acqua semplice* (tap water). You can also order *un bicchiere di acqua minerale* (a glass of mineral water) at any bar. If you are on a low-sodium diet, ask for everything (within reason) *senza sale* (without salt).

Lunch is served in Florence from 12:30 to 3:30, dinner from 7:30 to 10:30, or later in some restaurants. Service begins an hour earlier in smaller towns. Almost all eating places close one day a week and for vacations in summer and/or winter. *Buon appetito!*

Shopping

"Made in Italy" has become synonymous with style, quality, and craftsmanship whether it refers to high fashion or Maserati automobiles. The best buys are leather goods of all kinds—from gloves to bags to jackets—silk goods, knitwear, gold jewelry, ceramics, and local handicrafts. The most important thing to keep in mind when shopping in Italy is that every region has its specialties.

In general, the idea that bargaining is the rule in Italy is mistaken. There is no universal policy, but for the most part prices are fixed in the better shops. Where you see the sign PREZZI FISSI (fixed prices) you can be sure that there is no bargaining to be done. However, you can bargain to your heart's delight at outdoor markets and when buying from street vendors.

Unless your purchases are too bulky, avoid having them shipped home; if the shop seems extremely reliable about shipping, get a written statement of what will be sent, when, and how. (*See* Shopping *in* individual chapters for details.)

Spas

Thanks to its location in the Mediterranean region—one of the world's most active volcano belts—Italy is rich in thermo-mineral springs. Consequently, the Italians have developed a special attitude about what we call spas since the ancient Romans advanced the idea of *"mens sana in corpore sano"* (a sound mind in a healthy body). Perhaps old-fashioned today, taking the waters remains a unique part of Italian culture; it is state-supported and medically supervised. Never mind Greco-Roman worship of the body in temple-like baths, choices now range from antiaging cures to American-style aerobic workouts to fangotherapy (medicinal mud therapy). Today, more and more travelers are taking vacations from their vacations by visiting one of Italy's sybaritic spas.

But don't say spa (in Italian, s.p.a. denotes a business corporation). Forget the Roman origins: the term in Italy is *terme* (baths).

A peek into a typical Italian health resort can present an image worthy of Dante: a host of monkishly clad and mud-caked figures moving through mists of steam; these are health- and beauty-conscious aficionados enjoying a dizzying range of curative techniques. At over 200 of these centers, drinking and bathing cures are based on naturally produced thermal mineral waters, with mornings devoted to sipping and strolling as well as occasional forays into espresso bars. Then come hot mud packs, muscle massage, anticellulite treatments, and sinus-targeted steam inhalations.

Cura means "treatment," not miracle(s). After the obligatory evaluation by a staff doctor, a regimen is designed which allows plenty of time for sightseeing, jogging, and post-lunch shopping. If staying at a *terme* (spa) in places like Abano and Montecatini, you can add outings to nearby Etruscan ruins, country inns, and wineries.

Health Italian style comes in a variety of health, beauty, and antistress packages. Many of the new offerings at terme are based on old methods. Among them: therapeutic skin-care treatments using natural ingredients—flowers, fruits, muds, herbs, honey—in sophisticated salons devoted to *"benessere e bellezza"* (health and beauty); acupuncture, reflexology, shiatsu, facials, and colonic irrigations; longevity cures; and for *la buona figura* (healthy body), *dietetico* meals—based on light but delicious regional cuisine.

Increasingly, travelers to Italy are finding a visit to a thermal spa the best antidote for tourist fatigue, with many repeat visitors swearing by the benefits of particular waters (i.e. Terme Stabiane has 28 different springs). The pleasures at some are delightfully varied: you can sample the local acqua minerale while walking through a spa's park or garden accompanied by the strains of Puccini or Verdi. Here are some Tuscany's best healthy escapes.

Vineyards surround hillside terme where Tuscan food and wine can restore your spirits just in case the waters don't. Diversions range from golf to horse races, but hiking the unspoiled countryside—dotted with castles and Roman ruins—is the best way to discover the region's riches.

There is a wide range of spas from which to choose. Spadeus (⊠ Via le Piane 35, 53042 Chianciano Terme, ☎ 39/63232, FAX 39/64329) offers workouts with American fitness trainers and attracts people from all walks of life to Christina Newburgh's four-star hotel and Centro Benessere (Health Center). On site, you'll find an indoor Olympic-size pool, hydrotherapy, and medical services. With daily outings to ancient hill towns such as Montepulciano or Bagno Vignoni, you might forget to take the waters (closed mid-Dec.–Mar. 1). Grotta Giusti Terme (⊠ Via Grotta Giusti, 171, 51015 Monsummano, ☎ 39/51007) allows you to descend, dressed in a monk-like robe, to vapor caves that conjure up Dante's Inferno. Set in a vast park outside of Florence, the stone-arched villa has modern hydromassage, facials, and swimming pools. Here, the season runs from April to November.

The town of Montecatini Terme—Italy's most famous spa town—has it all: grand hotels and pensions, nightlife, sports, skin care, as well as traditional balneotherapy baths, fangotherapy, and drinking cures. Preventative and detoxicating treatments supervised by medical staff are optional, but don't miss the morning promenade at Tettuccio, one of the town's nine watering places and Italy's grandest temple of health. Perhaps the best place to stay is the five-star Grand Hotel e la Pace (⊠ Viale Delle Toretta 1, 51016, ☎ 39/75801, FAX 39/78451; closed November to March), where you can step back to a gilded age of princes and movie stars. Terme de Saturnia (⊠ 58050 Saturnia, ☎ 39/601061, FAX 39/601266) is set in a valley threaded with warm sulfuric waters. Here, aquarelaxation is combined with antistress programs; there are also new cosmetic treatments researched by staff scientists to ease the ravages of time. Thermal swimming pools and waterfalls, a gymnasium, and horseback excursions enhance this private retreat.

—*Bernard Burt*

Longtime spa buff, Bernard Burt is the author of Healthy Escapes: 240 Resorts and Retreats Where You Can Get Fit, Feel Good, Find Yourself and Get Away From It All *(Fodor's).*

NEW AND NOTEWORTHY

There's good news for those who plan to travel by rail or plane in Italy. FS, the Italian state railway, now provides **high-speed trains** for more destinations at reasonable rates. The ETR 460 Pendolino trains now serve Florence and other major cities, with additional destinations due to be added in 1997. The trains are fast and the fares are competitive. In the air, Alitalia's former monopoly on domestic travel has been shattered by some new and aggressively marketed airlines such as **Air One** and **Meridiana.** As a result, passengers are finding a wider range of bargain fares to choose from.

In **Florence,** the **Torre dei Pulci,** the 15th-century tower adjacent to the Uffizi that was gutted by a terrorist bomb in 1993, has been almost completely restored, and by 1997 it will once again house the headquarters of that historic cultural institution, the Accademia dei Georgofili. If you go to Florence, take a look at the tower, on a side street of Piazza degli Uffizi: Demolition work revealed that the exterior was originally painted to look like brickwork; restorers have reproduced the original effect.

The most popular after-dinner drink in 1997 will almost surely be the lemon-flavored liqueur called *limoncello,* available under many brand names in varying degrees of sweetness. Unknown to most until about a year ago, it is now the rage. The best comes from the Capri–Sorrento–Amalfi area, where it was originally made. It should be served ice-cold, and it supposedly aids digestion. In any case, it is delicious.

FODOR'S CHOICE

No two people agree on what makes a perfect vacation, but it's fun and helpful to know what others think. Here's a compendium drawn from the must-see lists of hundreds of Italian tourists. For detailed information about these memories-in-the-making, refer to the appropriate chapters in this book.

Quintessential Italy

★**Florence, Piazza della Signoria.** A Renaissance painting come to life, this piazza symbolizes all the grace, refinement, and power of the Renaissance. Nearby, discover Michelangelo's old neighborhood.

★**San Gimignano, Tuscany.** Stand on the steps of the Collegiata church at sunset as the swallows swoop in and out of the famous medieval towers, twittering softly as they coast on the air.

Dining Gem

★**Il Troia, Florence.** Florence has the best steaks in Italy and here you'll find the best *bistecca alla Fiorentina. $$*

Special Memory

★**Corso del Palio (Parade of the Banner), Siena.** Medieval pageantry and passion explode every July 2 and August 16 in this perfectly preserved city, when its historic Piazza del Campo becomes a racecourse for 17 horses.

Where Art Comes First

★**Accademia, Florence.** Compare the perfection of Michelangelo's *David* with the rough-hewn power of his struggling *Slaves.*

FESTIVALS AND SEASONAL EVENTS

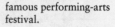

The region's top seasonal events are listed below, and any one of them could provide the stuff of lasting memories. Contact the **Italian Government Travel Office** for exact dates and further information.

WINTER

JAN. 5–6➣ **Epiphany Celebrations.** Roman Catholic Epiphany celebrations and decorations are evident throughout Italy.

SPRING

MAR. 30➣ The Easter Sunday **Scoppio del Carro,** or "Explosion of the Cart," in Florence, is the eruption of a cartful of fireworks in the Cathedral Square, set off by a mechanical dove released from the altar during High Mass.

LATE APR.–EARLY JULY➣ The **Florence May Music Festival** is the oldest and most prestigious Italian festival of the performing arts.

MID-MAY➣ **Race of the Candles.** This procession of bearers, in local costume, carrying towering wooden pillars, leads to the top of Mt. Ingino in Gubbio.

LATE MAY➣ The **Palio of the Archers** is a medieval crossbow contest in Gubbio.

SUMMER

EARLY JUNE➣ The **Battle of the Bridge,** in Pisa, is a medieval parade and contest.

LATE JUNE➣ **Soccer Games in 16th-Century Costume,** in Florence, commemorate a match played in 1530. Festivities include fireworks displays.

LATE JUNE–EARLY JULY➣ The **Festival of Two Worlds,** in Spoleto, is a famous performing-arts festival.

EARLY JULY AND MID-AUG.➣ The **Palio Horse Race,** in Siena, is a colorful bareback horse race with participants competing for the *palio* (banner).

EARLY AUG.➣ The **Joust of the Quintana** is a historical pageant in Ascoli Piceno.

LATE AUG.–EARLY SEPT.➣ The **Siena Music Week** features opera, concerts, and chamber music.

AUTUMN

EARLY SEPT.➣ The **Joust of the Saracen** is a tilting contest with knights in 13th-century armor in Arezzo.

MID-SEPT.➣ The **Joust of the Quintana** is a 17th-century-style joust and historical procession in Foligno.

OCT. 4➣ The **Feast of St. Francis** is celebrated in Assisi, his birthplace.

2　Florence

Birthplace of the Renaissance, Florence has been a mecca for travelers since the 19th century, when English ladies flocked here to stay in charming pensiones and paint romantic watercolors. They were captivated by a wistful Botticelli smile, impressed by the graceful dignity of Donatello's bronze David, *and moved by Michelangelo's provocative* Slaves *twisting restlessly in their marble prisons. Since then, millions have followed in their footsteps.*

FLORENCE IS ONE OF THE PREEMINENT TREASURES of Europe, and it is a time-honored mecca for sightseers from all over the world. But as a city, it can be surprisingly forbidding—at first glance. Its architecture is predominantly Early Renaissance and retains many of the implacable, fortresslike features of pre-Renaissance palazzi, whose facades were mostly meant to keep intruders out rather than to invite sightseers in. With the exception of a very few buildings, the classical dignity of the High Renaissance and the exuberant invention of the Baroque are not to be found here. The typical Florentine exterior gives nothing away, as if obsessively guarding secret treasures within.

The treasures, of course, are very real. And far from being a secret, they are famous the world over. The city is an artistic treasure trove of unique and incomparable proportions. A single historical fact explains the phenomenon: Florence gave birth to the Renaissance. In the early 15th century the study of antiquity—of the glory that was Greece and the grandeur that was Rome—became a Florentine passion, and with it came a new respect for learning and a new creativity in art and architecture. In Florence, that remarkable creativity is everywhere in evidence.

Though there had been a town here since Roman times, it wasn't until the 11th and 12th centuries that Florence started to make its mark. At this time Florentine cloth began to do particularly well in foreign markets, the various trades organized themselves in powerful unions (or *arti*), and the Florentines took over as the most important bankers in Europe thanks to their florin-based currency. They were perpetually at loggerheads with other Tuscan towns, such as Pisa and Siena, and this is why Florence has such a defensive air, and why its cathedral—the town's symbol—is so huge: It had to be bigger and more splendid than anyone else's. They kept expanding, despite periodic devastating plagues, and equally destructive civil strife. (One of the victims of the internal rift was the great poet Dante, author of the *Divine Comedy*, who happened to be on the losing side; he died in exile, cursing his native town.)

Meanwhile the banking families became more and more powerful, and in the early 15th century one of them, the Medici, began to outstrip all others. The most famous of them, Lorenzo de' Medici, was not only an astute politician, he was also a highly educated man and a great patron of the arts. He gathered around him, in the late 15th century, a court of poets, artists, philosophers, architects, and musicians, and organized all kinds of cultural events, festivals, and tournaments. It was Florence's golden period of creativity, when art made great leaps toward a new naturalism through the study of perspective and anatomy, when architects forged a new style based on the techniques used by the ancient Romans. The Renaissance man was born, a man who, like Leonardo da Vinci, could design a canal, paint a fresco, or solve a mathematical problem with equal ease.

Things changed with Lorenzo's death in 1492. First, his successor handed over most of Florence's key territories to the invading French king, Charles VIII, and then the city was sacked by the French army. A "republic" was set up, and one of its most vocal citizens was a charismatic, hellfire-preaching Dominican monk, Savonarola, who activated a moral cleanup operation to which the Florentines took with fanatical enthusiasm. He himself was accused of heresy and burned at the stake. After a decade or so of internal unrest, the Republic fell and the Medici were recalled to power. But even with the Medici back, Florence never regained its former prestige. By the 1530s all the major artistic talent had left the city—Michelangelo, for one, had settled in Rome. The now ineffectual Medici, calling themselves grand dukes, remained nominally in power until the line died out in 1737, and thereafter Florence passed from the Austrians to the French and back again, until the mid-19th-century unification of Italy, when for seven years it became the capital of Italy under King Vittorio Emanuele II.

Florence—Firenze in Italian—was "discovered" in the 19th century by the first art historians. It became a mecca for travelers, particularly the Romantics, including Keats and Shelley, who were inspired by the grandeur of its classicism and the elegance of its child, the Renaissance. It was also the favorite city of those English ladies of the *Room-with-a-View* type, who flocked here to stay in charming pensiones and paint romantic watercolors of the surrounding countryside. For them, the allure of Florence lay in its artistic treasures: They were captivated by a wistful Botticelli smile, impressed by the graceful dignity of Donatello's bronze *David,* and moved by Michelangelo's provocative Slaves twisting restlessly in their marble prisons. Today, millions of modern visitors follow in their footsteps. As the sun sets over the Arno and, as Mark Twain described it, "overwhelms Florence with tides of color that make all the sharp lines dim and faint and turn the solid city to a city of dreams," it's hard not to fall under the city's magic spell.

Pleasures and Pastimes

Art

No city in Italy can match Florence's astounding artistic wealth. Important paintings and sculptures are everywhere, and art scholars and connoisseurs have been investigating the subtleties and complexities of these works for hundreds of years. But what makes the art of Florence a revelation to the ordinary sightseer is a simple fact that scholarship often ignores: An astounding percentage of Florence's art is just plain beautiful. Nowhere in Italy—perhaps in all of Europe—is the act of looking at art more rewarding.

Dining

Florentines are justifiably proud of their robust food, claiming that it became the basis for French cuisine when Catherine de' Medici took a battery of Florentine chefs with her when she reluctantly relocated to become Queen of France in the 16th century. You can sample such specialties as *fagioli al fiasco* (slow-cooked beans) and *ribollita* (a thick soup of white beans, bread, cabbage, and onions) in bustling trattorias where you share long wooden tables set with paper place mats. The casual, convivial atmosphere in these places puts you in the Florentine mode. Like the Florentines, take a break at a wineshop during the day and discover some little-known but excellent types of Chianti.

Lodging

Whether you are in a five-star hotel or a more modest establishment you may have one of the greatest pleasures of all: a room with a view. Florence has so many famous landmarks that it's not hard to find lodgings with a vista to remember. And the equivalent of the genteel pensiones of yesteryear still exist, though they are now officially classified as hotels. Usually small and intimate, they often have a quaint appeal that fortunately does not preclude modern plumbing.

Shopping

Since the days of the medieval guilds, Florence has been synonymous with fine craftsmanship and good business. Such time-honored Florentine specialties as antiques (and reproductions), bookbinding, jewelry, lace, leather goods, silk, and straw attest to that. More recently, the Pitti fashion shows and the burgeoning textile industry in nearby Prato have added fine clothing to the long list of merchandise available in the shops of Florence.

Another medieval feature is the distinct feel of the different shopping areas, a throwback to the days when each district supplied a different product. Florence's most elegant shops are concentrated in the center of town, with Via Tornabuoni and the Galleria Tornabuoni, the world's chicest shopping mall, leading the list for designer clothing. Borgo Ognissanti and Via Maggio across the river have the city's largest concentration of antiques shops, and the Ponte Vecchio houses the city's jewelers, as it has since the 16th century. Boutiques abound on Via della Vigna Nuova and in the trendy area around the church of Santa Croce, heart of the leather merchants' district. In the less-specialized, more residential area near the Duomo and in Florence's trendiest area, the Oltrarno, just about everything goes on sale.

Those with a tight budget or a sense of adventure may want to take a look at the souvenir stands under the loggia of the Mercato Nuovo, the stalls that line the streets between the church of San Lorenzo and the Mercato Centrale, the Flea Market on Piazza dei Ciompi, or the open-air market that takes place in the Cascine park every Tuesday morning. A crafts fair is held in Piazza Santo Spirito on the first Sunday of the month.

EXPLORING FLORENCE

Sightseeing in Florence is space-intensive. Everything that you probably want to see is concentrated in a relatively small district in the historic core of the city. But there is so much packed into the area that you may find yourself slogging from one mind-boggling sight to another until your perception numbs and you become oblivious to beauty. A few words of warning are in order here. For some years now, Florentine psychiatrists have recognized a peculiar local malady to which foreign tourists are particularly susceptible. It's called "Stendhal's syndrome," after the 19th-century French novelist, who was the first to describe it in print. The symptoms can be severe: confusion, dizziness, disorientation, depression, and sometimes persecution anxiety and loss of identity. Some victims immediately suspect food poisoning, but the true diagnosis is far more outlandish. They are suffering from art poisoning, brought on by overexposure to so-called Important Works of High Culture. Consciously or unconsciously, they seem to view Florentine art as an exam (Aesthetics 101, 10 hours per day, self-taught, pass/fail), and they are terrified of flunking.

Obviously, the art of Florence should not be a test. So if you are not an inveterate museumgoer or church collector with established habits and methods, take it easy. Don't try to absorb every painting or fresco that comes into view. There is second-rate art even in the Uffizi and the Pitti (*especially* the Pitti), so find some favorites and enjoy them at your leisure. Getting to know a few paintings well will be far more enjoyable than seeing a vast number on the run.

And when fatigue begins to set in, stop. Take time off, and pay some attention to the city itself. Too many first-time visitors trudge dutifully from one museum to the next without really seeing what is in between. They fail to notice that Florence is a living, breathing phenomenon: a bustling metropolis that has managed to preserve its predominantly medieval street plan and predominantly Renaissance infrastructure while successfully adapting to the insistent demands of 20th-century

life. The resulting marriage between the very old and the very new is
not always tranquil, but it is always fascinating. Florence the city can
be chaotic, frenetic, and full of uniquely Italian noise, but it is alive in
a way that Florence the museum, however beautiful, is not. Do not
miss the forest for the trees. And, speaking of forests, during the
Guelph–Ghibelline conflict of the 13th and 14th centuries, Florence
was a forest of towers—more than 200 of them, if the smaller three-
and four-story towers are included. Today only a handful survive, but
if you look closely you'll find them as you explore the city's core.

Great Itineraries

You can see most of Florence's outstanding sights in three days. Plan
your day around the opening hours of museums and churches; to gain
a length on the tour groups in high season, go very early in the morning or toward closing time. If you can, allow a day to explore each of
the neighborhoods indicated in this chapter.

*Numbers in the text correspond to numbers in the margin and on the
Florence map.*

IF YOU HAVE 3 DAYS

Start from the Duomo, magnificent monument to Florentine pride, and
pause at the Battistero doors in which Michelangelo saw Paradise, before heading for the Museo dell'Opera del Duomo for a look at some
of the art that once graced the cathedral, including one of Michelangelo's three *Pietás*. Then head for Palazzo della Signoria and Palazzo
Vecchio, seat of civic power in Florence since the Middle Ages. From
there it's just a few steps to the Uffizi and its world-class collections
of Renaissance art. Walk across the Ponte Vecchio and back again to
the Mercato Nuovo for some shopping. On the second day, get an early
start, because the Medici Chapels and the Museo di San Marco close
at 2. Visit San Lorenzo and see Michelangelo's sculptures in the Cappelle Medicee (Medici Chapels) before making your way through the
San Lorenzo outdoor market (you can come back later; the stalls are
open in the afternoon) to Palazzo Medici-Riccardi, where you can ad-
mire the small but lavishly frescoed Cappella dei Magi (Chapel of Magi).
Then head for the Museo di San Marco and Fra Angelico's delightful
paintings of Madonnas, saints, and angels. By that time, the tour
groups should have thinned out at the Accademia, giving you an uncluttered view of Michelangelo's *David*. This leaves you much of the
afternoon for another walk, perhaps to Santa Croce, or Santa Maria
Novella. On the third day, cross the Arno on Ponte Vecchio and explore the Oltrarno district, starting with Pitti Palace and the Boboli Gardens and taking in the Brunelleschi-designed church of Santo Spirito
and Masaccio's frescoes in the church of Santa Maria del Carmine, along
with a lot of the local color of the trendy but unspoiled Oltrarno. In
the afternoon visit either Santa Croce or Santa Maria Novella.

IF YOU HAVE 5 DAYS

Break down the above itineraries into shorter ones, adding a few of
the optionals, such as Piazzale Michelangelo—where the picture-post-
card view of the city is yours to savor—and San Miniato, or the Cenacolo di Sant'Apollonia. When visiting the Duomo, climb Giotto's
Campanile, which also affords breathtaking views of the city. Take a
bus to Fiesole. Spend more time in the Uffizi and Bargello or one of
the smaller museums such as the Museo dell'Opificio delle Pietre Dure
and the Museo di Santa Maria Novella.

IF YOU HAVE 8 DAYS

Follow the five-day itinerary, but add an all-day excursion to Siena or
a couple of half-day trips to the Medici villas around Florence. Visit

more of Florence's interesting smaller churches, including Santa Maria Maddalena dei Pazzi and the Cenacolo di Sant'Appollonia.

The Historic Heart of Florence: From the Duomo to the Boboli Gardens

To say that Florence's historic center, stretching from the Piazza del Duomo in the north to the Boboli Gardens across the Arno to the south, is beautiful, could be misconstrued as an understatement. Indeed, this relatively small area is home to some of the most important artistic treasures in the world. This smorgasbord of churches, medieval towers, Renaissance *palazzi* (palaces), and world-class museums and galleries is not a static testimony to the artistic and architectural genius of the past millenium, but a living, breathing shrine to some of the most outstanding aesthetic achievements of Western history, challenging both the mind and the heart to come away untouched. Believe us, it cannot be done.

A Good Walk

Start at the **Duomo** ① and **Battistero** ②, climbing the **Campanile** ③ if you wish, then visit the **Museo dell'Opera del Duomo** ④, behind the Duomo. You can go directly to the Piazza della Signoria by way of Via Calzaiuoli, passing **Orsanmichele** ⑤, or make a detour along Via del Proconsolo to the **Bargello** ⑥ (opposite the ancient Badia Fiorentina, built in 1285), before discovering the architectural splendors of the **Piazza della Signoria** ⑦, including the Loggia dei Lanzi and the **Palazzo Vecchio** ⑧. The **Palazzo degli Uffizi** ⑨, Italy's most important art gallery, is just off the piazza. Leave the piazza from the southwest corner along Via Vacchereccia. At the corner with Via Por Santa Maria (which is lined with stores) is the **Mercato Nuovo** ⑩, whose stalls are packed with typical Florentine wares. Follow Via Por Santa Maria to the river and Florence's most famous bridge, the **Ponte Vecchio** ⑪.

TIMING

Before much of the historic heart of Florence was closed to traffic, you had to keep dodging passing cars and mopeds as you walked the narrow streets. Now you have to elbow your way through moving masses of fellow-tourists, especially in the neighborhood delimited by the Duomo, Piazza Signoria, Uffizi, and Ponte Vecchio. It takes about 40 minutes to walk the route, with 45 minutes to one hour each for the Museo dell'Opera del Duomo and for Palazzo della Signoria; one to 1½ hours for the Bargello and a minimum of two hours for the Uffizi. To avoid the crowds, you may want to make this walk in the afternoon, when all the sights and museums (except the Bargello) are open.

A special museum ticket valid for six months at seven city museums, including the Palazzo Vecchio, the Museum of Firenze Com'Era (Museum of Florentine History), and the Museum of Santa Maria Novella, costs 10,000 lire and is a good buy if you're planning to do some of these museums. Inquire at any city museum.

Sights to See

Badia Fiorentina. This ancient church was built in 1285; its graceful bell tower (best seen from the interior courtyard) is one of the most beautiful in Florence. The interior of the church proper was half-heartedly remodeled in the Baroque style during the 17th century; its best-known work of art is Filippino Lippi's delicate *Apparition of the Virgin to St. Bernard* (1486), on the left as you enter. The painting—one of Lippi's finest—is in superb condition and is worth exploring in detail. The Virgin's hands are perhaps the most beautiful in the city. (To illuminate, drop a coin in the box near the floor to the painting's right). ⊠ *Via del Proconsolo.*

18

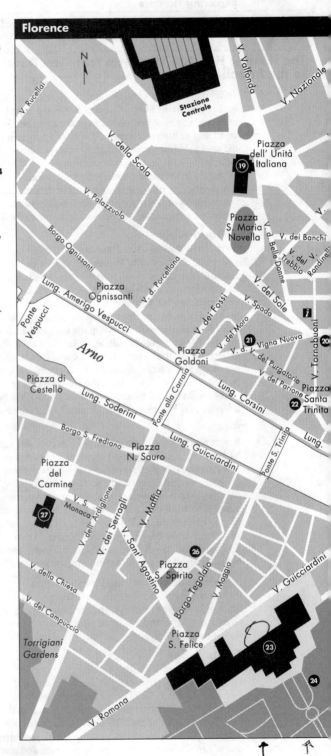

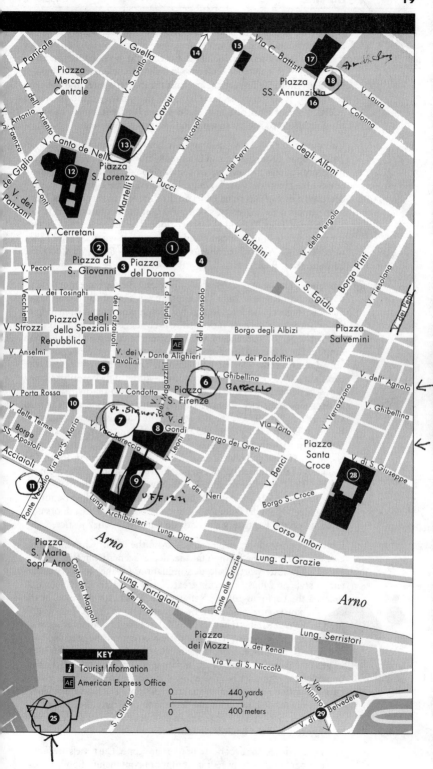

V. Panicale

V. Guelfa

V. C. Battisti

Via C. Battisti

14

15

17

Amlishog

Piazza
Mercato
Centrale

V. S. Gallo

18

Piazza
SS. Annunziata

V. Laura

V. dell' Ariento

V. S. Antonio

V. Faenza

V. Cavour

V. Ricasoli

16

V. Colonna

del Giglio

V. Canto de Nelli

12

Piazza
S. Lorenzo

13

V. dei Servi

V. degli Alfani

V. Conti

V. dei Panzani

V. Martelli

V. Pucci

V. della Pergola

V. Cerretani

V. Bufalini

Borgo Pinti

V. Fiesolana

1

V. Pecori

Piazza di
S. Giovanni

3

2

Piazza
del Duomo

4

Borgo degli Albizi

V. S. Egidio

Piazza
Salvemini

V. dei Tosinghi

V. Vecchietti

V. d. Studio

V. del Proconsolo

V. Strozzi

Piazza
della
Repubblica

V. degli
Speziali

V. dei Calzaioli

AE

V. Anselmi

V. dei
Tavolini

V. Dante Alighieri

V. dei Pandolfini

V. dell' Agnolo

5

6

Ghibellina

BARGELLO

V. Porta Rossa

V. Condotta

Piazza
S. Firenze

V. Ghibellina

10

PL. SIGNORIA

7

V. d.
Gondi

8

V. Leoni

Via Torta

V. Verrazzano

V. delle Terme

Borgo
SS. Apostoli

V. Vacchereccia

Borgo dei Greci

Piazza
Santa
Croce

V. di S. Giuseppe

Acciaioli

Via Por S. Maria

9

V. dei Neri

V. Benci

28

11

UFFIZI

Borgo S. Croce

Ponte Vecchio

Lung. Archibusieri

Lung. Diaz

Corso Tintori

Piazza
S. Maria
Sopr' Arno

Arno

Lung. d. Grazie

Costa dei Magnoli

Lung. Torrigiani

V. dei Bardi

Ponte alle Grazie

Arno

Lung. Serristori

Piazza
dei Mozzi

V. dei Renai

Via V. di S. Niccolò

V. S. Miniato

KEY

ℹ️ Tourist Information

AE American Express Office

0   440 yards

0   400 meters

V. S. Giorgio

25

V. del Belvedere

29

★ ❻ **Bargello.** During the Renaissance this building was used as a prison, and the exterior served as a "most-wanted" billboard: Effigies of notorious criminals and Medici enemies were painted on its walls. Today, it houses the **Museo Nazionale,** home to what is probably the finest collection of Renaissance sculpture in Italy. Michelangelo, Donatello, and Benvenuto Cellini are the preeminent masters here, and the concentration of masterworks is remarkable, though they stand among an eclectic array of arms, ceramics, and enamels. For Renaissance art lovers, the Bargello is to sculpture what the Uffizi is to painting.

One particular display—easily overlooked—should not be missed. In 1402 Filippo Brunelleschi and Lorenzo Ghiberti competed to earn the most prestigious commission of the day: the decoration of the north doors of the baptistery in Piazza del Duomo. For the competition, each designed a bronze bas-relief panel on the theme of the Sacrifice of Isaac; both panels are on display, side by side, in the room devoted to the sculpture of Donatello on the upper floor. The judges chose Ghiberti for the commission; you can decide for yourself whether or not they were right. ⊠ *Via del Proconsolo 4,* ☎ *055/238–8606.* ☞ *8,000 lire.* ☉ *Tues.–Sun. 9–2.*

★ ❷ **Battistero.** The octagonal baptistery is one of the supreme monuments of the Italian Romanesque. The Baptistery is one of the oldest buildings in Florence, and local legend has that it was once a Roman temple of Mars; modern excavations, however, suggest its foundation was laid in the 6th or 7th century AD, well after the collapse of the Roman Empire. The round-arched Romanesque decoration on the exterior probably dates from the 11th or 12th century. The interior ceiling mosaics (finished in 1297) are justly famous, but—glitteringly beautiful as they are—they could never outshine the building's most renowned feature: its bronze Renaissance doors decorated with panels crafted by Lorenzo Ghiberti (1378–1455). The doors, on which Ghiberti spent most of his adult life (from 1403 to 1452), are on the north and east sides of the baptistery—at least copies of them are—while the south door panels, in the Gothic style, were designed by Andrea Pisano in 1330. The originals of the Ghiberti doors were removed to protect them from the effects of pollution and acid rain and have been beautifully restored; some of the panels are now on display in the Cathedral Museum (☞ Museo dell'Opera del Duomo, *below*). The copy of the east doors now installed on the Baptistery does not do Ghiberti's work justice.

Ghiberti's north doors depict scenes from the life of Christ; his later east doors, facing the Duomo facade, depict scenes from the Old Testament. They are worth a close examination, for they are very different in style and illustrate with great clarity the artistic changes that marked the beginning of the Renaissance. Look, for instance, at the far right panel of the middle row on the earlier north doors (*Jesus Calming the Waters*). Ghiberti here captured the chaos of a storm at sea with great skill and economy, but the artistic conventions he used are basically pre-Renaissance: Jesus is the most important figure, so he is the largest; the disciples are next in size, being next in importance; the ship on which they founder is a mere toy. But you can sense Ghiberti's impatience with these artificial spatial conventions. The Cathedral Works Committee made him retain the decorative quatrefoil borders of the south doors for his panels here, and in this scene Ghiberti's storm seems to want to burst the bounds of its frame.

On the east doors, the decorative borders are gone. The panels are larger, more expansive, more sweeping, and more convincing. Look, for example, at the middle panel on the left-hand door. It tells the story of Jacob and Esau, and the various episodes of the story (the selling of the birthright, Isaac ordering Esau to go hunting, the blessing of Jacob, and so forth) have been merged into a single beautifully realized street scene. A perspective grid is employed to suggest depth, the background architecture looks far more convincing than on the north door panels, the figures in the foreground are grouped realistically, and the naturalism and grace of the poses (look at Esau's left leg) have nothing to do with the sacred message being conveyed. Although the religious content remains, man and his place in the natural world are given new prominence and are portrayed with a realism not seen in art since the fall of the Roman Empire, more than a thousand years before.

When Ghiberti was working on these panels, three of his artist friends were bringing the same new humanistic focus to their own very different work. In sculpture, Donato di Niccolò Betto Bardi, known as Donatello, was creating statuary for churches all over town; in painting, Tommaso di Ser Giovanni, known as Masaccio, was executing frescoes at the churches of Santa Maria del Carmine and Santa Maria Novella; in architecture, Filippo Brunelleschi was building the Duomo dome, the Ospedale degli Innocenti, and the church interiors of San Lorenzo and Santo Spirito. They are the fathers of the Renaissance in art and architecture—the four great geniuses who created a new artistic vision—and among them they began a revolution that was to make Florence the artistic capital of Italy for more than a hundred years.

As a footnote to Ghiberti's panels, one small detail of the east doors is worth a special look. Just to the lower left of the Jacob and Esau panel, Ghiberti placed a tiny self-portrait bust. From either side, the portrait is extremely appealing—Ghiberti looks like everyone's favorite uncle—but the bust is carefully placed so that there is a single spot in front of the doors from which you can make direct eye contact with the tiny head. When that contact is made, the impression of intelligent life—of *modern* intelligent life—is astonishing. It is no wonder that when these doors were completed, they received one of the most famous compliments in the history of art, from a competitor known to be notoriously stingy with praise: Michelangelo himself declared them so beautiful that they could serve as the Gates to Paradise. ⌂ *Free to Baptistery interior.* ☉ *Mon.–Sat. 1:30–6, Sun. 9–1:30.*

❸ **Campanile.** Giotto's bell tower is a shaft of multicolor marble decorated with reliefs now in the Museo dell'Opera del Duomo. A climb of 414 steps rewards you with a close-up of Brunelleschi's dome and a sweeping view of the city. ⌂ *8,000 lire* ☉ *Apr.–Oct., Mon–Sat. 9–6:30; Nov.–Mar. 9–4:20.*

★ ❶ **Duomo.** The historical heart of Florence is Piazza Duomo, the square surrounding the city's majestic Cathedral of Santa Maria del Fiore, more familiarly known as the Duomo. Don't be surprised if you feel overpowered on seeing the cathedral: it's the fourth largest in the world. In 1296 Arnolfo di Cambio was commissioned to build "the loftiest, most sumptuous edifice human invention could devise" in the newest Romanesque style on the site of the old church of Santa Reparata. The immense Duomo was not completed until 1436, the year when it was consecrated. The imposing facade dates only from the 19th century; it was added in the neo-Gothic style to complement Giotto's genuine Gothic (14th-century) campanile. The real glory of the Duomo, however, is Filippo Brunelleschi's dome, herald of the new Renaissance in architecture, which hovers over the cathedral (and the entire city, when seen from afar) with a dignity and grace that few domes, even to this day, can match. It was the first of its kind in the world, and for many people it is still the best.

Brunelleschi's **dome** was epoch-making as an engineering feat, as well. The space to be enclosed by the dome was so large and so high above the ground that traditional methods of dome construction—wooden centering and scaffolding—were of no use whatever. So Brunelleschi developed entirely new building methods, which he implemented with equipment of his own devising (including the modern crane). Beginning work in 1420, he built not one dome but two, one inside the other, and connected them with common ribbing that stretched across the intervening empty space, thereby considerably lessening the crushing weight of the structure. He also employed a new method of bricklaying, based on an ancient Roman herringbone pattern, interlocking each new course of bricks with the course below in a way that made the growing structure self-supporting. The result was one of the great engineering breakthroughs of all time: Most of Europe's great domes, including St. Peter's in Rome, were built employing Brunelleschi's methods, and today the Duomo has come to symbolize Florence in the same way that the Eiffel Tower symbolizes Paris. The Florentines are justly proud, and to this day the Florentine phrase for "homesick" is *nostalgia del cupolone* (homesick for the dome).

The interior is a fine example of Italian Gothic, although anyone who has seen the Gothic cathedrals of France will be disappointed by its lack of dramatic verticality. Italian architecture, even at the height of the Gothic era, never broke entirely free of the influence of Classical Rome, and its architects never learned (perhaps never wanted to learn) how to make their interiors soar like the cathedrals in the cities around Paris.

Much of the cathedral's best-known art has been moved to the nearby **Cathedral Museum** (☞ *below*). Notable among the works that remain, however, are two equestrian frescoes honoring famous soldiers: Andrea del Castagno's *Niccolò da Tolentino,* painted in 1456, and Paolo Uccello's *Sir John Hawkwood,* painted 20 years earlier; both are on the left-hand wall of the nave. *Niccolò da Tolentino* is particularly impressive: He rides his fine horse with military pride and wears his even finer hat—surely the best in town—with panache. It took restorers more than a decade from 1983 to 1995 to restore the structure of Brunelleschi's dome and clean the vast and crowded fresco of the *Last Judgment*—painted by Vasari and Zuccaro—on its interior. Originally, Brunelleschi wanted mosaics to cover the interior of the great ribbed cupola, but by the time the Florentines got around to commissioning the decoration, 150 years later, tastes had changed.

If time permits, you may want to explore the upper and lower reaches of the cathedral, as well. Ancient remains have been excavated beneath the nave; the stairway down is near the first pier on the right. The climb to the top of the dome (463 steps) is not for the fainthearted, but once there the view is superb; the entrance is on the left wall just before the crossing. ⊠ *Piazza del Duomo,* ☎ *055/230–2885. Duomo* ☉ *Weekdays 9–6, Sat. 8:30–5 (first Sat. of month 8:30–3:20).* ▣ *Excavation: 3,000 lire.* ☉ *Mon.–Sat. 10–5.* ▣ *Ascent to dome: 8,000 lire.* ☉ *Weekdays 9:30–5:30, Sat. 9:30–5 (first Sat. of month 9:30–3:20).*

⑩ Mercato Nuovo (New Market). This open-air loggia was new in 1551. Today it harbors mostly souvenir stands; its main attraction is Pietro Tacca's bronze *Porcellino* (Piglet) fountain on the south side, dating from around 1612 and copied from an earlier Roman work now in the Uffizi. Rubbing its drooling snout is a Florentine tradition—it is said to bring good luck. ⊠ *Corner of Via Por San Maria and Via Porta Rossa.*

★ **④ Museo dell'Opera del Duomo (Cathedral Museum).** The major attractions here—other than the originals of the Ghiberti door panels mentioned earlier and the *cantorie* (choir loft) reliefs by Donatello and Luca della Robbia—are two: Donatello's *Mary Magdalen* and Michelangelo's *Pietà* (not to be confused with his more famous *Pietà* in St. Peter's, in Rome). The High Renaissance in sculpture is in part defined by its revolutionary realism, but Donatello's *Magdalen* goes beyond realism: It is suffering incarnate. Michelangelo's heart-wrenching *Pietà* was unfinished at his death; the female figure supporting the body of Christ on the left was added by one Tiberio Calcagni, and never has the difference between competence and genius been manifested so clearly. ⊠ *Piazza del Duomo 9,* ☎ *055/230–2885.* ⊠ *8,000 lire.* ☉ *Mar.–Oct., Mon.–Sat. 9–6:50; Nov.–Feb., Mon.–Sat. 9–5:20.*

❺ Orsanmichele. This church, containing a beautifully detailed 14th-century Gothic tabernacle by Andrea Orcagna, was originally a granary. The building was transformed in 1336 into a church with 14 exterior niches. Each of the major Florentine trade guilds was assigned its own niche and paid for the sculpture the niche was to contain. The niches soon held works by Florence's most talented sculptors. Unfortunately, the best have been removed and replaced with copies. The originals will eventually be placed in a museum, perhaps even in Orsanmichele. Even so, all the statues are worth examining. One of those removed—Andrea del Verrocchio's *Doubting Thomas* (circa 1470)—was particularly deserving of scrutiny. Were the niche not empty, you would see Christ, like the building's other figures, entirely framed within the niche, and St. Thomas standing on its bottom ledge, with his right foot outside the niche frame. This one detail, the positioning of a single foot, brought the whole composition to life. It is particularly appropriate that this is the only niche to be topped with a Renaissance pediment, for it is the revolutionary vitality of sculpture like this that gave the Renaissance its name. ⊠ *Free.* ☉ *Daily, 9–12, 4–6.*

★ ❾ Palazzo degli Uffizi. The **Galleria degli Uffizi** occupies the top floor of this U-shape building fronting on the Arno, designed by Vasari in 1559 to hold the administrative offices of Medici duke Cosimo I—"*uffizi*" means "offices" in Italian. And here later Medicis installed their art collections, creating what was Europe's first modern museum, open to the public (at first only by request, of course) since 1591. Today the palazzo houses the finest collection of paintings in Italy. Hard-core museumgoers will want to pick up a complete guide to the collections, sold in bookshops and on newsstands, before they go.

The collection's highlights include Paolo Uccello's *Battle of San Romano* (its brutal chaos of lances is one of the finest visual metaphors for warfare ever committed to paint); Fra Filippino Lippi's *Madonna and Child with Two Angels* (the foreground angel's bold, impudent eye contact would have been unthinkable prior to the Renaissance); Sandro Botticelli's *Primavera* (its nonrealistic fairy-tale charm exhibits the painter's idiosyncratic genius at its zenith); Leonardo da Vinci's *Adoration of the Magi* (unfinished and perhaps the best opportunity in Europe to investigate the methods of a great artist at work); Raphael's *Madonna of the Goldfinch* (darkened by time, but the tenderness with which the figures in the painting touch each other is undimmed); Michelangelo's *Holy Family* (one of the very few easel works in oil he ever painted, clearly reflecting his stated belief that draftsmanship is a necessary ingredient of great painting); Rembrandt's *Self-Portrait as an Old Man* (which proves that even Michelangelo could, on occasion, be wrong); Titian's *Venus of Urbino* and Caravaggio's *Bacchus* (two very great paintings whose attitudes toward myth and sexuality are—to put it mildly—diametrically opposed); and many, many more. If panic sets in at the prospect of absorbing all this art at one go, bear in mind that the Uffizi is, except on Sunday, open late and isn't usually crowded in the late afternoon. The coffee bar inside the Uffizi has a terrace with a fine close-up view of Palazzo Vecchio. ⊠ *Piazzale degli Uffizi 6,* ☎ *055/23885.* 🎫 *12,000 lire.* ⊘ *Tues.–Sat. 9–7, Sun. 9–2.*

❽ Palazzo Vecchio. Looming over Piazza della Signoria is Florence's forbidding, fortresslike city hall. The palazzo was begun in 1299 and designed (probably) by Arnolfo di Cambio, and its massive bulk and towering campanile dominate the piazza. It was built as a meeting place for the heads of the seven major guilds that governed the city at the time; over the centuries it has served lesser purposes, but today it is once again the City Hall of Florence. The interior courtyard is a good deal less severe, having been remodeled by Michelozzo in 1453; the copy of Verrocchio's bronze *puttino,* topping the central fountain, softens the effect considerably.

Although most of the interior public rooms are well worth exploring, the main attraction is on the second floor: two adjoining rooms that supply one of the most startling contrasts in Florence. The first is the vast **Sala dei Cinquecento** (Room of the Five Hundred), named for the 500-member Great Council, the people's assembly established by Savonarola, which met here. The Sala was decorated by Giorgio Vasari, around 1570, with huge frescoes celebrating Florentine history; depictions of battles with neighboring cities predominate. Continuing the martial theme, the Sala also contains Michelangelo's *Victory* group, intended for the never-completed tomb of Pope Julius II, plus others' miscellaneous sculptures of decidedly lesser quality.

The second room is the little **Studiolo,** entered to the right of the Sala's entrance. The study of Cosimo de' Medici's son, the melancholy Francesco I, it was designed by Vasari and decorated by Vasari and Agnolo Bronzino. It is intimate, civilized, and filled with complex, questioning, allegorical art. It makes the vainglorious proclamations next door ring more than a little hollow. ⊠ *Piazza della Signoria,* ☎ *055/276–8465.* 🎫 *10,000 lire.* ⊘ *Mon.–Wed., Fri.–Sat. 9–7, Sun. 8–1.*

Piazza della Repubblica. This square marks the site of the ancient forum that was the core of the original Roman settlement The street plan in the area around the piazza still reflects the carefully plotted orthogonal grid of the Roman military encampment. The Mercato Vecchio (Old Market), located here since the Middle Ages, was demolished at the end of the last century, and the current piazza was constructed between 1890 and 1917 as a neoclassical showpiece. Nominally the center of town, it has yet to earn the love of most Florentines.

★ ❼ Piazza della Signoria. This is by far the most striking square in Florence. It was here, in 1497, that the famous "bonfire of the vanities" took place, when the fanatical monk Savonarola induced his followers to hurl their worldly goods into the flames; it was also here, a year later, that he was hanged as a heretic and, ironically, burned. A bronze plaque in the piazza pavement marks the exact spot of his execution.

The statues in the square and in the 14th-century **Loggia dei Lanzi** on the south side vary in quality. Cellini's famous bronze *Perseus Holding the Head of Medusa* is his masterpiece; even the pedestal is superbly executed. Other works in the loggia include *The Rape of the Sabine Women* and *Hercules and the Centaur,* both late–16th-century works by Giambologna, and, in the back, a row of sober matrons that date from Roman times. When the loggia underwent a lengthy structural restoration a few years ago, many of the statues were replaced by copies.

In the square, Bartolomeo Ammannati's Neptune Fountain, dating from 1565, takes something of a booby prize. Even Ammannati himself considered it a failure, and the Florentines call it *Il Biancone*, which may be translated as "the big white man" or "the big white lump," depending on your point of view. Giambologna's equestrian statue, to the left of the fountain, pays tribute to the Medici Grand Duke Cosimo I. Occupying the steps of the Palazzo Vecchio are a copy of Donatello's proud heraldic lion of Florence, known as the *Marzocco* (the original is now in the Bargello); a copy of Donatello's *Judith and Holofernes* (the original is inside the Palazzo Vecchio); a copy of Michelangelo's *David* (the original is now in the Accademia); and Baccio Bandinelli's *Hercules* (1534).

NEED A
BREAK?

At the west end of Piazza della Signoria, facing the statuary on the steps of the Palazzo Vecchio, is **Rivoire,** a café famous for its chocolate (both packaged and hot). Its outdoor tables and somewhat less expensive indoor counter are stylish, if pricey, places from which to observe the busy piazza.

★ ⑪ **Ponte Vecchio (Old Bridge).** This elegant bridge is to Florence what Tower Bridge is to London. It was built in 1345 to replace an earlier bridge that was swept away by flood, and its shops housed first butchers, then grocers, blacksmiths, and other merchants. But in 1593 the Medici Grand Duke Ferdinando I, whose private corridor linking the Medici palace (the Palazzo Pitti) with the Medici offices (the Uffizi) crossed the bridge atop the shops, decided that all this plebeian commerce under his feet was unseemly. So he threw out all the butchers and blacksmiths and installed 41 goldsmiths and eight jewelers. The bridge has been devoted solely to these two trades ever since.

In the middle of the bridge, take a moment to study the **Ponte Santa Trinitá,** the next bridge downriver. It was designed by Bartolomeo Ammannati in 1567 (possibly from sketches by Michelangelo), blown up by the retreating Germans during World War II, and painstakingly reconstructed after the war ended. Florentines like to claim it is the most beautiful bridge in the world. Given its simplicity, this may sound like idle Tuscan boasting. But if you commit its graceful arc and delicate curves to memory and then begin to compare these characteristics with those of other bridges encountered in your travels, you may well conclude that the boast is justified. The Ponte Santa Trinita is a beautiful piece of architecture.

Michelangelo Country: From San Lorenzo to the Accademia

Poet, painter, sculptor, and architect, Michelangelo was a consummate genius. His prodigious energy and virtuoso technique overcame the political and artistic vicissitudes of almost a century to produce some of the greatest sculpture of his—or any—age. This itinerary takes us to some of his most important creations, from the Biblioteca Laurenziana, perhaps his most intuitive work of architecture; to the Cappelle Medicee, whose magnificent sculptures are a key to understanding Michelangelo's genius; and to the Galleria dell'Accademia, home to his most recognized work (including even the Sistine Chapel), the towering and beautiful *David*.

A Good Walk

Start at the church of **San Lorenzo** ⑫, visiting the **Biblioteca Laurenziana** and its famous anteroom, before circling the church and making your way through the San Lorenzo outdoor market on Via del Canto de' Nelli to the entrance of the **Cappelle Medicee** to see the tombs Michelangelo sculpted for his Medici patrons. Retrace your steps through the market and take Via dei Gori to Via Cavour and the **Palazzo Medici-Riccardi** ⑬, home to Florence's most important family throughout the Renaissance. Follow Via Cavour two blocks north to Piazza San Marco and the church of the same name, attached to which is the **Museo San Marco** ⑭, a memorial to the pious and exceptionally talented painter-monk, Fra Angelico. From Piazza San Marco, take a short detour a half-block down Via Ricasoli (which runs back toward the Duomo) to the **Galleria dell'Accademia** ⑮, where Michelangelo's most recognizable masterpiece, *David,* looks down on the admiring crowds. If you have time to make a detour, return to Piazza San Marco and take Via Cesare Battisti into Piazza della Santissima Annunziata, one of Florence's prettiest squares, site of the **Ospedale degli Innocenti** ⑯ and, at the north end of the square, the church of **Santissima Annunziata** ⑰. One block southeast of the entrance to Santissima Annunziata, through the arch and on the left side of Via della Colonna, is the **Museo Archeologico** ⑱.

TIMING

The walk alone takes about one hour, plus 45 minutes for the Cappelle Medicee, 20 minutes for the Palazzo Medici-Riccardi, 40 minutes for the Museo di San Marco, 30 minutes for the Accademia (*David*), and 40 minutes for the Museo Archeologico. After visiting San Lorenzo, resist the temptation to explore the clothes' market that surrounds the church before going to the Palazzo Medici-Riccardi; you can always come back later, when the churches and museums have closed; the market is open until 7 PM.

Sights to See

Biblioteca Laurenziana. The Laurentian Library and its famous anteroom, adjacent to the church of San Lorenzo, were designed by Michelangelo. The entrance to the library is to the left of the church facade. Michelangelo the architect was every bit as original as Michelangelo the sculptor. Unlike Brunelleschi (the architect of San Lorenzo), however, he was not interested in expressing the ordered harmony of the spheres in his architecture. He was interested in experimentation and invention and in expressing a personal vision that was at times highly idiosyncratic.

It was never more idiosyncratic than here. This strangely shaped anteroom has had scholars scratching their heads for centuries. In a space more than two stories high, why did Michelangelo limit his use of columns and pilasters to the upper two-thirds of the wall? Why didn't he rest them on strong pedestals instead of on huge, decorative curlicue scrolls, which rob them of all visual support? Why did he recess them into the wall, which makes them look weaker still? The architectural elements here do not stand firm and strong and tall, as inside the church next door; instead, they seem to be pressed into the wall as if into putty, giving the room a soft, rubbery look that is one of the strangest effects ever achieved by Classical architecture. It is almost as if Michelangelo purposely set out to defy his predecessors—intentionally to flout the conventions of the High Renaissance in order to see what kind of bizarre, mannered effect might result. His innovations were tremendously influential and produced a period of architectural experimentation—the Mannerist era in architecture—that eventually evolved into the Baroque. As his contemporary Giorgio Vasari (the first art historian) put it, "Artisans have been infinitely and perpetually indebted to him because he broke the bonds and chains of a way of working that had become habitual by common usage."

Many critics have thought the anteroom a failure and ha[ve]
that Michelangelo's experiment here was willful and perve[rse.]
body has ever complained about the room's staircase (best view[ed]
on), which emerges from the library with the visual force o[f an]
unstoppable flow of lava. In its highly sculptural conception and ex
ecution, it is quite simply one of the most original and beautiful stair-
cases in the world. ⊠ *Free.* ☉ *Mon.–Sat. 9–1.*

★ **Cappelle Medicee.** This magnificent complex includes the **Cappella dei
Principi**, the Medici chapel and mausoleum that was begun in 1605
and kept marble workers busy for several hundred years, and the **New
Sacristy,** designed by Michelangelo, so called to distinguish it from
Brunelleschi's Old Sacristy. Both are part of the San Lorenzo complex.

Michelangelo received the commission for the New Sacristy in 1520
from Cardinal Giulio de' Medici, who later became Pope Clement VII
and who wanted a new burial chapel for his father, Giuliano, his uncle
Lorenzo the Magnificent, and two recently deceased cousins. The result was a tour de force of architecture and sculpture. Architecturally,
Michelangelo was as original and inventive here as ever, but it is—quite
properly—the powerful sculptural compositions of the side wall tombs
that dominate the room. The scheme is allegorical: On the wall tomb
to the right are figures representing day and night, and on the wall tomb
to the left are figures representing dawn and dusk; above them are ide-
alized portraits of the two cousins, usually interpreted to represent the
active life and the contemplative life. But the allegorical meanings are
secondary; what is most important is the intense presence of the sculptural figures, the force with which they hit the viewer. Michelangelo's
contemporaries were so awed by the impact of this force (in his sculpture here and elsewhere) that they invented an entirely new word to
describe the phenomenon: *terribilità* (dreadfulness). To this day it is
used only when describing his work, and it is in evidence here at the
peak of its power. ⊠ *Piazza di Madonna degli Aldobrandini,* ☏
055/213206. ⊠ *10,000 lire.* ☉ *Tues.–Sun. 9–2.*

★ ⓯ **Galleria dell'Accademia.** This is the home of the statue that everyone
comes to Florence to see. The museum contains a notable collection
of Florentine paintings dating from the 13th to the 18th centuries, but
it is most famous for its collection of statues by Michelangelo, including
the unfinished *Slaves*—which were meant for the tomb of Michelangelo's patron and nemesis Pope Julius II (and which seem to be fight-
ing their way out of the marble)—and the original *David,* which was
moved here from Piazza della Signoria in 1873. The *David* was
commissioned in 1501 by the Opera del Duomo (Cathedral Works Committee), which gave the 26-year-old sculptor a leftover block of marble
that had been ruined by another artist. Michelangelo's success with the
defective block was so dramatic that the city showered him with hon-
ors, and the Opera del Duomo voted to build him a house and a studio in which to live and work.

Today the *David* is beset not by Goliath but by tourists, and seeing
the statue at all—much less really studying it—can be a trial. After a
1991 attack upon it by a hammer-wielding frustrated artist who,
luckily, inflicted only a few minor nicks on the toes, the sculpture is
surrounded by a plexiglass barrier. But a close look is worth the effort it takes to combat the crowd. The statue is not quite what it seems.
It is so poised and graceful and alert—so miraculously *alive*—that it
is often considered the definitive embodiment of the ideals of the
High Renaissance in sculpture. But its true place in the history of art
is a bit more complicated.

angelo well knew, the Renaissance painting and sculpture ...ded his work were deeply concerned with ideal form. Per... proportion was the ever-sought Holy Grail; during the Re..., ideal proportion was equated with ideal beauty, and ideal ...vas equated with spiritual perfection. In painting, Raphael's ...Madonnas are perhaps the preeminent expression of this phi...: They are meant to embody a perfect beauty that is at once physical and spiritual.

But Michelangelo's *David*, despite its supremely calm and dignified pose, departs from these ideals. As a moment's study will show, Michelangelo did not give the statue ideal proportions. The head is slightly too large for the body, the arms are slightly too large for the torso, and the hands are dramatically too large for the arms. By High Renaissance standards these are defects, but the impact and beauty of the *David* are such that it is the *standards* that must be called into question, not the statue. Michelangelo was a revolutionary artist (and the first Mannerist) because he brought a new expressiveness to art: He created the "defects" of the *David* intentionally. He knew exactly what he was doing, calculating that the perspective of the viewer would be such that, in order for the statue to appear proportioned, the upper body, head, and arms would have to be bigger as they are further away from the viewer's line of vision. But he also did it in order to express and embody, as powerfully as possible in a single figure, an entire biblical story. David's hands *are* too big, but so was Goliath, and these are the hands that slew him. ⊠ *Via Ricasoli 60*, ☎ *055/214375.* ▢ *12,000 lire.* ☉ *Tues.–Sat. 9–7, Sun. 9–2.*

OFF THE
BEATEN PATH

MUSEO DELL'OPIFICIO DELLE PIETRE DURE – This is one of Florence's many fascinating small museums. It is attached to an Opificio, or workshop, which was established in 1588 by Ferdinando I de' Medici to train craftsmen in the art of working with precious and semiprecious stones and marble, with an eye to the future decoration of the Cappella dei Principi. The institute is now known internationally, especially as a center for the restoration of mosaics and inlays in semiprecious stones. The informative exhibits include some magnificent antique examples of this highly specialized craft. ⊠ *Via degli Alfani 78.* ▢ *4,000 lire.* ☉ *Tues.–Sat. 9–7, Sun. 9–2.*

⑱ Museo Archeologico This interesting museum contains Etruscan, Egyptian, and Greco-Roman antiquities; guidebooks in English are available. The Etruscan collection is particularly notable—the largest in northern Italy—and includes the famous bronze *Chimera,* which was discovered (without the tail, which is a reconstruction) in the 16th century. ⊠ *Via della Colonna 36*, ☎ *055/247–8641.* ▢ *8,000 lire.* ☉ *Tues.–Sat. 9–2, Sun. 9–1.*

OFF THE
BEATEN PATH

SANTA MARIA MADDALENA DEI PAZZI – One of Florence's hidden treasures, Perugino's cool and composed *Crucifixion,* is in the chapter hall of the monastery adjacent to this church. ⊠ *Borgo Pinti 58.* ▢ *Donation requested.* ☉ *Daily 9–12, 5–7.*

TORRE DEI CORBIZI – The tower at the south end of the small Piazza San Pier Maggiore (from the Museo Archeologico, follow Via della Colonna east to Borgo Pinti and turn right, following Borgo Pinti through the arch of San Piero into the piazza) dates from the Middle Ages, when, during the Guelph–Ghibelline conflict of the 13th and 14th centuries, Florence was awash with such towers—more than 200 of them. Today only a handful survive. ⊠ *Piazza San Pier Maggiore.*

⑭ Museo San Marco. A former Dominican monastery adjacent to the church of San Marco now houses this museum, which—in fact, the entire monastery—is a memorial to Fra Angelico, the Dominican monk who, when he was alive, was as famous for his piety as for his painting. When the monastery was built in 1437, he decorated it with his frescoes, which were meant to spur religious contemplation; when the building was turned into a museum, other works of his from all over the city were brought here for display. His paintings are simple and direct and furnish a compelling contrast to the Palazzo Medici-Riccardi chapel (☞ *below*). Fra Angelico probably would have considered the glitter of Gozzoli's work there worldly and blasphemous). The entire monastery is worth exploring, for Fra Angelico's paintings are everywhere, including the Chapter House, at the top of the stairs leading to the upper floor (the famous *Annunciation*), in the upper-floor monks' cells (each monk was given a different religious subject for contemplation), and in the gallery just off the cloister as you enter. The latter room contains, among many other works, his beautiful *Last Judgment;* as usual with Last Judgments, the tortures of the damned are far more inventive than the pleasures of the redeemed. ⊠ *Piazza San Marco 1,* ☎ *055/238–8608.* ⊡ *8,000 lire.* ☉ *Tues.–Sun. 9–2.*

OFF THE BEATEN PATH | **CENACOLO DI SANT'APOLLONIA –** This refectory of a former Benedictine monastery is worth a visit for the frescoes painted in sinewy style on its wall by Andrea del Castagno, a follower of Masaccio. The *Last Supper* is a powerful version of this typical refectory theme. From the Cenacolo entrance, walk around the corner to Via San Gallo 25 and take a peek at the lovely 15th-century cloister which belonged to the same monastery but is now part of the University of Florence. ⊠ *Via XXVII Aprile 1,* ⊡ *Free.* ☉ *Tues.–Sun. 9–2.*

⑯ Ospedale degli Innocenti. Built by Brunelleschi in 1419 to serve as a foundling hospital, it takes the historical prize as the very first Renaissance building. Brunelleschi designed the building's portico with his usual rigor, building it out of the two shapes he considered mathematically (and therefore philosophically and aesthetically) perfect: the square and the circle. Below the level of the arches, the portico encloses a row of perfect cubes; above the level of the arches, the portico encloses a row of intersecting hemispheres. The whole geometric scheme is articulated with Corinthian columns, capitals, and arches borrowed directly from antiquity. At the time he designed the portico, Brunelleschi was also designing the interior of San Lorenzo, using the same basic ideas. But since the portico was finished before San Lorenzo, the Ospedale degli Innocenti can claim the honor of ushering in Renaissance architecture. The 10 ceramic medallions depicting swaddled infants that decorate the portico are by Andrea della Robbia, done approximately in 1487.

★ ⑬ Palazzo Medici-Riccardi. The main attraction of this palace, begun in 1444 by Michelozzo for Cosimo de' Medici, is the interior chapel, the so-called **Capella dei Magi** on the upper floor. Painted on its walls is Benozzo Gozzoli's famous Procession of the Magi, finished in 1460 and celebrating both the birth of Christ and the greatness of the Medici family, whose portraits it contains. Like his contemporary Ghirlandaio, Gozzoli was not a revolutionary painter and is today considered less than first rate because of his technique, old-fashioned even for his day. Gozzoli's gift, however, was for entrancing the eye, not challenging the mind, and on those terms his success here is beyond question. The paintings are full of activity yet somehow frozen in time in a way that fails utterly as realism, but succeeds triumphantly as soon as the demand for realism is set aside. Entering the chapel is like walking into the middle of a magnificently illustrated child's storybook, and the beauty of the illustrations makes this one of the most unpretentiously enjoyable rooms in the entire city. ⊠ *Via Cavour 1,* ☎ *055/276–0340.* ▧ *6,000 lire.* ⊙ *Mon., Tues., Thurs.–Sat. 9–1 and 3–6; Sun. 9–1.*

⑫ **San Lorenzo.** The facade of this church was never finished. Like Santo Spirito on the other side of the Arno, the interior of San Lorenzo was designed by Filippo Brunelleschi in the early 15th century. The two church interiors are similar in design and effect and proclaim with ringing clarity the beginning of the Renaissance in architecture. You may want to read the entry on Santo Spirito now; it describes the nature of Brunelleschi's architectural breakthrough, and its main points apply equally well here (☞ The Pitti Palace, Boboli, and Oltrarno, *below*). San Lorenzo possesses one feature that Santo Spirito lacks, however, which considerably heightens the dramatic effect of the interior: the grid of dark, inlaid marble lines on the floor. The grid makes the rigorous regularity with which the interior was designed immediately visible and offers an illuminating lesson on the laws of perspective. If you stand in the middle of the nave at the church entrance, on the line that stretches to the high altar, every element in the church—the grid, the nave columns, the side aisles, the coffered nave ceiling—seems to march inexorably toward a hypothetical vanishing point beyond the high altar, exactly as in a single-point-perspective painting. Brunelleschi's **Old Sacristy** has stucco decorations by Donatello; the entrance is at the end of the left transept.

OFF THE
BEATEN PATH

MERCATO CENTRALE – Florence's busy main food market is a reminder that Florence is more than just a museum. In this huge, two-story market hall, food is everywhere, some of it remarkably exotic, and many of the displays verge on the magnificent. At the Mercato Nuovo, near the Ponte Vecchio, you will see tourists petting the snout of the bronze piglet for good luck; here you will see Florentines petting the snout of a real one, very recently deceased and available for tonight's dinner. The Mercato Centrale has a number of small coffee bars scattered about; there is even one upstairs among the mountains of vegetables. The square, too, has a full complement of cafés and down-to-earth trattorias. Have a coffee, watch the activity, and enjoy the fact that for once there is not a painting in sight.

⑰ **Santissima Annunziata.** This church was designed in 1447 by Michelozzo, who gave it an uncommon (and lovely) entrance cloister. The interior is an extreme rarity for Florence: a sumptuous example of the Baroque. But it is not really a fair example, since it is merely 17th-century Baroque decoration applied willy-nilly to an earlier structure—exactly the sort of violent remodeling exercise that has given the Baroque a bad name ever since. The **Tabernacle of the Annunziata,** immediately inside the entrance to the left, illustrates the point. The lower half, with its stately Corinthian columns and carved frieze bearing the Medici arms, was built at the same time as the church; the upper half, with its erupting curves and impish sculpted cherubs, was added 200 years later. Each is effective in its own way, but together they serve only to prove that dignity is rarely comfortable wearing a party hat.

Around Santa Maria Novella

Piazza Santa Maria Novella is near the train station, and like the train stations of most other European cities, it is an area pervaded by a certain squalor, especially at night. Nevertheless, the streets in and around the piazza are an architectural treasure-trove, lined with some of Florence's most elegant palazzi. This walk ends at Santa Trinità, home of Ghirlandaio's fresco cycle.

A Good Walk

Start in the Piazza Santa Maria Novella, dominated by the church of **Santa Maria Novella** ⑲ on the north side, then take Via delle Belle Donne, which leads to a minuscule square, at the center of which a curious shrine, known as the Croce al Trebbio, stands. Take Via del Trebbio and turn right onto **Via Tornabuoni,** Florence's finest shopping street. At the intersection of Via Tornabuoni and Via Strozzi is the classical **Palazzo Strozzi** ⑳. One block west, down Via della Vigna Nuova, is Alberti's High Renaissance-style **Palazzo Rucellai** ㉑. Follow the narrow street opposite the palazzo (Via del Purgatorio) almost to its end, then zigzag right and left to reach Piazza di Santa Trinita, where, in the middle, stands the **Colonna della Giustizia,** erected by Cosimo de' Medici in 1537. Halfway down the block to the right (toward the Arno) is the church of **Santa Trinita** ㉒, home to Ghirlandaio's glowing frescoes. Then follow Borgo Santi Apostoli, a typical medieval street flanked by tower-houses, to Via Por Santa Maria. Alternatively, from Piazza Santa Trinita you can cross Ponte Santa Trinita and head into the Oltrarno neighborhood.

TIMING

The walk takes about 30 minutes, plus 30 minutes for Santa Maria Novella and 15 minutes for Santa Trinita. A visit to the Santa Maria Novella museum and cloister takes about 30 minutes. Allow 30 minutes for the museum.

Sights to See

Croce al Trebbio. This roofed crucifix was erected in 1308 by the Dominican friars (nearby Santa Maria Novella is a Dominican church) to commemorate a victory famous locally: It was here that they defeated their avowed enemies, the Patarene heretics, in a bloody street brawl. ⊠ *Via del Trebbio.*

㉑ **Palazzo Rucellai.** Architect Leon Battista Alberti designed perhaps the very first private residence done in High Renaissance style—which goes a step further than the Palazzo Strozzi. A comparison between the two is illuminating. Evident on the facade of the Palazzo Rucellai is the ordered arrangement of windows and rusticated stonework seen on the Palazzo Strozzi, but Alberti's facade is far less forbidding. Alberti devoted a far larger proportion of his wall space to windows, which soften the facade's appearance, and filled in the remainder with rigorously ordered classical elements borrowed from antiquity. The end result, though still severe, is less fortresslike, and Alberti strove for this effect purposely (he is on record as stating that only tyrants need fortresses). Ironically, the Palazzo Rucellai was built some 30 years *before* the Palazzo Strozzi. Alberti's civilizing ideas here, it turned out, had little influence on the Florentine palazzi that followed. To the Renaissance Florentines, power—in architecture, as in life—was just as impressive as beauty. ⊠ *Via della Vigna Nuova.* ☉ *Mon., Tues., Thurs., and Sun. 10–7:30, Fri.–Sat. 10–11:30* PM.

⑳ **Palazzo Strozzi.** This is the most imposing palazzo on Via Tornabuoni. Designed (probably) by Giuliano da Sangallo around 1489 and modeled after Michelozzo's earlier Palazzo Medici-Riccardi (☞ Michelangelo Country, *above*), the exterior of the palazzo is simple and severe; it is not the use of classical detail but the regularity of its features, the stately march of its windows, that marks it as a product of the early Renaissance. The interior courtyard (entered from the rear of the palazzo) is another matter altogether. It is here that the classical vocabulary—columns, capitals, pilasters, arches, and cornices—is given uninhibited and powerful expression. Unfortunately, the courtyard's effectiveness is all but destroyed by the addition of a brutal metal fire escape. Its introduction here is one of the most disgraceful acts of 20th-century vandalism in the entire city. ✉ *Via Tornabuoni.*

⑲ Santa Maria Novella. The facade of this church looks distinctly clumsy by later Renaissance standards, and with good reason: It is an architectural hybrid. The lower half of the facade was completed mostly in the 14th century; its pointed-arch niches and decorative marble patterns reflect the Gothic style of the day. About a hundred years later (around 1456), architect Leon Battista Alberti was called in to complete the job. The marble decoration of his upper story clearly defers to the already existing work below, but the architectural features he added evince an entirely different style. The central doorway, the four ground-floor half-columns with Corinthian capitals, the triangular pediment atop the second story, the inscribed frieze immediately below the pediment—these are classical features borrowed from antiquity, and they reflect the new Renaissance era in architecture, born some 35 years earlier at the Ospedale degli Innocenti (☞ Michelangelo Country, *above*). Alberti's most important addition, however, the S-curve scrolls that surmount the decorative circles on either side of the upper story, had no precedent whatever in antiquity. The problem was to soften the abrupt transition between wide ground floor and narrow upper story. Alberti's solution turned out to be definitive. Once you start to look for them, you will find scrolls such as these (or sculptural variations of them) on churches all over Italy, and every one of them derives from Alberti's example here.

The architecture of the interior is, like the Duomo, a dignified but somber example of Italian Gothic. Exploration is essential, however, because the church's store of art treasures is remarkable. Highlights include the 14th-century stained-glass rose window depicting *The Coronation of the Virgin* (above the central entrance door); the Filippo Strozzi Chapel (to the right of the altar), containing late–15th-century frescoes and stained glass by Filippino Lippi; the chancel (the area around the altar), containing frescoes by Domenico Ghirlandaio (1485); and the Gondi Chapel (to the left of the altar), containing Filippo Brunelleschi's famous wooden crucifix, carved around 1410 and said to have so stunned the great Donatello when he first saw it that he dropped a basket of eggs.

One other work in the church is worth special attention, for it possesses great historical importance as well as beauty. It is Masaccio's *Holy Trinity with Two Donors,* on the left-hand wall, almost halfway down the nave. Painted around 1425 (at the same time Masaccio was working on his frescoes in Santa Maria del Carmine, ☞ The Pitti Palace, Boboli, and Oltrarno, *below*), it unequivocally announced the arrival of the Renaissance era. The realism of the figure of Christ was revolutionary in itself, but what was probably even more startling to contemporary Florentines was the coffered ceiling in the background. The mathematical rules for employing perspective in painting had just been discovered (probably by Brunelleschi), and this was one of the first paintings to employ them with utterly convincing success. As art historian E. H. Gombrich expressed it, "We can imagine how amazed the Florentines must have been when this wall-painting was unveiled and seemed to have made a hole in the wall through which they could look into a new burial chapel in Brunelleschi's modern style." ✉ *Piazza Santa Maria Novella.* 🎫 *5,000 lire.* ⏰ *Sat.–Thurs. 9–2, Sun. 8–1.*

....

OFF THE
BEATEN PATH   **MUSEO DI SANTA MARIA NOVELLA** – This museum, entered to the left of the church, includes the church's cloisters, interesting for the faded fresco cycle by Paolo Uccello depicting tales from Genesis, with a dramatic vision of the Deluge. There are more, earlier and better preserved

frescoes, painted by Andrea di Firenze in the 1360s in the chapter hall, or Cappella degli Spagnoli, off the cloisters. ☒ *The church of Santa Maria Novella.*

㉒ **Santa Trinita.** Originally built in the Romanesque style, the church underwent a Gothic remodeling during the 14th century (remains of the Romanesque construction are visible on the interior front wall). Its major artistic attraction is the cycle of frescoes and the altarpiece in the Sassetti Chapel, the second to the altar's right, painted by Domenico Ghirlandaio, around 1485. Ghirlandaio was a conservative painter for his day, and generally his paintings exhibit little interest in the investigations into the laws of perspective that had been going on in Florentine painting for more than 50 years. But his work here possesses such graceful decorative appeal that his lack of interest in rigorous perspective hardly seems to matter. The wall frescoes illustrate the life of St. Francis, and the altarpiece, *The Adoration of the Shepherds,* seems to stop just short of glowing.

In the center of Piazza Santa Trinita is a column from the Baths of Caracalla, in Rome, given to the Medici Grand Duke Cosimo I by Pope Pius IV in 1560. The column was raised here by Cosimo in 1565, to mark the spot where he heard the news, in 1537, that his exiled Ghibelline enemies had been defeated at Montemurlo, near Prato; the victory made his power in Florence unchallengeable and all but absolute. The column is called, with typical Medici self-assurance, the **Colonna della Giustizia,** the Column of Justice.

Via Tornabuoni. For those who can afford it, this is probably Florence's finest shopping street, and it supplies an interesting contrast to the nearby Piazza della Repubblica (☞ The Historic Heart of Florence, *above*). There, at the turn of the century, the old was leveled to make way for the new; here, past and present cohabit easily and efficiently, with the oldest buildings housing the newest shops. Ironically, the "modern" Piazza della Repubblica now looks dated and more than a little dowdy, and it is the unrenewed Via Tornabuoni, lined with Renaissance buildings, bustling with activity, that seems up-to-the-minute.

NEED A BREAK? For a midmorning pickup in the company of stylish Florentines, try **Giacosa,** at No. 83 Via Tornabuoni, for excellent coffee, cappuccino, and pastries, or **Procacci,** at No. 64, for finger sandwiches and cold drinks. (Both closed Mon.)

The Pitti Palace, Boboli, and Oltrarno

This walk takes in two very different aspects of Florence: the splendor of the Medicis, manifest in the riches of mammoth Pitti Palace and the gracious Boboli gardens; and the charm of the Oltrarno, literally, "beyond the Arno," a now-gentrified neighborhood of artisans and antique shops.

A Good Walk

If you start from Santa Trinita, cross the Arno over Ponte Santa Trinita and continue down Via Maggio until you reach the crossroads of Sdrucciolo dei Pitti (on the left) and the short Via Michelozzi (on the right). Turn left onto the Sdrucciolo dei Pitti. **Palazzo Pitti** ㉓, Florence's largest architectural set piece, lies before you as you emerge onto Piazza Pitti. Behind the palace are the **Boboli Gardens** ㉔. If you have time, walk uphill in the gardens all the way to the **Belvedere Fortress** ㉕, which is worth it for the view. Return to Via Maggio from the Pitti, take Via Michelozzi to Piazza Santo Spirito, dominated at its north end by the unassuming facade of the church of **Santo Spirito** ㉖. After your visit to perhaps Italy's most important architectural interior, take Via Sant'Agostino, diagonally across the square from the church entrance, and follow it to Via dei Serragli. Cross and follow Via Santa Monaca to Piazza del Carmine and the church of **Santa Maria del Carmine** ㉗, where, in the attached Brancacci Chapel, is the Masaccio cycle that is famous throughout the world. Go to the far end of Piazza del Carmine and turn right onto Borgo San Frediano, then follow Via di Santo Spirito and Borgo San Jacopo to reach the Ponte Vecchio.

TIMING

The walk alone takes about 45 minutes; allow one hour to visit the Galleria Palatina in the Pitti Palace, or more if you visit the other galleries. Spend at least 30 minutes to an hour savoring the graceful elegance of the Boboli gardens. When you reach the crossroads of the Sdrucciolo dei Pitti and Via Michelozzi, you have a choice. If the noon hour approaches, you may want to postpone the next stop temporarily to see the churches of Santo Spirito and Santa Maria del Carmine before they close for the afternoon. Otherwise, proceed to the Palazzo Pitti, where you should bank on spending at least 30 minutes visiting the palace. The churches of Santo Spirito and Santa Maria del Carmine can be visited in 15 minutes each, but we strongly recommend that if you have the time, linger a while in either church to soak up the sheer historical and artistic grandeur that is the essence of Florence's beauty.

Sights to See

㉕ **Belvedere Fortress.** This imposing structure was built in 1429 to help defend the city against siege. But time has effected an ironic transformation, and what was once a first-rate fortification is now a first-rate picnic ground. Buses carry view-seeking tourists farther up the hill to the Piazzale Michelangelo, but, as the natives know, the best views of Florence are right here. To the north, all the city's monuments are spread out in a breathtaking cinemascopic panorama, framed by the rolling Tuscan hills beyond: the squat dome of Santa Maria Novella, Giotto's proud campanile, the soaring dome of the Duomo, the forbidding medieval tower of the Palazzo Vecchio, the delicate Gothic spire of the Badia, and the crenellated tower of the Bargello. It is one of the best city views in Italy. To the south the nearby hills furnish a complementary rural view, in its way equally memorable. If time and weather permit, a picnic lunch here on the last day of your stay is the perfect way to review the city's splendors and fix them forever in your memory. The fortress is connected with the gardens by a secondary entrance. ▨ *Free.* ☉ *Daily 9–sunset.*

㉔ **Boboli Gardens.** The main entrance to these landscaped gardens is in the right wing of the Pitti Palace. The gardens began to take shape in 1549, when the Pitti family sold the palazzo to Eleanor of Toledo, wife of the Medici Grand Duke Cosimo I. The initial landscaping plans were laid out by Niccolò Pericoli Tribolo. After his death in 1550 development was continued by Bernardo Buontalenti, Giulio, and Alfonso Parigi, and, over the years, many others, who produced the most spectacular backyard in Florence. The Italian gift for landscaping—less formal than the French but still full of sweeping drama—is displayed here at its best. A description of the gardens' beauties would fill a page but would be self-defeating, for the best way to enjoy a pleasure garden is to wan-

der about, discovering its pleasures for yourself. [...]
deserves special note, however: the famous *Bacch[...]*
entrance. It is a copy of the original, showing Pietro [...]
favorite dwarf, astride a particularly unhappy tort[...]
illustrating—very graphically, indeed—the perils [...]
At the top of the gardens, a gate gives access to the Belvedere Fortress.
✉ *4,000 lire.* ⊘ *Daily, except first and last Mon. of each month, 9–1 hr before sunset.*

㉓ Palazzo Pitti. This enormous palace is one of Florence's largest—if not one of its best—architectural set pieces. The original palazzo, built for the Pitti family around 1460, comprised only the middle cube (the width of the middle seven windows on the upper floors) of the present building. In 1549 the property was sold to the Medicis, and Bartolomeo Ammannati was called in to make substantial additions. Although he apparently operated on the principle that more is better, he succeeded only in producing proof that more is just that, more.

Today the immense building houses several museums: the former **Royal Apartments,** containing furnishings from a remodeling done in the 19th century; the **Museo degli Argenti,** containing a vast collection of Medici household treasures; the **Galleria del Costume,** a showcase of the fashions of the past 300 years; the **Galleria d'Arte Moderna,** containing a collection of 19th- and 20th-century paintings, mostly Tuscan; and, most famous of all, the **Galleria Palatina,** containing a broad collection of 16th- and 17th-century paintings. The rooms of the latter remain much as the Medici family left them, but, as Mary McCarthy pointed out, the Florentines invented modern bad taste, and many art lovers view the floor-to-ceiling painting displays here as Italy's most egregious exercise in conspicuous consumption, aesthetic overkill, and trumpery. Still, the collection possesses high points that are very high indeed, including a number of portraits by Titian and an unparalleled collection of paintings by Raphael, among them the famous *Madonna of the Chair.* ✉ *Piazza Pitti,* ☎ *055/210323.* ✉ *Royal Apartments: 8,000 lire; Museo degli Argenti and Galleria del Costume: 8,000 lire (valid for both); Galleria d'Arte Moderna: 4,000 lire; Galleria Palatina: 12,000 lire.* ⊘ *Tues.–Sun. 9–2.*

㉗ Santa Maria del Carmine. The **Brancacci Chapel,** at the end of the right transept of this church, a masterpiece of Renaissance painting: a fresco cycle that changed the course of art forever. Fire almost destroyed the church in the 18th century; miraculously, the Brancacci Chapel survived almost intact.

The cycle is the work of three artists: Masaccio and Masolino, who began it in 1423, and Filippino Lippi, who finished it, after a long interruption during which the sponsoring Brancacci family was exiled, some 50 years later. It was Masaccio's work that opened a new frontier for painting; tragically, he did not live to experience the revolution his innovations caused, as he died in 1428 at the age of 27.

Masaccio collaborated with Masolino on several of the paintings, but by himself he painted *The Tribute Money* on the upper-left wall; *Peter Baptizing the Neophytes* on the upper altar wall; *The Distribution of the Goods of the Church* on the lower altar wall; and, most famous, *The Expulsion of Adam and Eve* on the chapel's upper-left entrance pier. If you look closely at the latter painting and compare it with some of the chapel's other works, you will see a pronounced difference. The figures of Adam and Eve possess a startling presence, a presence primarily due to the dramatic way in which their bodies seem to reflect light. Masaccio here shaded his figures consistently, so as to suggest emphatically a single, strong source of light within the world of the painting but outside its frame. In so doing, he succeeded in imitating with paint the real-world effect of light on mass, and he thereby imparted to his figures a sculptural reality unprecedented in its day. To contemporary Florentines his Adam and Eve must have seemed surrounded by light and air in a way that was almost magical. All the painters of Florence came to look.

These matters have to do with technique, but with *The Expulsion of Adam and Eve,* his skill went beyond technical innovation, and if you look hard at the faces of Adam and Eve, you will see more than just finely modeled figures. You will see terrible shame and terrible suffering, and you will see them depicted with a humanity rarely achieved in art. ⊠ *Brancacci Chapel.* 🖾 *5,000 lire.* ☉ *Mon. and Wed.–Sat. 10–5, Sun. 1–5.*

NEED A
BREAK?

A popular spot for lunch on Piazza del Carmine is **Carmine,** a moderately priced restaurant with outdoor tables during the warmer months. It is at the end of the piazza's northern extension. ⊠ *Piazza del Carmine. Closed Sun.*

㉖ Santo Spirito. The plain, unfinished facade gives nothing away, but, in fact, the interior, although it appears chilly (cold, even) compared with later churches, is one of the most important pieces of architecture in all Italy. One of a pair of Florentine church interiors designed by Filippo Brunelleschi in the early 15th century (the other is San Lorenzo, ☞ Michelangelo Country, *above*) it was here that Brunelleschi supplied definitive solutions to the two main problems of interior Renaissance church design: how to build a cross-shaped interior using classical architectural elements borrowed from antiquity and how to reflect in that interior the order and regularity that Renaissance scientists (of which Brunelleschi was one) were at the time discovering in the natural world around them.

Brunelleschi's solution to the first problem was brilliantly simple: Turn a Greek temple inside out. To see this clearly, look at one of the stately arch-topped arcades that separate the side aisles from the central nave. Whereas the ancient Greek temples were walled buildings surrounded by classical colonnades, Brunelleschi's churches were classical arcades surrounded by walled buildings. This was perhaps the single most brilliant architectural idea of the early Renaissance, and its brilliance overthrew the previous era's religious taboo against pagan architecture once and for all, triumphantly reclaiming that architecture for Christian use.

Brunelleschi's solution to the second problem—making the entire interior orderly and regular—was mathematically precise: He designed the ground plan of the church so that all its parts are proportionally related. The transepts and nave have exactly the same width; the side aisles are exactly half as wide as the nave; the little chapels off the side aisles are exactly half as deep as the side aisles; the chancel and transepts are exactly one-eighth the depth of the nave; and so on, with dizzying exactitude. For Brunelleschi, such a design technique would have been far more than a convenience; it would have been a matter of passionate conviction. Like most theoreticians of his day, he believed that mathematical regularity and aesthetic beauty were opposite sides of the same coin, that one was not possible without the other. The conviction stood unchallenged for a hundred years, until Michelangelo turned his hand to architecture and designed the Medici Chapel and the Biblioteca Laurenziana in San Lorenzo across town (☞ Michelangelo Country, *above*), and thereby unleashed a revolution of his own that spelled the end of the Renaissance in architecture and the beginning of the Baroque. ⊠ *Piazza Santo Spirito.* ☉ *Thurs.–Tues. 8–12, 4–6; Wed. 8–12*

From Santa Croce to San Miniato

The Santa Croce neighborhood, on the southwest fringe of the historic center of Florence, was built up in the Middle Ages just outside the medieval city walls. The centerpiece of the neighborhood was the church of Santa Croce, which could hold great numbers of worshipers and accommodate the overflow in the vast piazza, which also served as a fairground and playing field for traditional, no-holds-barred football games. A center of leather-working since the Middle Ages, the neighborhood is still packed with leather craftsmen and shops selling leather goods.

A Good Walk

Begin your walk at the church of **Santa Croce** ㉘, take Via de' Benci and cross the Arno over Ponte alle Grazie. Turn left onto Lungarno Serristori and continue to Piazza Poggi, where a series of ramps and stairs climbs to **Piazzale Michelangelo,** where the city lies before you like a painting. From Piazzale Michelangelo, climb the stairs to the church of San Salvatore al Monte, and follow the lane to the stairs that climb to **San Miniato al Monte** ㉙, cutting through the fortifications hurriedly built by Michelangelo in 1529 when Florence was threatened by Emperor Charles V's troops. If you prefer, you can avoid the long walk by taking Bus 12 or 13 at the west end of Ponte alle Grazie and get off at the stop after Piazzale Michelangelo. You still have to climb the monumental stairs to San Miniato, but then the rest of your itinerary will be downhill. From San Miniato descend to San Salvatore al Monte and then to Piazzale Michelangelo, where you can get a bus back to the center of town.

TIMING

The walk alone takes about 1½ hours one way, plus 30 minutes in Santa Croce, 30 minutes in the Museo di Santa Croce, and 30 minutes in San Miniato. Depending on the amount of time you have, you can limit your sightseeing to Santa Croce or continue on to Piazzale Michelangelo. The walk to Piazzale Michelangelo is a long uphill hike, with the prospect of another climb to San Miniato from there. If you decide to take a bus, remember to buy your ticket before you board. Finally, since you go to Piazzale Michelangelo for the view, skip that stop on the itinerary if it's a hazy day.

Sights to See

Piazzale Michelangelo. From this lookout, you have a marvelous view of Florence and the hills around it, rivaling the vista from the Belvedere Fortress (☞ The Pitti Palace, Boboli, and Oltrarno, *above*). It has a copy of Michelangelo's *David* and outdoor cafés that are packed with tourists during the day and with Florentines in the evening. In May, the Iris Garden off the piazza is abloom with more than 2,500 varieties of the flower that has been Florence's symbol since 1251, and it is open to the public. The Rose Garden on the terraces below the piazza is also open in May and June.

NEED A
BREAK?

After seeing the light of the setting sun cast a glow on Florence's domes and towers from a vantage point on Piazzale Michelangelo, have supper or a snack at the **Antico Vineria** on Via San Nicolò, off Piazza Poggi at the foot of the hill. It's a busy wineshop-trattoria with atmosphere. ✉ *Via San Nicolò 60/r. Closed Sun.*

㉙ **San Miniato al Monte.** This church, like the Baptistery (☞ The Historic Heart of Florence, *above*), is a fine example of Romanesque architecture and is one of the oldest churches in Florence, dating from the 11th century. The lively green and white marble facade has a 12th-century mosaic topped by a gilded bronze eagle, emblem of San Miniato's sponsors, the Calimala (Wool Merchant's Guild). Inside are a 13th-century inlaid marble floor and apse mosaic. Artist Spinello Aretino covered the walls of the Sacristy with frescoes of the life of St. Benedict. The adjacent Chapel of the Portuguese Cardinal is one of the richest Renaissance works in Florence. Built to hold the tomb of a Portuguese cardinal, Prince James of Lusitania, who died young in Florence in 1459, it has a glorious ceiling by Luca della Robbia, a sculptured tomb by Antonio Rossellini and inlaid pavement in multicolored marble.

★ ㉘ **Santa Croce.** Like the Duomo, this church is Gothic, but (also like the Duomo) its facade dates only from the 19th century. The interior is most famous for its art and its tombs. As a burial place, the church is a Florentine pantheon and probably contains a larger number of important skeletons than any church in Italy. Among others, the tomb of Michelangelo is immediately to the right as you enter (he is said to have chosen this spot so that the first thing he would see on Judgment Day, when the graves of the dead fly open, would be Brunelleschi's Duomo dome through Santa Croce's open doors); the tomb of Galileo Galilei, who produced evidence that the earth is not the center of the universe (and who was not granted a Christian burial until 100 years after his death because of it), is on the left wall, opposite Michelangelo; the tomb of Niccolò Machiavelli, the Renaissance political theoretician whose brutally pragmatic philosophy so influenced the Medici, is halfway down the nave on the right; the grave of Lorenzo Ghiberti, creator of the Gates of Paradise doors to the Baptistery, is halfway down the nave on the left; the tomb of composer Gioacchino Rossini, of "William Tell Overture" fame, is at the end of the nave on the right. The monument to Dante Alighieri, the greatest Italian poet, is a memorial rather than a tomb (he is actually buried in Ravenna); it is on the right wall near the tomb of Michelangelo.

The collection of art within the church and church complex is by far the most important of that in any church in Florence. Historically, the most significant works are probably the Giotto frescoes in the two adjacent chapels immediately to the right of the altar. They illustrate scenes from the lives of St. John the Evangelist and St. John the Baptist (in the right-hand chapel) and scenes from the life of St. Francis (in the left-hand chapel). Time has not been kind to them; over the centuries, wall tombs were introduced into the middle of them, whitewash and plaster covered them, and in the 19th century they underwent a clumsy restoration. But the reality that Giotto introduced into painting can still be seen. He did not paint beautifully stylized symbols of religion, as the Byzantine style that preceded him prescribed; he instead painted drama—St. Francis surrounded by grieving monks at the very moment of his death. This was a radical shift in emphasis, and it changed the course of art. Before him, the role of painting was to symbolize the attributes of God; after him, it was to imitate life. The style of his work is indeed primitive, compared with later painting, but in the proto-Renaissance of the early 14th century, it caused a sensation that was not equalled for another 100 years. He was, for his time, the equal of both Masaccio and Michelangelo.

Among the church's other highlights are Donatello's *Annunciation,* one of the most tender and eloquent expressions of surprise ever sculpted (on the right wall two-thirds of the way down the nave); Taddeo Gaddi's 14th-century frescoes illustrating the life of the Virgin, clearly showing the influence of Giotto (in the chapel at the end of the right transept); and Donatello's *Crucifix,* criticized by Brunelleschi for making Christ look like a peasant (in the chapel at the end of the left transept). Outside the church proper, in the **Museo dell'Opera di Santa Croce** off the cloister, is Giovanni Cimabue's 13th-century *Triumphal Cross,* badly damaged by the flood of 1966. The **Pazzi Chapel,** yet another of Brunelleschi's crisp exercises in architectural geometry, is at the end of the cloister. ✉ *Piazza Santa Croce 16,* ☎ *055/244619. Church:* ☉ *Apr.–Sept., Mon.–Sat. 8–6:30, Sun. 8–12:30, 3–6:30; Oct.–Mar., Mon.–Sat. 8–12:30, 3–6:30, Sun. 3–6. Church cloister and museum:* ⛶ *3,000 lire.* ☉ *Apr.–Sept., Thurs.–Tues. 10–12:30, 2:30–6:30; Oct.–Mar., Thurs.–Tues. 10–12:30, 3–5.*

NEED A BREAK? The Santa Croce neighborhood has some sweet surprises hidden among its byways: **Vivoli** (✉ Via Isola delle Stinche 7/r, off Via dell'Anguillara, one of the streets opposite the facade of Santa Croce) is Florence's most famous *gelateria* (ice-cream parlor). If you're homesick for brownies and chocolate-chip cookies, find your way to **Carlie's American Bakery.** ✉ *Via della Brache, also known as Via dei Legnaioli 12/r, a narrow street off Via dei Neri between Via dei Benci and Via dei Rustici; open 10– 1:30 and 3:30–7:30.*

DINING

A typical Tuscan repast starts with an antipasto of *crostini* (toasted bread spread with a chicken liver pâté) or cured meats such as prosciutto *crudo* (a salty prosciutto), *finocchiona* (salami seasoned with fennel), and *salsiccia di cinghiale* (sausage made from wild boar). This is the time to start right in on the local wine—Chianti, *naturalmente.* Don't be surprised if the waiter brings an entire flask to the table. Customers are charged only for what they consume (*al consumo,* the arrangement is called), but it's wise to ask for a flask or bottle to be opened then and there, since leftover wines are often mixed together.

Primi piatti (first courses) can consist of excellent local versions of risotto or pasta dishes available throughout Italy. Peculiar to Florence, however, are the vegetable-and-bread soups such as *pappa al pomodoro* (tomatoes, bread, olive oil, onions, and basil), ribollita, or, in the summer, a salad called *panzanella* (tomatoes, onions, vinegar, oil, and bread). Before they are eaten, these are often christened with *un "C" d'olio,* a generous C-shape drizzle of the excellent local olive oil from the ever-present tabletop cruet.

Second to none among the *secondi piatti* (main courses) is *bistecca alla fiorentina*—a thick slab of local Chianina beef, grilled over charcoal, seasoned with olive oil, salt, and pepper, and served rare. *Trippa alla fiorentina* (tripe stewed with tomatoes in a meat sauce) and *arista* (roast loin of pork seasoned with rosemary) are also regional specialties, as are many other roasted meats that go especially well with the Chianti. These are usually served with a *contorno* (side dish) of white beans, sautéed greens, or artichokes in season, all of which can be drizzled with more of that wonderful olive oil.

Tuscan desserts are typically spartan. The cheese is the hard pecorino, and locals like to go for the even tougher *biscottini di Prato,* a caramelized cookie, which provide an excuse to dunk them in the potent, sweet dessert wine called *vin santo,* made of dried grapes, which they say will bring the dead back to life!

Remember that dining hours are earlier here than in Rome, starting at 12:30 for the midday meal and at 7:30 for dinner. Many of Florence's

40

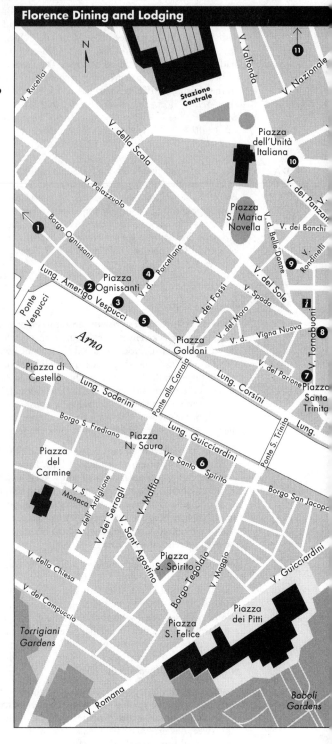

Florence Dining and Lodging

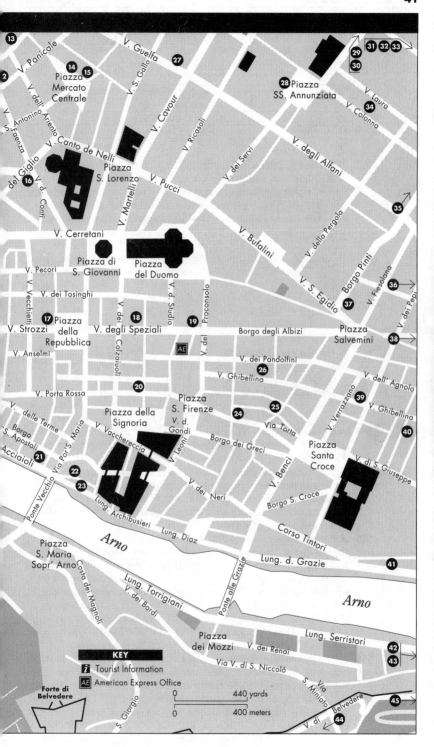

Piazza
Mercato
Centrale

V. Panicale

V. Guelfa

V. Cavour

Piazza
SS. Annunziata

V. Laura

V. Colonna

V. del Giglio

V. Canto de Nelli

Piazza
S. Lorenzo

V. Martelli

V. Pucci

V. Ricasoli

V. dei Servi

V. degli Alfani

V. Cerretani

Piazza di
S. Giovanni

Piazza
del Duomo

V. Bufalini

V. della Pergola

Borgo Pinti

V. Fiesolana

V. Pecori

V. dei Tosinghi

V. S. Egidio

V. Vecchietti

V. Strozzi

Piazza
della
Repubblica

V. degli Speziali

V. d. Studio

Proconsolo

Borgo degli Albizi

Piazza
Salvemini

V. dei Pepi

V. Anselmi

V. dei Calzaiuoli

V. del

V. dei Pandolfini

V. dell' Agnolo

V. Porta Rossa

V. Ghibellina

Piazza
S. Firenze

V. Ghibellina

V. delle Terme

Piazza della
Signoria

V. Vacchereccia

V. d.
Gondi

Via Torta

V. Verrazzano

Borgo
S. Apostoli

V. Leoni

Borgo dei Greci

Piazza
Santa
Croce

V. di S. Giuseppe

Acciaioli

Ponte Vecchio

Lung. Archibusieri

V. dei Neri

V. Benci

Borgo S. Croce

Corso Tintori

Lung. Diaz

Arno

Piazza
S. Maria
Sopr' Arno

Costa dei Magnoli

Lung. d. Grazie

Lung. Torrigiani

V. dei Bardi

Ponte alle Grazie

Arno

Lung. Serristori

Piazza
dei Mozzi

V. dei Renai

Via V. di S. Niccolò

Via
S. Miniato

Forte di
Belvedere

S. Giorgio

KEY

i Tourist Information

AE American Express Office

0   440 yards

0   400 meters

V. di Belvedere

restaurants are small, so reservations are a must. Note that the *r* in some of the following addresses indicates the red numbering system used for Florentine businesses, which differs from the black numbers used for residences.

CATEGORY	COST*
$$$$	over 110,000 lire
$$$	80,000–110,000 lire
$$	35,000–80,000 lire
$	under 35,000 lire

per person, for a three-course meal, including house wine and taxes

$$$$ ✕ **Enoteca Pinchiorri.** A sumptuous Renaissance palace with high, fres-
★ coed ceilings and bouquets in silver vases is the setting for this restaurant, one of the most expensive in Italy, and also considered one of the best (though it has been known to have its off days). The "enoteca" part of the name comes from its former incarnation as a wineshop under owner Giorgio Pinchiorri, who still keeps a stock of vintage bottles in the cellar. Wife Annie Feolde has added her refined interpretations of Tuscan cuisine—*triglie alla viareggina* (mullet with tomato sauce) and *arrosto di coniglio* (roast rabbit)—to a nouvelle menu that includes *cannelloni di astice* (pasta stuffed with lobster), *filetto d'agnello con melanzane e pomodori canditi* (filet of lamb with eggplant and candied tomatoes). ⊠ *Via Ghibellina 87,* ☎ *055/242777. Reservations essential. Jacket and tie. AE, MC, V. Closed Sun., Mon., Aug., and 1 wk in Dec. No lunch Wed.*

$$$ ✕ **Harry's Bar.** Americans love it, and it *is* the only place in town to get a perfect martini or a hamburger or a club sandwich, but it offers two typical Tuscan dishes every day. The small menu also has well-prepared international offerings, and the bar is open until midnight. ⊠ *Lungarno Vespucci 22/r,* ☎ *055/239–6700. Reservations essential. AE, MC, V. Closed Sun. and Dec. 15–Jan. 8.*

$$$ ✕ **Il Cestello.** Across the Arno from the church of San Frediano in Cestello, the restaurant is part of the Excelsior hotel and moves to the roof during the warmer months to enjoy a stupendous view of the city. The Tuscan-based menu features delicious risotto and pasta dishes, including an exemplary pasta *e fagioli* (with beans), a rare selection of seafood, and an ever-changing sampling of whatever is fresh from the market. ⊠ *Hotel Excelsior, Piazza Ognissanti 3,* ☎ *055/264201. Jacket and tie. AE, DC, MC, V.*

$$$ ✕ **Il Verrocchio.** In an elegant 18th-century villa, now a deluxe hotel, the restaurant is about 20 minutes from downtown Florence by car or taxi, and well worth the ride. The dining room has a huge fireplace, columns, and a high, vaulted ceiling. Outdoors you dine on a terrace overlooking the Arno. The menu changes with the seasons but can be described as Tuscan-creative, with such offerings as *agnello con salsa di albicocche* (lamb with apricot sauce) and delicate, fresh pasta dishes. ⊠ *Villa La Massa, Via La Massa 6, Candeli,* ☎ *055/651–0101. Jacket and tie. AE, DC, MC, V. Closed Mon. and Tues. Nov.–Mar.*

$$$ ✕ **La Capannina di Sante.** Florence's best fish restaurant is situated,
★ not surprisingly, along a quiet stretch of the Arno, with indoor tables in an ample, unpretentious trattoria setting and tables outdoors on the terrace during the warmer months. Risotto and various types of pasta are combined with seafood, and the *grigliata mista di pesce* (mixed grill of fish) is among the standouts. ⊠ *Piazza Ravenna,* ☎ *055/688345. AE, DC, MC, V. Closed Sun., 10 days in Aug., Dec. 23–30. No lunch.*

$$$ ✕ **La Loggia.** The view of Florence from the glassed-in veranda or dining terrace of a century-old mansion on Piazzale Michelangelo is what you and all the other tourists come for, but the relatively new management wants you to remember the food, too. Along with Florentine classics, host Gaetano offers seafood and southern Italian dishes, using produce from his farm in Impruneta. ✉ *Piazzale Michelangelo 1,* ☎ *055/234–2832. Jacket and tie. AE, DC, MC, V. Closed Wed.*

$$$ ✕ **Relais le Jardin.** Another hotel restaurant, this one with a turn-of-the-century, stained-glass-and-wood-paneling setting, stands on its own. This is gourmet cooking at its most refined, including such dishes as *fagottino di vitello* (veal roulade), stuffed with eggplant and cheese in wine sauce, or *calamari farciti* (shrimp-stuffed cuttlefish) with seafood sauce. ✉ *Hotel Regency, Piazza Massimo D'Azeglio 3,* ☎ *055/245247. Reservations essential. Jacket and tie. AE, DC, MC, V. Closed Sun.*

$$$ ✕ **Terrazza Brunelleschi.** The rooftop restaurant of the Hotel Baglioni
★ has the best view in town. The dining room, decorated in pale blue and creamy tones, has wraparound picture windows framing a close-up of Brunelleschi's dome. The summer terrace outside is charming, with tables placed under arbors and with turrets for guests to climb to get an even better view. The menu offers some traditional Tuscan dishes, such as pappa al pomodoro and *tagliata* (sliced Tuscan steak garnished with arugula and aromatic olive oil). If you order carefully, your check may be in the $$ category. ✉ *Hotel Baglioni, Piazza Unità Italiana 6,* ☎ *055/215642. Jacket and tie. AE, DC, MC, V.*

$$ ✕ **Acqua al Due.** You'll find this tiny restaurant near the Bargello. It serves an array of Florentine specialties in a lively, very casual setting. Acqua al Due is popular with young Florentines, partly because it's air-conditioned in the summer and always open late. It's known for pastas and salads, even if some customers find its clubby atmosphere downright frosty. ✉ *Via della Vigna Vecchia 40/r,* ☎ *055/284170. Reservations not accepted. AE, MC, V. Closed Mon. and Aug.*

$$ ✕ **Alle Murate.** Situated between the Duomo and Santa Croce, this is a sophisticated but informal restaurant. The menu features creative versions of classic Tuscan dishes—*anatra alle erbe* (duck with herb and orange sauce)—but also southern Italian specialties such as *cavatelli con broccoli* (homemade pasta with broccoli and cheese). The main dining room has an elegant, uncluttered look, with warm wood floors and paneling and soft lights. In a smaller adjacent room called the *vineria,* table settings are simpler and the menu more limited. Since the Murate is known for its wine list, this is the place to splurge on a good vintage. ✉ *Via Ghibellina 52/r,* ☎ *055/240618. No credit cards. Closed Mon. No lunch.*

$$ ✕ **Angiolino.** This bustling little trattoria in the Oltrarno district is pop-
★ ular with locals and visitors. It has a real charcoal grill and an old wood-burning stove to keep customers warm on nippy days. The menu offers Tuscan specialties such as ribollita and a classic bistecca alla fiorentina. The bistecca can push the check up, as you pay by weight (order one for two people). ✉ *Via Santo Spirito 36/r,* ☎ *055/239–8976. AE, DC, MC, V. Closed Mon. and last 3 wks in July. No dinner Sun.*

$$ ✕ **Buca dell'Orafo.** One of the best of the Florentine *buca,* meaning hole-in-the-wall, restaurants, Buca dell'Orafo is set in the cellar of a former goldsmith's shop near the Ponte Vecchio. It offers all the Florentine specialties and prides itself on its bistecca. ✉ *Via dei Girolami 28,* ☎ *055/213619. No credit cards. Closed Sun., Mon., and Aug.*

$$ ✕ **Cantinetta Antinori.** Set on the ground floor of a Renaissance palace, this is an elegant place for lunch after shopping in nearby Via Tornabuoni. The Antinori family is best known as wine producers, and their wares may be sampled with light salads, bread, sausage, and cheese snacks or more complete meals. ✉ *Piazza Antinori 3,* ☎ *055/292234. AE, DC, MC, V. Closed Sat., Sun., and Aug.*

$$ ✕ **Hosteria da Ganino.** On a side street between the Duomo and Palazzo Vecchio, this trattoria is informal, rustic, and cheerful. The menu features homemade pasta, and the fettuccine with porcini mushrooms is a specialty. Main courses uphold Florentine tradition, with grilled steak and chops and bean dishes. Get there early: It seats only about 35; double that number in good weather at outside tables. ⊠ *Piazza dei Cimatori 4/r,* ☎ *055/214125. AE, DC, V. Closed Sun. and Aug. 15–25.*

$$ ✕ **Il Cibreo.** Trendsetter that he is, chef Fabrio Picchi has made Cibreo
★ into Florence's newest pilgrimage spot for gourmands. His menu of Tuscan country dishes relies less on his memories than on his lively imagination, which has created updated versions of Florentine classics, such as pappa al pomodoro, presented as a thick red dollop on a sparkling white Ginori plate, and *anatra farcita di pinoli e uvetta* (duck stuffed with pine nuts and raisins). Don't miss the yellow-pepper soup—made, thanks to the restaurant's location near the Sant'-Ambrogio market, with the freshest ingredients available. You'll dine in an upscale trattoria-style dining room or, during warmer weather, in a piazza overlooking the market. A café annex across the street serves drinks and snacks all day. There is also a small, inconspicuous, and inexpensive tavern annex around the corner. ⊠ *Via dei Macci 118/r,* ☎ *055/234–1100. Reservations essential. AE, DC, MC, V. Closed Sun., Mon., July 25–Sept. 5, and Dec. 31–Jan. 7.*

$$ ✕ **La Giostra.** Only about five minutes from the cathedral or from Santa Croce, the Giostra has the typically unpretentious look of a trattoria, but with a difference: the gourmet touch of the courteous owner-chef. Try his fusilli *del Boboli* (with fresh vegetables and mozzarella cheese). Like the menu, the wine list offers good value. Service is informal, and the restaurant is open until midnight, a rarity in Florence. ⊠ *Borgo Pinti 10/r,* ☎ *055/241341. AE, DC, MC, V.*

$$ ✕ **Le Fonticine.** Owner Silvano Bruci is from Tuscany, wife Gianna
★ from Emilia-Romagna, and the restaurant combines the best of both worlds in a setting liberally hung with their extensive collection of paintings. Emilia-Romagna specialties such as tortellini ready the taste buds for Tuscan grilled porcini mushrooms so meaty they provide serious competition for the bistecca alla fiorentina. ⊠ *Via Nazionale 79/r,* ☎ *055/282106. AE, DC, MC, V. Closed Sun., Mon, and July 25–Aug. 25.*

$$ ✕ **Pallottino.** Pallottino has the look of a typical Florentine trattoria, with dark wood tables and benches and copper utensils and old photos on the walls, but here the decor is somehow improved. The menu features traditional fare, from bread or bean soup to spaghetti *alla fiaccheraia* (with piquant fresh tomato sauce). Meat courses are varied; try *involtini alla pallottino* (beef roulades with a creamy sauce). Prices are at the low end of this category. For dessert go down the street for ice cream at Vivoli. ⊠ *Via Isola delle Stinche 1/r,* ☎ *055/289573. AE, DC, MC, V. Closed Mon. and Aug. 1–20.*

$$ ✕ **Sostanza (a.k.a. Il Troia).** Il Troia is Florence's oldest restaurant,
★ founded in 1869. Travelers usually love it, in spite of, or perhaps because of, the no-frills decor and the brusque service. Why? Along with a quintessential bistecca alla fiorentina with a hefty price tag, within this small room you'll be sure to find an entire world of Florence aficionados. The waiters may be surly but the new friends you'll make at the communal tables—chances are you'll sit next to an art historian from Vassar or a bookstore owner from London—will more than make up for it. ⊠ *Via del Porcellana 25/r,* ☎ *055/212691. No credit cards. Closed Sun. and Aug. No dinner Sat.*

$$ ✕ **Toscano.** A small table attractively set in a show window identifies this restaurant, located about five minutes from Palazzo Medici-Riccardi. It lives up to its name in ambience and cuisine. The cold-cuts counter at the entrance, terra-cotta tile floors, and beamed ceilings typify a Tuscan trattoria, but the pink tablecloths, arty photos on the walls, and a touch of creative cuisine take it out of the ordinary. The kitchen prides itself on top-quality meat; this is the place to try tagliata or *spezzatino peposo* (beef stew with lots of black pepper and a wine sauce). The fixed-price menu is a good value, at about 35,000 lire. ⊠ *Via Guelfa 70/r, ☎ 055/215475. AE, DC, MC, V. Closed Tues. and Aug.*

$ ✕ La Maremmana. A display of garden-fresh vegetables and fruit catches your eye as you enter this popular trattoria near Santa Croce. Authentic Tuscan cuisine is offered in the dining room, which has the usual wood paneling and long tables that you will probably be asked to share. The fixed-price menu offers generous servings and good value, and it may include ribollita and *stracotto* (beef stew). ⊠ *Via dei Macci 77/r, ☎ 055/241226. DC, MC, V. Closed Sun. and Aug.*

$ ✕ Mario. Clean and classic, this family-run trattoria on the corner of Piazza del Mercato near San Lorenzo offers genuine Florentine atmosphere and cooking, with no frills. Open for lunch only, it's just around the corner from Za-Za (☞ *below*). ⊠ *Via Rosina 2/r (Piazza del Mercato Centrale), ☎ 055/218550. Reservations not accepted. No credit cards. Closed Sun. No dinner.*

$ ✕ Mossacce. You share a heavy wooden trattoria table here and watch the cook in the glassed-in kitchen prepare your order, chosen from a menu of Florentine classics. ⊠ *Via del Proconsolo 55/r, ☎ 055/294361. Reservations not accepted. AE, MC, V. Closed weekends and Aug.*

$ ✕ Za-Za. Slightly more upscale than neighboring trattorias, Za-Za attracts white-collar workers and theater people. Posters of movie stars hang on wood-paneled walls, but you couldn't ask for a more typically Florentine dining experience, with traditional atmosphere and food. ⊠ *Piazza Mercato Centrale 16/r, ☎ 055/215411. AE, DC, MC, V. Closed Sun.*

Wineshops

Don't have time for a trattoria? Head for one of Florence's wine bars for a fast focaccia, sandwich or snack, and a glass of Chianti Classico. Of these, **Le Cantine** (⊠ Via dei Pucci) is stylish and popular, as is **Cantinone del Gallo Nero** (⊠ Via Santo Spirito 6), which also serves meals in a brick-vaulted wine cellar; **Le Volpi e l'Uva** (⊠ Piazza de' Rossi 1), and—the city's best, although a 15-minute walk from the center of town—**Fuori Porta** (⊠ Via dei Monte all Croci 10). More modest are **Borgioli** (⊠ Piazza dell'Olio), **Fiaschetteria** (⊠ Via dei Neri 2, corner of Via dei Benci), **Fratellini** (⊠ Via dei Cimatori), **Nicolino** (⊠ Volta dei Mercanti), and **Piccolo Vinaio** (⊠ Via Castellani).

LODGING

Florence's importance not only as a tourist city but as a convention center and the site of the Pitti fashion collections throughout the year has guaranteed a variety of accommodations, many in former villas and palazzos. However, these very factors mean that, except during the winter, reservations are a must.

Near the A1 autostrada exits, drivers will find the **Sheraton Firenze** (☎ 055/64901, FAX 055/680747, $$$$), the **Holiday Inn** (☎ 055/653–1841, FAX 055/653–1806, $$$), and the **Forte Agip** (☎ 055/420–5081, FAX 055/421–9015, $$$).

If you do find yourself in Florence with no reservations, go to the **Consorzio ITA** office in the train station. It's open every day from 8:20 AM to 9 PM. If the office is shut, your best bet is to try some of the inexpensive (but clean) accommodations at a one- or two-star hotel; many are on **Via Nazionale** (which leads east from Piazza Stazione) and on **Via Faenza,** the second left off Via Nazionale.

CATEGORY	COST*
$$$$	over 450,000 lire
$$$	280,000–450,000 lire
$$	190,000–280,000 lire
$	under 190,000 lire

All prices are for a double room for two, including tax and service.

$$$$ **Excelsior.** Traditional Old World charm finds a regal setting at the
★   Excelsior, a neo-Renaissance palace complete with painted wooden ceilings, stained glass, and acres of Oriental carpets strewn over marble floors in the public rooms. The rooms are furnished with the opulence of 19th-century Florentine antiques and sumptuous fabrics, set off by charming old prints of the city and long mirrors of the Empire style. Plush touches include wall-to-wall carpeting in the rooms and thick terry-cloth towels on heated racks in the bathrooms. Try to get a room facing the Piazza Ognissanti. The Il Cestello restaurant serves excellent food, and in summer moves up to the roof for a wonderful view. ✉ *Piazza Ognissanti 3,* ☎ *055/264201,* ℻ *055/210278. 177 rooms with bath. Restaurant, piano bar. AE, DC, MC, V.*

$$$$ **Grand Hotel.** Across the piazza from the Excelsior, this Florentine classic, also owned by the CIGA chain, provides all the luxurious amenities of its sister. Most rooms and public areas are decorated in sumptuous Renaissance style, many with frescoes. Baths are in marble. Some rooms have balconies overlooking the Arno. ✉ *Piazza Ognissanti 1,* ☎ *055/288781,* ℻ *055/217400. 107 rooms with bath. Restaurant, bar, parking (fee). AE, DC, MC, V.*

$$$$ **Grand Hotel Villa Cora.** Built near the Boboli Gardens and Piazzale Michelangelo in 1750, the Villa Cora retains the opulence of the 18th and 19th centuries. The decor of its remarkable public and private rooms runs the gamut from neoclassical to rococo and even Moorish, and reflects the splendor of such former guests as the Empress Eugénie, wife of Napoléon III, and Madame Von Meck, Tchaikovsky's mysterious benefactress. ✉ *Viale Machiavelli 18,* ☎ *055/229–8451,* ℻ *055/229–086. 48 rooms with bath. Restaurant, piano bar, pool. AE, DC, MC, V.*

$$$$ **Regency.** In this stylish hotel in a respectable residential district near the synagogue, the noise and crowds of Florence seem far away, though you are less than 10 minutes away from the Accademia and Michelangelo's *David.* The rooms are decorated in richly colored and tasteful fabrics and antique-style furniture faithful to the hotel's 19th-century origins as a private mansion. It has one of Florence's best hotel restaurants (☞ *above*). ✉ *Piazza Massimo D'Azeglio 3,* ☎ *055/245247,* ℻ *055/234–6735. 34 rooms with bath. Restaurant, parking (fee). AE, DC, MC, V.*

$$$$ **Villa San Michele.** The setting for this hideaway is so romantic—nestled in the hills of nearby Fiesole—that it once attracted Brigitte Bardot for her honeymoon. The villa was originally a monastery whose facade and loggia have been attributed to Michelangelo. Many of the rooms now contain sumptuous statuary, paintings, and whirlpool baths. Many have a panoramic view of Florence, while others look onto the former cloister. A luxurious garden surrounds the whole affair. The restaurant is excellent. This is one of Italy's costliest hotels. ✉ *Via Doccia 4, Fiesole,* ☎ *055/59451,* ℻ *055/598734. 36 rooms with bath. Restaurant, piano bar, pool. AE, DC, MC, V. Closed Dec.–mid-Mar.*

$$$ **Baglioni.** This large turn-of-the-century building was conceived in the European tradition of grand hotels; it's between the train station and the cathedral. The charming roof terrace has the best view in Florence and is home to the Terrazza Brunelleschi restaurant. The hotel has well-proportioned rooms, some decorated in antique Florentine style, and many with leaded-glass windows. Most rooms have been done in pastel tones harmonizing with the carpeting or mellow parquet. There

is a full range of conference facilities, which makes it a favorite of businesspeople. ⊠ *Piazza dell'Unità Italiana 6*, ☎ *055/23580*, ℻ *055/235–8895. 195 rooms with bath. Restaurant. AE, DC, MC, V.*

$$$ ⊞ **Beacci Tornabuoni.** This is perhaps *the* classic Florentine pensione (although by law all lodgings have been reclassified as hotels of various categories). Set in a 14th-century palazzo, it has old-fashioned style and just enough modern comfort to keep today's guests happy. Half board is required, but the food is good and can also be served in the rooms, most of which have views of the red-tile roofs in the neighboring downtown area. ⊠ *Via Tornabuoni 3*, ☎ *055/212645*, ℻ *055/283594. 30 rooms with bath. Restaurant, bar. AE, DC, MC, V.*

$$$ ⊞ **Brunelleschi.** Architects united a Byzantine tower, a medieval church,
★ and a later building in a stunning structure in the very heart of Renaissance Florence to make this the city's most unique hotel. This remarkable place even has its own museum displaying the ancient Roman foundations and pottery shards found during restoration. Medieval stone walls and brick arches contrast pleasingly with the plush, contemporary decor. The comfortable, soundproof bedrooms, many with good views, are done in coordinated patterns and soft colors; the ample bathrooms feature beige travertine marble. Brunelleschi ranks high for atmosphere, interest, and comfort. ⊠ *Piazza Sant'Elisabetta (Via dei Calzaiuoli)*, ☎ *055/562068*, ℻ *055/219653. 96 rooms with bath, 7 junior suites. Restaurant, bar, meeting rooms. AE, DC, MC, V.*

$$$ ⊞ **J&J.** Away from the crowds, on a quiet street within walking distance of the sights, this unusual hotel is a converted 16th-century monastery. Its large, suitelike rooms are ideal for honeymooners, families, and small groups of friends traveling together. Some rooms are on two levels, and all are imaginatively arranged around a central courtyard and decorated with flair. There are also smaller, more intimate rooms, some opening onto their own little courtyard. The gracious owners chat with guests in the elegant lounge; breakfast is served in a glassed-in Renaissance loggia or in the central courtyard. ⊠ *Via di Mezzo 20*, ☎ *055/234–5005*, ℻ *055/240282. 20 rooms with bath. Bar. AE, DC, MC, V.*

$$$ ⊞ **Kraft.** The efficient and comfortable Kraft is modern, but it has many period-style rooms, some with balconies and a rooftop terrace café. Its location near the Teatro Comunale (it is also next to the U.S. consulate) gives it a clientele from the music world. ⊠ *Via Solferino 2*, ☎ *055/284273*, ℻ *055/239–8267. 78 rooms with bath. Pool. AE, DC, MC, V.*

$$$ ⊞ **Monna Lisa.** Housed in a Renaissance palazzo, the hotel retains its
★ original marble staircase, terra-cotta floors, and painted ceilings. Its rooms still have a rather homey quality, and though on the small side, many have contemplative views of a lovely garden. The ground-floor lounges give you the feel of living in an aristocratic town house. ⊠ *Borgo Pinti 27*, ☎ *055/247–9751*, ℻ *055/247–9755. 30 rooms with bath. Bar. AE, DC, MC, V.*

$$$ ⊞ **Plaza Hotel Lucchesi.** Elegant without being ostentatious, this hotel
★ is right on the Arno near Santa Croce. Front bedrooms have views of the river and hills beyond; rear rooms on the top floor have balconies and knockout views of Santa Croce. Spacious, quiet bedrooms (double glazing throughout) are furnished comfortably in mahogany and pastel fabrics against creamy white walls. The roomy, welcoming lounges and piano bar are favorite meeting places for Florentines. ⊠ *Lungarno della Zecca Vecchia 38*, ☎ *055/26236*, ℻ *055/248–0921. 97 rooms with bath. Restaurant, piano bar, parking (fee). AE, DC, MC, V.*

$$ ⊞ **Bencistà.** Below the luxurious Villa San Michele in Fiesole, this hotel has the same tranquil setting and is even two centuries older. The rooms are furnished with antiques, and half board is required. ⊠ *Via Benedetto da Maiano 4, Fiesole*, ☎ *055/59163*, ℻ *055/59163. 40 rooms, 30 with bath. No credit cards.*

$$ 🏨 **Hermitage.** Comfortable and charming are suitable adjectives for this hotel occupying the top two floors of a palazzo next to Ponte Vecchio and the Uffizi. Inviting living rooms overlooking the Arno, bright breakfast rooms, flowered roof terrace, and well-lighted bedrooms have the decor and atmosphere of a well-kept Florentine home. Double glazing, air-conditioning, and attentive maintenance sustain the relaxing ambience. (The hotel has an elevator at the top of a short flight of stairs from the street.) ⊠ *Vicolo Marzio 1 (Piazza del Pesce, Ponte Vecchio),* ☎ *055/287216,* 𝔽𝔸𝕏 *055/212208. 29 rooms with bath. MC, V.*

$$ 🏨 **La Residenza.** Centrally located on Florence's most elegant shopping street, on the upper floors of a restored 15th-century building, La Residenza has character and comfort. The roof garden and adjacent sitting room are added attractions. Paintings and etchings add interest to the room decor, while soundproofing and satellite TV help guests to relax. ⊠ *Via Tornabuoni 8,* ☎ *055/218684,* 𝔽𝔸𝕏 *055/284197. 24 rooms, 20 with bath. Restaurant, parking (fee). AE, DC, MC, V.*

$$ 🏨 **Loggiato dei Serviti.** This hotel was not designed by Brunelleschi,
★   Florence's architectural genius, but it might as well have been. A mirror image of the architect's famous Ospedale degli Innocenti across the way, the Loggiato is tucked away on one of the city's quietest and loveliest squares. Occupying a 16th-century former monastery, the building was originally a refuge for traveling priests. Vaulted ceilings and tasteful furnishings, some of them antiques, make this a place for those who want to get the feel of Florence in a spare, Renaissance building while enjoying modern creature comforts. The hotel has no restaurant. ⊠ *Piazza Santissima Annunziata 3,* ☎ *055/289592,* 𝔽𝔸𝕏 *055/289595. 29 rooms with bath. AE, DC, MC, V.*

$$ 🏨 **Morandi alla Crocetta.** Near Piazza Santissima Annunziata, this is
★   a charming and distinguished residence in which guests are made to feel like privileged friends of the family. It is close to the sights but very quiet, in a former monastery, and is furnished comfortably in the classic style of a gracious Florentine home. The Morandi is not only an exceptional hotel but also a good value. Very small, it is worth booking well in advance. ⊠ *Via Laura 50,* ☎ *055/234–4747,* 𝔽𝔸𝕏 *055/248–0954. 10 rooms with bath. AE, DC, MC, V.*

$$ 🏨 **Pendini.** The atmosphere of an old-fashioned Florentine pensione is intact here, though most bedrooms have been freshly renovated. Public rooms are delightful; furnishings throughout are early 19th-century antiques or reproductions. Most bedrooms have brass or walnut beds, pretty floral wallpaper, and pastel carpeting; baths are modern. Many rooms can accommodate extra beds. The location is central, and rates are low for the category. Off season rates are a real bargain. ⊠ *Via Strozzi 2,* ☎ *055/211170,* 𝔽𝔸𝕏 *055/281807. 42 rooms with bath. AE, DC, MC, V.*

$ 🏨 **Alessandra.** The location, a block from the Ponte Vecchio, and clean, ample rooms make this a good choice. The English-speaking staff is friendly and helpful. ⊠ *Borgo Santi Apostoli 17,* ☎ *055/283438. 25 rooms, 18 with bath. AE, MC, V.*

$ 🏨 **Apollo.** A friendly Italian-Canadian couple owns and manages this conveniently located hotel near the station, offering good value in spacious rooms decorated in Florentine style. The gleaming new bathrooms, though compact, have such amenities as hair dryers. The staff is helpful and attentive to guests' needs. ⊠ *Via Faenza 77,* ☎ *055/284119,* 𝔽𝔸𝕏 *055/210101. 15 rooms with bath. Parking (fee). AE, DC, MC, V.*

$ 🏨 **Bellettini.** You couldn't ask for anything more central; this small hotel
★   is on three floors (the top floor has two nice rooms with a view) of a palazzo near the Duomo. The cordial family management takes good care of guests, providing a relaxed atmosphere and attractive public rooms with a scattering of antiques. Breakfast, with homemade cakes, and air-conditioning are included in the low room rate. The good-size

rooms have Venetian or Tuscan provincial decor; bathrooms are bright and modern. ⊠ *Via dei Conti 7,* ☎ *055/213561,* ☏ *055/283551. 28 rooms with bath. Bar, parking (fee). AE, DC, MC, V.*

$ ⊞ **Liana.** This small hotel near the English Cemetery is in a quiet 19th-century villa that formerly housed the British Embassy. Its clean and pleasant rooms all face a stately garden. ⊠ *Via Vittorio Alfieri 18,* ☎ *055/245303,* ☏ *055/234–4596. 17 rooms with bath or shower. AE, MC, V.*

$ ⊞ **Nuova Italia.** Near the train station and within walking distance of the sights, this hotel is run by a genial English-speaking family. It has a homey atmosphere; rooms are clean and simply furnished, bright with pictures and posters, and all with private baths. Some rooms can accommodate extra beds. Low bargain rates include breakfast. ⊠ *Via Faenza 26,* ☎ *055/268430,* ☏ *055/210941. 20 rooms with bath. AE, DC, MC, V.*

NIGHTLIFE AND THE ARTS

The Arts

Concerts

The **Maggio Musicale Fiorentina** series of internationally acclaimed concerts and recitals is held in the Teatro Comunale (⊠ Corso Italia 16, ☎ 055/277–9236) from late April through June. From December to early June, there is a concert season of the **Orchestra Regionale Toscana** in the church of Santo Stefano al Ponte Vecchio (☎ 055/210804). **Amici della Musica** organizes concerts at the Teatro della Pergola (⊠ Box office, Via della Pergola 10/r, ☎ 055/247–9652).

Opera

Operas are performed in the Teatro Comunale from December through February.

Film

English-language films are shown at the **Cinema Astro** on Piazza San Simone near Santa Croce. There are two shows every evening, Tuesday through Sunday (closed in July).

Festival del Popolo. This festival, held each December, is devoted to documentaries and is held in the Fortezza da Basso.

Florence Film Festival. An international panel of judges gathers in late spring at the Forte di Belvedere to preside over a wide selection of new releases.

Nightlife

Unlike the Romans and Milanese, the frugal and reserved Florentines do not have a reputation for an active nightlife; however, the following places attract a mixed crowd of Florentines and visitors.

Piano Bars

Many of the more expensive hotels have their own piano bars, where nonguests are welcome to come for an *aperitivo* or an after-dinner drink. The best view is from the bar at the **Excelsior** (⊠ Piazza Ognissanti 3, ☎ 055/264201), on a roof garden overlooking the Arno. The accent is on Brazil at **Caffè Voltaire** (⊠ Via della Scala 9/r, ☎ 055/218255), where there's Latin food and music. Music is on tape at the **Champagneria** (⊠ Via Lambruschini 15/r, ☎ 055/490804), a bistro-type watering hole (closed Sun.).

Nightclub

River Club (⊠ Lungarno Corsini 8, ☎ 055/282465) has winter-garden decor and a large dance floor (closed Sun.).

Discos

The two largest discos, with the youngest crowds, are **Yab** (⊠ Via Sassetti 5r, ☎ 055/282018) and **Space Electronic** (⊠ Via Palazzuolo 37, ☎ 055/239–3082). Less frenetic alternatives are **Jackie O'** (⊠ Via Erta Canina 24, ☎ 055/234–4904) and **Full Up** (⊠ Via della Vigna Vecchia 21/r, ☎ 055/293006). **Meccanò** (⊠ Viale degli Olmi 1, in Cascine Park, ☎ 055/331371) is a multimedia experience in a high-tech disco with a late-night restaurant (closed Mon.).

OUTDOOR ACTIVITIES AND SPORTS

Participant Sports

Bicycling

Bikes are a good way of getting out into the hills, but the scope for biking is limited in the center of town. *See* Getting Around *in* Florence A to Z, *below,* for information on where to rent bicycles.

Canoeing

Those who get the urge to paddle on the Arno can try **Società Canottieri Firenze** (⊠ Lungarno dei Medici 8, ☎ 055/282130) near the Uffizi.

Golf

Golf Club Ugolino (⊠ Via Chiantigiana 3, Impruneta, ☎ 055/230–1009) is a hilly 18-hole course in the heart of Chianti country just outside town. It is open to the public.

Jogging

Don't even think of jogging on city streets, where tour buses and triple-parked Alfa Romeos leave precious little space for pedestrians. Instead, head for the **Cascine,** the park along the Arno at the western end of the city. You can jog to the Cascine along the Lungarno (stay on the sidewalk), or take Bus 17 from the Duomo. A cinder track lies on the hillside just below **Piazzale Michelangelo,** across the Arno from the city center. The views of the Florence skyline are inspirational, but the locker rooms are reserved for members, so come ready to run.

Swimming

There are a number of pools open to foreigners who want to beat the Florentine heat, among them **Bellariva** (⊠ Lungarno Colombo 6, ☎ 055/677521), **Circolo Tennis alle Cascine** (⊠ Viale Visarno 1, ☎ 055/356651), **Costoli** (Viale Paoli, ☎ 055/675–744), and **Le Pavoniere** (⊠ Viale degli Olmi, ☎ 055/367506).

Tennis

The best spot for an open court is **Circolo Tennis alle Cascine** (⊠ Viale Visarno 1, ☎ 055/356651). Other centers include **Tennis Club Rifredi** (⊠ Via Facibeni, ☎ 055/432552) and **Il Poggetto** (⊠ Via Mercati 24/b, ☎ 055/460127).

Spectator Sports

Horse Racing

You can make your bets at the **Ippodromo Visarno** (⊠ Piazzale delle Cascine, ☎ 055/360056). Check the local papers to see when they're running.

Soccer

Calcio (soccer) is a passion with the Italians, and the Florentines are no exception; indeed, *tifosi* (fans) of the Fiorentina team are renowned for their passionate support. The team plays its home games at the Stadio Comunale (Municipal Stadium) at the top of Viale Manfredo Fanti. Tickets for all games (which are played on Sunday afternoons) except those against their biggest rivals, Juventus of Turin and A. C. Milan, are difficult but not impossible to come by; try the Chiosco degli Sportivi, a ticket booth on the north side of Piazza della Repubblica. The season runs from about late August to May. A medieval version of the game is played in costume each year on or around June 24, feast day of St. John the Baptist.

SHOPPING

Shops in Florence are generally open from 9 to 1 and 3:30 to 7:30 and closed Sundays and Monday mornings most of the year. During the summer the hours are usually 9 to 1 and 4 to 8, with closings on Saturday afternoons but not Monday mornings. When locating the stores, remember that the addresses with *r* in them, which stands for *rosso* (red), and indicates a commercial address, follow a separate numbering system from the black residential addresses. A rule of thumb for shopping in Florence is that if it *looks* expensive, it will more than likely be *more* expensive than you had anticipated. Most shops take major credit cards and will ship purchases, though it's wiser to take your purchases with you.

Borgo Ognissanti

Alberto Pierini (⊠ Borgo Ognissanti 22/r). The rustic Tuscan furniture here is all antique, and much of it dates back to the days of the Medici.
Fallani Best (⊠ Borgo Ognissanti 15/r). The eclectic collection of antiques, although it concentrates on 18th- and 19th-century Italian paintings, has enough variety to appeal to an international clientele.
Giotti (⊠ Piazza Ognissanti 3/r). The largest selection of Bottega Veneta's woven-leather bags are stocked at this shop, which carries a full line of the firm's other leather goods, as well as its own leather clothing.
Loretta Caponi (⊠ Borgo Ognissanti 12/r). Signora Caponi is synonymous with Florentine embroidery, and her luxury lace, linens, and lingerie have earned her a worldwide reputation.
Paolo Ventura (⊠ Borgo Ognissanti 16/r). Specialties here are antique ceramics from all periods and places of origin. As with the other shops, the rule of thumb is that the Italian goods are best.
Pratesi (⊠ Lungarno Amerigo Vespucci 8/r). The name Pratesi is a byword for luxury, in this case linens that have lined the beds of the rich and famous, with an emphasis on the former.

Duomo

Bartolini (⊠ Via dei Servi 30/r). For housewares, nothing beats this shop, which has a wide selection of well-designed, practical items.
Calamai (⊠ Via Cavour 78/r). One of Florence's largest gift shops, Calamai carries everything from inexpensive stationery to housewares in bright, bold colors and designs in its largest of three stores.
Casa dello Sport (⊠ Via dei Tosinghi 8/r). Here you'll find casual wear for the entire family—sporty clothes by some of Italy's most famous manufacturers.
Emilio Pucci (⊠ Via dei Pucci 6/r). A member of an aristocratic Italian family, the Marchese di Barsento was a household name in Florence, and until his death in 1992, he presided over the opening of the Renaissance *Calcio in Costume* festivities each year. He became an in-

ternational name during the early 1960s, when the stretch ski clothes he designed for himself caught on with the dolce vita crowd. His prints and "palazzo pajamas" then became the rage. The shop in the family palazzo still sells the celebrated Pucci prints, along with a line of wines from the family estate in Chianti.

Pineider (✉ Piazza della Signoria 14/r and Via Tornabuoni 76/r). Pineider now has shops throughout the world, but it began in Florence and still does all its printing here. Personalized stationery and business cards are its main business, but the stores also sell fine desk accessories.

Ponte Vecchio

Della Loggia (✉ Via Por Santa Maria 29/r). For a contemporary look, try this store, which combines precious and semiprecious stones in settings made of precious and nonprecious metals, such as the gold and steel pieces usually on display in its windows.

Gherardi (✉ Ponte Vecchio 5). The king of coral in Florence has the city's largest selection of finely crafted and encased specimens, as well as other precious materials such as cultured pearls, jade, and turquoise.

Melli (✉ Ponte Vecchio 44/r). Antique jewelry is the specialty here; it is displayed alongside period porcelains, clocks, and other museum-quality objects.

Piccini (✉ Ponte Vecchio 23/r). This venerable shop has literally been crowning the heads of Europe for almost a century, and combines its taste for the antique with contemporary jewelry.

Oltrarno

Centro Di (✉ Piazza dei Mozzi 1). Its name stands for Centro di Documentazione Internazionale, and it publishes art books and exhibition catalogues for some of the most important organizations in Europe. Centro Di stocks its own publications along with many others.

Galleria Luigi Bellini (✉ Lungarno Soderini 5). The Galleria claims to be Italy's oldest antiques dealer, which may be true, since father Mario Bellini was responsible for instituting Florence's international antiques biennial. At any rate, what matters is that the merchandise is genuine.

Giannini (✉ Piazza Pitti 37/r). One of Florence's oldest paper-goods stores, Giannini is *the* place to buy the marbleized versions, which come in a variety of forms, from flat sheets to boxes and even pencils.

Santa Croce

I Maschereri (✉ Borgo Pinti 18/r). Spurred on by the revival of Carnival in recent years, I Maschereri has begun to produce fanciful masks in commedia dell'arte and contemporary styles.

Leather Guild (✉ Piazza Santa Croce 20/r). This is one of many such shops throughout the area that produce inexpensive, antique-looking leather goods of mass appeal, but here you can see the craftspersons at work, a reassuring experience.

Salimbeni (✉ Via Matteo Palmieri 14/r). Long one of Florence's best art bookshops, Salimbeni specializes in publications on Tuscany; it publishes many itself.

Sbigoli Terrecotte (✉ Via Sant'Egidio 4/r). This crafts shop carries a wide selection of terra-cotta and ceramic vases, pots, cups, and saucers.

Via Maggio

Giovanni Pratesi (✉ Via Maggio 13/r). This shop specializes in Italian antiques, in this case furniture, with some fine paintings, sculpture, and decorative objects turning up from time to time.

Guido Bartolozzi (✉ Via Maggio 18/r). Vying with Luigi Bellini as one of Florence's oldest antiques dealers, Bartolozzi's collection of predominately Florentine objects from all periods is as highly selected as it is priced.

Paolo Paoletti (⊠ Via Maggio 30/r). Look for Florentine antiques, with an emphasis on Medici-era objects from the 15th and 16th centuries.

Soluzioni (⊠ Via Maggio 82/r). This offbeat store displays some of the most unusual items on this staid street, ranging from clocks to compacts, all selected with an eye for the eccentric.

Via della Vigna Nuova

Alinari (⊠ Via della Vigna Nuova 46/r). This outlet is one of Florence's oldest and most prestigious photographers, and in this store, next to its museum, prints of its historic photographs are sold along with books and posters.

Antico Setificio Fiorentino (⊠ Via della Vigna Nuova 97/r). This fabric outlet really *is* antique, as it has produced antique fabrics for over half a millennium. Swaths of handmade material of every style and description are for sale, and the decorative tassels make lovely typically Florentine presents as well.

Et Cetera (⊠ Via della Vigna Nuova 82/r). In a city of papermakers, this store has some of the most unusual such items, most of which are handmade and some of which have made it into the design collection of New York's Museum of Modern Art.

Filpucci (⊠ Via della Vigna Nuova 14/r). This is Italy's largest manufacturer of yarns. Nearby factories produce skeins of the stuff for Italy's top designers, and the extensive stock of its retail outlet in Florence encourages the talented to create their own designs.

Il Bisonte (⊠ Via del Parione 31/r). The street address is just off Via della Vigna Nuova; Il Bisonte is known for its natural-look leather goods, all stamped with the store's bison symbol.

Laurèl (⊠ Via della Vigna Nuova 67/r). An elegant boutique, Laurèl has a reputation for the quality and understatement that is the hallmark of Florentine women's fashions.

Via Tornabuoni

Casadei (⊠ Via Tornabuoni 33/r). The ultimate fine leathers are crafted into classic shapes here, winding up as women's shoes and bags.

Ferragamo (⊠ Via Tornabuoni 16/r). Born near Naples, the late Salvatore Ferragamo made his fortune custom-making exotic shoes for famous feet, especially Hollywood stars, and so this establishment knows about less-than-delicate shoe sizes. His palace at the end of the street has since passed on to his wife, Wanda, and displays designer clothing, but elegant footwear still underlies the Ferragamo success.

Gucci (⊠ Via Tornabuoni 73/r). The Gucci family is practically single-handedly responsible for making designers' initials (in this case the two interlocking *G*s) a status symbol. This Florence store is the one that started it all, and prices on the clothing and leather goods are slightly better here than elsewhere.

Settepassi-Faraone (⊠ Via Tornabuoni 25/r). One of Florence's oldest jewelers, Settepassi-Faraone has supplied Italian (and other) royalty with finely crafted gems for centuries. Its selection of antique-looking classics has been updated with a choice of contemporary silver.

Ugolini (⊠ Via Tornabuoni 20/r). This shop once made gloves for the Italian royal family, but now anyone who can afford it can have the luxury of its exotic leathers, as well as silk and cashmere ties and scarves.

SIDE TRIPS

Fiesole

An excursion to the ancient Roman town of **Fiesole,** set in the hills 8 kilometers (5 miles) above Florence, gives you a respite from museums and breaks up the inevitable monotony of city sightseeing. Fiesole began life as an ancient Etruscan and later Roman village that held some power until it succumbed to the barbarian invasions and eventually gave up its independence in exchange for Florence's protection. The medieval cathedral, some other old churches, the ancient Roman amphitheater, and lovely old villas behind garden walls are clustered on a series of hilltops. Fiesole is a place for walking and admiring the views; a nice half-day jaunt in fair weather.

The ride from Florence by car or bus takes about 20 minutes. A walk around Fiesole can take from one to two or three hours, depending on how far you stroll from the main piazza.

Take city Bus 7 from the Santa Maria Novella train station, Piazza San Marco, or the Duomo to Fiesole. The cathedral and other old buildings are on the main piazza, and the Roman amphitheater is about 30 yards away. Climb the hill to the church of San Francesco to get to the terrace for a good view of Florence and the plain below. The air is usually clearest early in the morning or late in the afternoon. If you really want to stretch your legs, walk along Via Vecchia Fiesolana, a narrow lane, to the church of San Domenico and the Badia Fiesolana, Fiesole's cathedral, 4 kilometers (2½ miles) southwest of Fiesole.

The **Duomo** has a stark medieval interior. In the raised presbytery, the Salutati Chapel was frescoed by 15th-century artist Cosimo Rosselli, but it was his contemporary, sculptor Mino da Fiesole, who put the town on the artistic map. The Madonna on the altarpiece and the tomb of Bishop Salutati are his work.

Nightlife and the Arts
Estate Fiesolana. From June through August, this festival of theater, music, dance, and film takes place in the churches and the archaeological area of Fiesole (⊠ Teatro Romano, Fiesole, ☎ 055/599931).

FLORENCE A TO Z

Arriving and Departing
By Bus
Long-distance buses run by **SITA** (⊠ Via Santa Caterina da Siena 15/r, ☎ 055/483651 weekdays, 211487 on weekends) and **Lazzi Eurolines** (⊠ Via Mercadante 2, ☎ 055/215154) offer inexpensive if somewhat claustrophobic service between Florence and other cities in Italy and Europe.

By Car
Florence is connected to the north and south of Italy by the Autostrada del Sole (A1). It is about an hour's scenic drive from Bologna (although heavy truck traffic over the Apennines often makes for slower going) and about three hours from Rome. The Tyrrhenian coast is an hour away on A11 West. In the city, abandon all hope of using a car, since most of the downtown area is a pedestrian zone. For traffic information in Florence, call 055/577–777.

By Plane
The A. Vespucci Airport, called **Peretola** (☎ 055/333–498), is 10 kilometers (6 miles) northwest of Florence. Although it accommodates flights from Milan, Rome, and some European cities, it is still a relatively minor airport. **Galileo Galilei Airport** in Pisa (☎ 050/500–707) is 80 kilometers (50 miles) west of Florence and is used by most international carriers; for flight information, call the Florence Air Ter-

minal at Santa Maria Novella train station (☎ 055/216–073) or Galilei airport information.

International travelers flying on Alitalia to Rome's **Leonardo da Vinci Airport** and headed directly for Florence can make connections at the airport for a flight to Florence, but if the layover is a long one, consider taking the FS airport train to Termini station in Rome, where fast trains for Florence are frequent during the day.

BETWEEN THE AIRPORTS AND DOWNTOWN

By Bus. There is no direct bus service from Pisa's airport to Florence. Buses do go to Pisa itself, but then you have to change to a slow train service. There is a local bus service from Peretola to Florence.

By Car. From Peretola take autostrada A11 directly into the city. Driving from the airport in Pisa, take S67, a direct route to Florence.

By Train. A scheduled service connects the station at Pisa's Galileo Galilei Airport with Santa Maria Novella Station in Florence, roughly a one-hour trip. Trains start running about 7 AM from the airport, 6 AM from Florence, and continue service every hour until about 11:30 PM from the airport, 8 PM from Florence. You can check in for departing flights at the air terminal at Track 5 of the train station (☎ 055/216–073).

By Train

Florence is on the principal Italian train route between most European capitals and Rome and within Italy is served quite frequently from Milan, Venice, and Rome by nonstop Intercity (IC) trains. The **Santa Maria Novella Station** is near the downtown area; avoid trains that stop only at the Campo di Marte Station in an inconvenient location on the east side of the city. For train information in Florence, call 055/288–785.

Getting Around

By Bicycle

Brave souls (cycling in Florence is difficult, at best) may rent bicycles at easy-to-spot locations at Fortezza da Basso, the Santa Maria Novella train station, and Piazza Pitti, from **Alinari** (✉ Via San Zanobi 9/r, ☎ 055/490–113) or **Motorent** (✉ Via Guelfa 85/r, ☎ 055/280–500), or from **Ciao e Basta** (✉ Lungarno Pecori Girardi 1, ☎ 055/234–2726).

By Bus

Maps and timetables are available for a small fee at the **ATAF** booth next to the train station or at the office at Piazza del Duomo 57/r, or for free at visitor information offices (☞ Contacts and Resources, *below*). Tickets must be bought in advance and can be purchased at tobacco stores, newsstands, from automatic ticket machines near main stops, or at ATAF booths (next to the station and at strategic locations throughout the city). The ticket must be canceled in the small validation machine immediately upon boarding. Two types of tickets are available, both valid for one or more rides on all lines. One costs 1,400 lire and is valid for 60 minutes from the time it is first canceled; the other costs 1,900 lire and is valid for 120 minutes. A multiple ticket—four tickets each valid for 60 minutes—costs 5,400 lire. A 24-hour tourist ticket costs 5,000 lire. Long-term visitors or frequent users of the bus should consider a monthly pass, which is sold at the ATAF office.

By Moped

Those who want to go native and rent a noisy Vespa (Italian for "wasp") or other make of motorcycle or moped may do so at **Motorent** or **Alinari** (☞ By Bicycle, *above*). Helmets are mandatory and can be rented at either place.

By Taxi

Taxis usually wait at stands throughout the city (such as in front of the train station and in Piazza della Repubblica), or they can be called (☎ 055/4390 or 055/4798). The meter starts at 4,000 lire.

Contacts and Resources

Consulates

U.S. Consulate. (✉ Lungarno Vespucci 38, ☎ 055/239–8276. ◷ Weekdays 8:30–noon and 2–4). **U.K. Consulate.** (✉ Lungarno Corsini 2, ☎ 055/284133. ◷ Weekdays 9:30–12:30 and 2:30–4:30). **Canadians** should contact their embassy in Rome.

Doctors and Dentists

For English-speaking doctors and dentists, get a list from the U.S. consulate, or contact **Tourist Medical Service** (✉ Viale Lorenzo Il Magnifico, ☎ 055/475411).

Emergencies

Police: (☎ 113); main police station (✉ Via Zara 2, near Piazza della Libertà). **Ambulance:** (☎ 118), or Misericordia (✉ Piazza del Duomo 20, ☎ 055/212222). If you need hospital treatment—and an interpreter—you can call AVO, a group of volunteer interpreters who offer their services free (☎ 055/403126; Mon., Wed., Fri. 4–6 PM, ☎ 055/234–4567).

English-Language Bookstores

Paperback Exchange (✉ Via Fiesolana 31/r, ☎ 055/247–8154) will do just that, besides selling books outright. **BM Bookshop** (✉ Borgo Ognissanti 4/r, ☎ 055/294575) has a fine selection of books on Florence. **Seeber** (✉ Via Tornabuoni 68, ☎ 055/215697) has English-language books alongside the other titles. ◷ *All are open 9–1 and 3:30–7:30. Closed Sun. and Mon. morning.*

Guided Tours

EXCURSIONS

Contact bus operators (☞ Arriving and Departing, *above*) a day in advance, if possible, because excursions are popular. Comfortable buses with English-speaking guides make full-day trips from Florence to Siena and San Gimignano (departure 9 AM, return 6 PM, lunch not included) and afternoon excursions to Pisa (departure 2 PM, return 7 PM), with pickup and return from the main hotels. The Siena excursion costs about 68,000 lire, the Pisa excursion about 48,000 lire. Good bus and train connections make it easy for you to do these on your own, however.

ORIENTATION TOURS

Visitors who have a limited amount of time in Florence may find guided tours an efficient way of covering the city's major sights. The major bus operators (☞ Arriving and Departing, *above*) offer half-day itineraries, all of which generally follow the same plan, using comfortable buses staffed with English-speaking guides. Morning tours begin at 9, when buses pick visitors up at the main hotels. Stops include the cathedral complex, the Accademia, Piazzale Michelangelo, and the Pitti Palace (or, on Mondays, the Museo dell'Opera del Duomo). Afternoon tours stop at the main hotels at 2 PM and take in Piazza della Signoria, the Uffizi Gallery (or the Palazzo Vecchio on Monday, when the Uffizi is closed), the nearby town of Fiesole, and, on the return, the church of Santa Croce. A half-day tour costs about 48,000 lire, including museum admissions.

Late-Night Pharmacies

The following are open 24 hours a day, seven days a week. (For others, ☎ 055/110.)

Comunale No. 13 (✉ Santa Maria Novella Station, ☎ 055/289435). **Molteni** (✉ Via Calzaiuoli 7/r, ☎ 055/289490). **Taverna** (✉ Piazza San Giovanni 20/r, ☎ 055/284013).

Travel Agencies

American Express (✉ Via Guicciardini 49/r, near Piazza Pitti, ☎ 055/288751; ✉ Via Dante Alighiere 20/r, ☎ 055/50981) is also represented by **Universalturismo** (✉ Via Speziali 7/r, off Piazza della Repubblica, ☎ 055/217241). **CIT** (✉ Via Cavour 56, ☎ 055/294306; ✉ Piazza Stazione 51, ☎ 055/239–6963). **Thomas Cook** is represented by **World Vision** (✉ Via Cavour 154/r, ☎ 055/579294). All agencies are open weekdays 9–12:30 and 3:30–7:30, Saturday 9–noon.

Visitor Information

The city information office is open from 8:30 to 7 Via Cavour 1/r (✉ next to Palazzo Medici–Riccardi, ☎ 055/290–832). Another municipal information office is next to the train station (☎ 055/212245; closed after 2 PM in winter). There is another information office near Piazza della Signoria (✉ Chiasso dei Baroncelli 17/r, ☎ 055/230–2124).

The **APT** (tourist office) is just off Piazza Beccaria (✉ Via Manzoni 16, ☎ 055/234–6284. ⊙ Mon.–Sat. 8:30–1:30).

3 Tuscany

Lucca, Siena, and the Hill Towns

Without a doubt, Nature outdid herself in Tuscany. Punctuated by thickly wooded hills, snowcapped peaks, sun-warmed vineyards, olive groves, and dramatic hill towns, Tuscany's milk-and-honey vistas have changed little since Renaissance artists first beheld them.

In case you want to see the world.

At American Express, we're here to make your journey a smooth one. So we have over 1,700 travel service locations in over 120 countries ready to help. What else would you expect from the world's largest travel agency?

do more ®

Travel

In case you want to be welcomed there.

We're here to see that you're always welcomed at establishments everywhere. That's why millions of people carry the American Express® Card – for peace of mind, confidence, and security, around the world or just around the corner.

do more®

Cards

In case you're running low.

We're here to help with more than 118,000 Express Cash locations around the world. In order to enroll, just call American Express before you start your vacation.

do more

Express Cash

And just in case.

We're here with American Express® Travelers Cheques and Cheques *for Two*® They're the safest way to carry money on your vacation and the surest way to get a refund, practically anywhere, anytime.
Another way we help you...

do more®

Travelers Cheques

ROME MAY BE THE CAPITAL OF ITALY, but Tuscany is its heart. Stretching from the Apennines to the sea, midway between Milan and Rome, the region is quintessentially Italian, in both its appearance and its history. Its scenic variety is unmatched in Italy; its past has been ignoble (it produced the Guelph–Ghibelline conflict of the Middle Ages) and glorious (it gave birth to the Renaissance). Its towns are justly famous for their wealth of fine architecture and art, but visitors often go home even more enthusiastic about Tuscany's unspoiled hilly landscapes, about the delicious Chianti wines produced by vineyards on those hills, and about the robust and flavorful Tuscan cooking. Be sure to allot some portion of your time here for leisurely strolls, unhurried meals, and aimless wandering around this peerless countryside, where the true soul of Tuscany is to be found.

Tuscany also produced the Italian language. Thanks to the eminence of their writings, it was the Tuscan dialect of Dante, Petrarch, and Boccaccio, all native sons, that grew to be the national tongue, a fact of which the Tuscans are rightly proud. Today the purest Italian is said to be spoken in the area between Siena and Arezzo, and even visitors with limited textbook Italian can often hear the difference. As they enter the region, the language suddenly becomes much easier to understand and takes on a bell-like clarity and mellifluous beauty unequaled throughout the rest of Italy.

It also takes on a notorious wit. As a common proverb has it, "Tuscans have Paradise in their eyes and the Inferno in their mouths" (a wry reference to Dante), and the sting of their wit is as famous throughout Italy as is the beauty of their speech. Happily, the Tuscans usually reserve their wit for each other and treat visitors with complete and sincere courtesy.

For a long time, the Tuscan hill towns were notorious as well. Even their earliest civilized settlers, the Etruscans, chose their city-sites for defensive purposes (the fortress-town of Fiesole, above Florence, is a fine surviving example). With the end of the Roman Empire, the region fell into disunity, and by the 11th century, Tuscany had evolved into a collection of independent city-states, each city seeking to dominate, and sometimes forcibly overpower, its neighbors. The region then became embroiled in an apparently endless international quarrel between a long succession of popes and Holy Roman Emperors. By the 13th century, Tuscany had become a battleground: The infamous conflict between the Guelphs and the Ghibellines had begun.

The Guelphs and the Ghibellines are the bane of Italian schoolchildren; their infinitely complicated, bloody history is to Italy what the Wars of the Roses are to England. To oversimplify grossly, the Ghibellines were mostly allied with both the Holy Roman Emperor (headquartered over the Alps in Germany) and the local aristocracy (dominated by feudal lords); the Guelphs were mostly allied with both the pope (headquartered in Rome) and the emerging middle class (dominated by the new trade guilds). Florence, flourishing as a trade center, was (most of the time) Guelph; its neighboring city-states Pisa and Siena were (most of the time) Ghibelline. But the bitter struggles that resulted were so byzantine in their complexity, so full of factional disputes and treachery, that a dizzying series of conflicts within conflicts resulted. (Dante, for instance, was banished from Florence not for being a Ghibelline but for being the wrong brand of Guelph.)

Eventually the Florentine Guelphs emerged victorious, and in the 15th century the region was united to become the Grand Duchy of Tuscany, controlled from Florence by the Medici grand dukes. Today the hill towns are no longer fierce, although they retain a uniquely medieval air, and in most of them the citizens walk the same narrow streets and inhabit the same houses that their ancestors did 600 years ago.

Tuscan art, to most people, means Florence, and understandably so. The city is unique and incomparable, and an astonishing percentage of the great artists of the Renaissance lived and worked there. But there is art elsewhere in Tuscany, and too often it is overlooked in favor of another trip to the Uffizi. Siena, particularly, possesses its own style of architecture and art quite different from the Florentine variety; the contrast is both surprising and illuminating. And even the smallest of the hill towns can possess hidden treasures, for the artists of the Middle Ages and the Renaissance took their work where they could find it. Piero della Francesca's fresco cycle in the church of San Francesco in Arezzo is perhaps the preeminent hidden treasure. Tucked away in a small church in a small town, and, sadly, faded, the frescoes are artistically the equal of almost everything Florence has to offer and are all the more appealing for their uncrowded setting.

Pleasures and Pastimes

Dining

Though Florentine cuisine now predominates throughout Tuscany, the Etruscan influence on regional food still persists after more than three millennia. Just as the ancient Etruscans were responsible for the introduction of the cypress to the Tuscan landscape, so they are also credited with the use of herbs in cooking. Basic ingredients such as tarragon, sage, rosemary, and thyme appear frequently, happily coupled with game, Chianina beef, or even seafood. Each region has its own specialties, usually based on simple ingredients, and Tuscans are disparagingly called *mangiafagioli*, or bean eaters, by other Italians. However, Tuscan chefs have recently discovered the rest of the world, and for better or worse, an "international cuisine" has been gradually making its appearance throughout the region.

Fortunately, Tuscany's wines remain unaltered. Grapes have been cultivated here since Etruscan times, and Chianti still rules the roost (almost literally when selected by the Gallo Nero Black Rooster label, a symbol of one of the region's most powerful wine-growing consortiums; the other is a putto, or cherub). The robust red wine is still a staple on most tables, and the discerning can select from a multitude of other varieties, including such reds as Brunello di Montalcino and Vino Nobile di Montepulciano, and whites such as Valdinievole and Vergine della Valdichiana. The dessert wine *vin santo* is produced throughout the region and is often enjoyed with *biscottini di Prato*, (caramelized cookies which are perfect for dunking)

CATEGORY	COST*
$$$$	over 110,000 lire
$$$	60,000 lire–110,000 lire
$$	35,000 lire–60,000 lire
$	under 35,000 lire

per person, for a three-course meal, including house wine and taxes

Lodging

Tuscany is not an inexpensive place to stay, especially the main towns and tourist centers. But the selection of options includes some wonderful properties, including some fine Renaissance hotels and even medieval palazzi where you'll feel more like Lorenzo de Medici than a 20th-century tourists. To keep costs down, stick to less-visited towns and farmhouse lodgings.

CATEGORY	COST*
$$$$	over 300,000 lire
$$$	220,000 lire–300,000 lire
$$	100,000 lire–220,000 lire
$	under 100,000 lire

All prices are for a double room for two, including tax and service.

Exploring Tuscany

Tuscany has two basic geographical regions—the area immediately to the south of Florence, which contains the famous Tuscan hill towns, and the area immediately to the west, a string of cities that were historically the enemies of Florence, which fought to control them in order to have access to the sea. We describe each of these regions in its own section, below.

Great Itineraries

Although Tuscany is relatively small—no sight of importance is more than a few hours' drive from Florence—the desire to linger is strong: Can anyone ever really get enough of sitting on a hillside *terrazza* (terraces) with a good espresso or a robust chianti and watch the evening settle over a landscape of soft-edged hills, proud medieval towns, quiet villages, and cypress-ringed villas?

It only takes a few days for the region to leave an indelible mark on the memory and, for many, the soul. Ten days would allow for leisurely explorations of the main towns and for meandering along country roads to rustic-elegant estates and wineries. If you have five days, you can see the most interesting towns, but you'll need to stick to the main sights and move briskly between destinations. In three days, you can take in all the highlights, if not the small corners.

Numbers in the text correspond to numbers in the margin and on the Tuscany, Lucca, and Siena maps.

IF YOU HAVE 3 DAYS

See **Lucca** ④–⑪ and the Leaning Tower in **Pisa** ⑫, then head for 🏨 **San Gimignano** ⑭ to overnight. The next day, spend a few hours in **Siena** ⑮–⑳, then move on to 🏨 **Montepulciano** ㉔ for the night; the following day, see **Arezzo** ㉖ and head back to Florence, your starting point, via the A1.

IF YOU HAVE 5 DAYS

Florence makes a good starting point. From there, head for industrial **Prato** ① to see its striking medieval core; historic **Pistoia** ②, site of bitter Guelph–Ghibelline feuding; and **Montecatini** ③, one of Europe's most famous spas. Overnight in 🏨 **Lucca** ④–⑪ and spend part of the next day exploring this most elegant of cities, then head for **Pisa** ⑫; see the Leaning Tower and then move on to hilltop **Volterra** ⑬, a fortress town, and beautiful 🏨 **San Gimignano** ⑭ the archetypal Tuscan town and a good place to spend your second night. On the third day, while away the morning in **Siena** ⑮–⑳, perhaps Italy's loveliest medieval city, before heading for the **Abbey of Monte Oliveto Maggiore** ㉑, **Montalcino** ㉒ of wine-growing fame, the **Abbey of Sant'Antimo**, and then 🏨 **Montepulciano** ㉔, where you should overnight. Trace your road back on the morning of your fourth day for a tour of **Pienza** ㉓, designed for Pope Pius II to be the perfect Renaissance town. Move on to handsome but underappreciated **Arezzo** ㉖ and 🏨 **Cortona** ㉕, where there are galleries and lodging, visiting **Chiusi** and **Chianciano** along the way. Spend part of your fifth day in Cortona or Arezzo before returning to Florence.

IF YOU HAVE 7 DAYS

More time allows you to see more towns and more in those you visit. Be sure to rent a car if your goal is to soak up the essence of Tuscany— it's the only way to get to many of the vineyards and estates.

As you approach **Prato** ①, you'll have time to visit the Pecci Center of Contemporary Art. In **Montecatini Terme** ③ ride the funicular up to older Montecatini Alto. If you're an architecture buff, extend your visit to **Pisa** ⑫ beyond the main square to include the Renaissance buildings of the Piazza dei Cavalieri. To really see the Tuscan countryside, don't travel south to **Volterra** ⑬ when leaving Pisa; instead, continue toward Florence on the S67 and turn south on the meandering S222, which leads through a region that's perfect for leisurely exploration—for the best experience, always take winding smaller roads to and from the towns of interest. The S222 is also known as the Strada Chiantigiana because it runs through the heart of the Chianti wine-producing country; the most scenic section runs between Strada in Chianti, 16 kilometers (10 miles) south of Florence, and Greve in Chianti, 11 kilometers (7 miles) farther south, where rolling hillsides are planted with vineyards and olive groves. On your way, be sure to visit **Monteriggioni,** a hilltop hamlet encircled by formidable 13th-century walls.

Take time to make the lengthy detour around Colle Val d'Elsa's workaday lower town up to the ridge, where the medieval center remains practically intact. Break the drive to **Arezzo** ㉖ at prosperous-looking **Monte San Savino** and the tiny nearby fortified village of **Gargonza.** For more Tuscan countryside, don't return yet to Florence but instead detour through the Casentino, a mountainous region smothered in a huge forest that is a far cry from the pastoral images often associated with Tuscany. Return to Florence along the winding S67, known in Tuscany as the splendidly scenic Consuma, or "consumer," as it is a road wrought with hairpin turns and blind corners that require even the best driver to be alert.

When to Tour Tuscany

In summer, try to arrive in towns early in the morning. Italians are early risers, and most shops and museums open by 8:30. If you get up at cockcrow, you can avoid both the crowds and the often oppressive heat. In any case, Tuscany is not about late nights; most bars close their shutters at midnight.

If you plan to visit the frescoes in the Palazzo Pubblico in Siena at midday, be prepared to wait in line and, once inside, to be shuffled along by iron-willed guardians eager to see you in and out in the fastest time possible. If you want to photograph the towers of San Gimignano from a distance, do it in early morning, when the light is good and lines of neon-colored, diesel-spewing tour buses snaking up the hill will not ruin a perfect picture.

WESTERN TUSCANY

Tuscan Gateway: Prato, Pistoia, Lucca, and Pisa

Set in the shadows of the rugged coastal Alpi Apuane, where Michelangelo quarried his marble, this area isn't as lush as the south and lacks its vineyards and olive groves. The population centers here are real cities, with some rather unattractive suburbs in addition to their stunning medieval and Renaissance centers.

Prato

❶ *17 km (10.5 mi) northwest of Florence, 60 km (37 mi) east of Lucca.*

The wool industry in this city, one of the world's largest manufacturers of cloth, was known throughout Europe as early as the 13th century. It was further stimulated in the 14th century by a local cloth merchant, Francesco di Marco Datini, who built his business, according to one of his surviving ledgers, "in the name of God and of profit."

Prato's main attraction is its 11th-century **Duomo.** Romanesque in style, it is famous for its Chapel of the Holy Girdle (to the left of the entrance), which enshrines the sash of the Virgin; it is said that the girdle was given to the apostle Thomas by the Virgin herself, when she miraculously appeared after her Assumption. The Duomo also contains 16th-century frescoes by Prato's most famous son, the libertine monk Fra Filippo Lippi; the best known depict Herod's banquet and Salome's dance. ⊠ *Piazza del Duomo.* ☉ *Daily May–Oct. 6:30–noon and 4–7; Nov.–Apr. 6:30–noon, 3:30–6:30.*

Sculpture by Donatello that originally adorned the Duomo's exterior pulpit is now on display in the **Museo dell'Opera del Duomo.** ⊠ *Piazza del Duomo 49,* ☎ *0574/29339.* 🎟 *5,000 lire (includes Galleria Comunale).* ☉ *Mon., Wed.–Sat. 9:30–12:30, 3–6:30; Sun. 9:30–12:30.*

The **Galleria Comunale** contains a good collection of Tuscan and Sienese paintings, mainly from the 14th century. ⊠ *Palazzo Pretorio, Piazza del Comune,* ☎ *0574/452302.* 🎟 *5,000 lire (includes Museo dell'Opera del Duomo).* ☉ *Mon., Wed.–Sat. 9:30–12:30, 3–6:30; Sun. 9:30–12:30.*

Prato's **Pecci Center of Contemporary Art** has a burgeoning collection of works by Italian and other artists. ⊠ *Viale della Repubblica,* ☎ *0574/570620.* 🎟 *10,000 lire.* ☉ *Wed.–Sun. 10–7.*

For a look at gracious country living, Medici style, detour 7 kilometers (4 miles) south of Prato to the elegant **Villa Medici in Poggio a Caiano.** The villa was built by Giuliano da Sangallo for Lorenzo the Magnificent and lavished with frescoes by Andrea del Sarto and Pontormo, among others. 🎟 *4,000 lire.* ☉ *Apr.–May and Sept., Mon.–Sat. 9–5:30; June–Aug., Mon.–Sat. 9–6:30; Mar. and Oct., Mon.–Sat. 9–4:30; Nov.–Feb., Mon.–Sat. 9–3:30. Closed 2nd and 3rd Mon. of month. Ticket office closes 1 hr before closing time.*

Dining

$$$ ✕ **Piraña.** Oddly named for the cannibalistic fish swimming in an aquarium in full view of diners, this sophisticated restaurant, decorated in shades of blue with steely accents, is a local favorite. Seafood is the specialty and may take the form of *bavettine in cacciucco* (linguine with seafood) or *branzine in crosta di sale* (sea bass baked in salt). It's a bit out of the way for sightseers but handy if you have a car, as it's near the Prato Est autostrada exit. ⊠ *Via G. Valentini 110,* ☎ *0574/25746. AE, DC, MC, V. Closed Sun. and Aug. No lunch Sat.*

$$ ✕ **La Veranda.** A large antipasto buffet greets you just inside the door of this restaurant near Prato's 13th-century Castello dell'Imperatore. Although it's an elegant place with its pale pink walls, terra-cotta tiled floors, and Venetian glass chandeliers, the atmosphere is friendly and

Tuscany

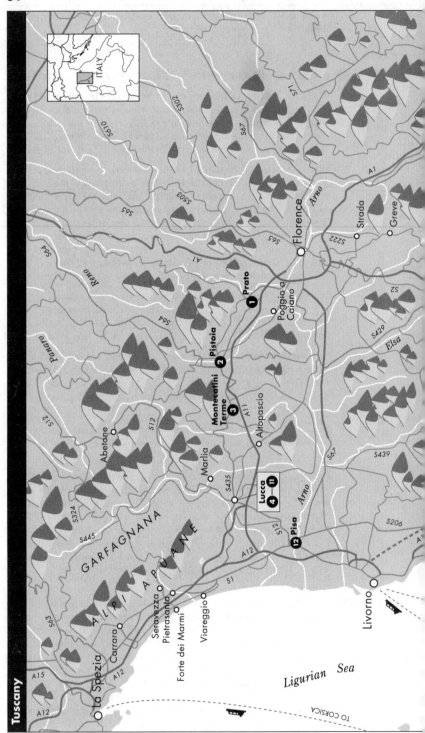

ITALY

Florence

Arno

Strada

Greve

S222

S2

S429

Elsa

S67

S439

A1

Prato

1

Poggio a
Caiano

Pistoia **2**

Montecatini
Terme **3**

Altopascio

A11

Lucca **4—11**

12 Pisa

Arno

S206

A

Livorno

S302

S610

S635

S503

S65

S67

S564

Reno

Panaro

S64

S12

Abetone

S12

Marlia

S435

S12

GARFAGNANA

S324

S445

A L P I   A P U A N E

S63

Carrara

Seravezza
Pietrasanta

Forte dei Marmi

Viareggio

S1

A12

A12

La Spezia

A15

A12

Ligurian   Sea

TO CORSICA

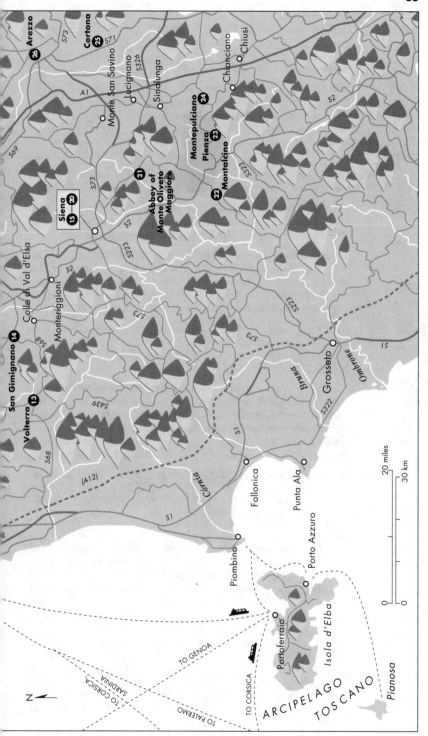

family oriented. The large menu offers several international dishes, including Spanish paella, but never ignores Tuscan specialties, such as *agnello alla cacciatora* (lamb with a tangy wine-vinegar sauce). ⊠ *Via dell'Arco 10,* ☎ *0574/38235. AE, DC, MC, V. Closed Sun. and Aug. No lunch Sat.*

Shopping
Prato makes hard almond cookies called *biscottini,* ideal for dunking in the beverage of one's choice. They're available at bakeries and food stores around town.

Pistoia

❷ *18 km (11mi) northwest of Prato, 36 km (20 mi) northwest of Florence, 40 km (25 mi) east of Lucca, 108 km (67 mi) north of Siena.*

The town saw the beginning of the bitter Guelph-Ghibelline conflict of the Middle Ages. Reconstructed after heavy bombing during World War II, it contains some fine Romanesque architecture.

The **Cathedral of San Zeno** in the main square (⊠ Piazza del Duomo) houses the *Dossale di San Jacopo,* a magnificent silver altarpiece. The two half-figures on its left side are by Filippo Brunelleschi (1377–1446), better known as the first Renaissance architect (and designer of Florence's magnificent Duomo dome). ☜ *Illumination of altarpiece: 2,000 lire.*

The 14th-century Palazzo del Comune houses the **Museo Civico,** containing medieval art. ⊠ *Museo Civico, Piazza del Duomo,* ☎ *0573/ 371275.* ☜ *5,000 lire; free Sat. 3–7.* ☉ *Tues.–Sat. 9–1 and 3–7, Sun. 9–12:30.*

Also in Pistoia are several other attractions. The **Ospedale del Ceppo** (⊠ Piazza Ospedale, a short way down Via Pacini from Piazza del Duomo), a hospital founded during the 14th century, has a superb early 16th-century terra-cotta frieze by Giovanni della Robbia. In the church of **Sant'Andrea** (⊠ Via Pappe to Via Sant'Andrea), the fine early 14th-century pulpit by Giovanni Pisano depicts the life of Christ.

Ⓒ Just outside town is the **Giardino Zoologico,** especially laid out to accommodate the wiles of both animals and children. ⊠ *Via Pieve a Celle 160, Pistoia,* ☎ *0573/939219.* ☜ *13,000.* ☉ *Apr.–Sept., daily 9– 7; Oct.–Mar., daily 9–5.*

Dining
$$ ✕ **La Casa degli Amici.** The name means "the house of friends," and that's the atmosphere that the two industrious ladies who own it succeed in creating in this restaurant outside Pistoia's old walls, on the road toward the exit of the A11 autostrada. They offer homey specialties such as *ribollita* (a thick soup of white beans, bread, cabbage, and onions), pasta *e fagioli* (with beans), and some creative dishes, too. In summer, you can dine outdoors on the terrace. ⊠ *Via Bonellina 111,* ☎ *0573/ 380305. AE, DC, MC, V. Closed Tues. and Aug. No dinner Sun.*

$$ ✕ **Leon Rosso.** To find this small and usually crowded restaurant, walk straight down Via Roma off the Piazza del Duomo. You'll find Tuscan cuisine, starting with appetizing crostini and *fusilli all'orto* (corkscrew pasta with seasonal vegetables). For dessert try *panna cotta* (milk custard) with caramel sauce. ⊠ *Via Panciatichi 4,* ☎ *0573/29230. AE, DC, MC, V. Closed Sun. and Aug.*

$$ ✕ **Rafanelli.** *Maccheroni all'anatra* (pasta with duck sauce) and other game dishes, the specialties, have been served with careful attention to tradition and quality for more than half a century by the same family. The restaurant is just outside the old city walls in a garden setting that allows for alfresco dining during summer. ⊠ *Via Sant'Agostino*

47, ☎ 0573/532046. AE, DC, MC, V. Closed Mon. and Aug. No dinner Sun.

Montecatini Terme

❸ *16 km (10 mi) west of Pistoia, 48 km (30 mi) west of Florence, 55 km (34 mi) northeast of Pisa.*

Immortalized in Fellini's 8½, Montecatini Terme is Italy's premier spa, both for its reputed curative powers and, at least once upon a time, for its great popularity with the wealthy. It is renowned for its mineral springs, which flow from five sources and are used to treat liver and skin disorders. Those "taking the cure" report each morning to one of the town's *stabilimenti termali* (thermal establishments) to drink their prescribed cupful of water, whose curative effects became known in the 1800s. The town's wealth of Art Nouveau buildings went up during its most active period of development, at the beginning of this century. Of these structures, the most attractive is the **Stabilimento Tettuccio,** a neoclassical edifice with colonnades. Here Montecatini's healthful water spouts from fountains set up on marble counters, the walls are decorated with bucolic scenes depicted on painted ceramic tiles, and an orchestra plays under a frescoed dome.

An older town of Montecatini, called **Montecatini Alto,** sits on top of a hill near the spa town and is reached by a funicular.

Lucca

★ **❹** *27 km (17 mi) west of Montecatini Terme, 74 km (46 mi) southeast of La Spezia.*

It was in this picturesque fortress town that Caesar, Pompey, and Crassus agreed to rule Rome as a triumvirate in 56 BC; it was later the first town in Tuscany to accept Christianity. Today it still has a mind of its own, and when most of Tuscany was voting communist as a matter of course, its citizens rarely followed suit. It is well worth exploring on foot.

★ **❺** The main attraction is the **Duomo** (⊠ Piazza del Duomo) on the southern side of town. Its round-arched facade is a fine example of the rigorously ordered Pisan Romanesque style, in this case happily enlivened by an extremely disordered collection of carved columns. The decoration of the facade and of the porch below are worth a close look; they make this one of the most entertaining church fronts in Tuscany. The Gothic interior contains a moving Byzantine crucifix (called the Volto Santo, or Holy Face), brought here in the 8th century, and the masterpiece of the Sienese sculptor Jacopo della Quercia, the marble *Tomb of Ilaria del Caretto* (1406).

❻ Slightly west of the center of town is the church of **San Michele** (⊠ Piazza San Michele), with a facade even more fanciful than the Duomo's; it was heavily restored in the 19th century, however, and somewhat jarringly displays busts of modern Italian patriots such as Garibaldi and Cavour.

NEED A
BREAK?

For dessert, try *buccellato*—a sweet, anise-flavored bread with raisins that is a specialty of Lucca, available at **Pasticceria Taddeucci** (⊠ Piazza San Michele 34)—or a coffee or ice cream at the venerable **Caffè di Simo** (⊠ Via Fillungo), a favorite of Giacomo Puccini, composer of some of the world's best-loved operas.

❼ The church of **San Frediano** (⊠ Piazza San Frediano) is just inside the middle of the north town wall; it contains more works by Jacopo della Quercia, and, bizarrely, the lace-clad mummy of the patron saint of domestic servants, Santa Zita. To the southeast of the north town wall

❽ is **Piazza del Mercato,** where the **Anfiteatro Romano,** or Roman Amphitheater, once stood. The piazza takes its oval shape from the theater, but the tiers disappeared when medieval houses were built on top of them.

❾ Near the west walls of the old city, the **Pinacoteca Nazionale** is worth a visit to see the Mannerist, Baroque, and Rococo art on display. ⊠ *Palazzo Mansi, Via Galli Tassi 43,* ☎ *0583/55570.* 🖃 *8,000 lire.* ☉ *Tues.–Sat. 9–7, Sun. 9–2.*

NEED A BREAK?   For an inexpensive lunch in pleasant surroundings, try **Trattoria da Giulio** (⊠ Via delle Conce 47, near Porta San Donato; closed Sun. and Mon.), which serves orzo and *porri* (leek) soups, roasted meats, and other simple Lucchese specialties.

---

❿ On the eastern end of the historic center, the **Museo Nazionale** houses an extensive collection of local Romanesque and Renaissance art. ⊠ *Villa Guinigi, Via della Quarquonia,* ☎ *0583/46033.* 🖃 *4,000 lire.* ☉ *May–Sept., Tues.–Sun. 9–7; Oct.–Apr., Tues.–Sun. 9–2.*

⓫ Finally, the tower of the medieval **Palazzo Guinigi,** near the center of town, contains one of the city's most curious oddities: a grove of ilex trees has grown at the top of the tower, and its roots have grown into the room below. From the top, you will have a magnificent view of the city and the surrounding countryside. 🖃 *4,500 lire.* ☉ *10–sunset, 9–sunset in summer.*

OFF THE BEATEN PATH   **MARLIA –** The Villa Reale is 8 kilometers (5 miles) north of Lucca in Marlia. Once the home of Napoléon's sister, Princess Elisa, and recently restored by the Counts Pecci-Blunt, this estate is celebrated for its spectacular gardens, laid out in the 18th and 19th centuries. Gardening buffs adore the legendary *teatro di verdura,* a theater carved out of hedges and topiaries; concerts are occasionally offered here. ⊠ *Villa Reale,* ☎ *0583/30108.* 🖃 *8,000 lire.* ☉ *Guided tours, July–Sept., Tues.–Sun. 10, 11, 4, 5, 6; Oct.–Nov. and Mar.–June, Tues.–Sun., 10, 11, 3, 4, 5. Closed Dec.–Feb.*

FESTIVAL DI MARLIA – Held in July and August, this is one of the most popular among Tuscany's many summer music events.

Dining and Lodging

$$$ ✕ **Solferino.** About 6 kilometers (4 miles) outside town, on the road to Viareggio, this pleasant restaurant serves exquisite variations of regional favorites, such as *faraona cotta nella creta* (guinea hen baked in a clay oven, made with ingredients from the family farm. Ask for a piece of buccellato, Lucca's celebrated dessert bread. ⊠ *San Macario in Piano,* ☎ *0583/59118. Reservations essential. AE, DC, MC, V. Closed Wed. and Jan. 7–15. No lunch Thurs.*

$$–$$$ ✕ **La Mora.** This former country inn 9 kilometers (6 miles) outside Lucca
★ is worth a detour. The menu offers a range of local specialties, from *minestra di farro* (wheat soup) with beans to *tacconi* (homemade pasta) with rabbit sauce and lamb from the nearby Garfagnana hills. You'll be tempted by the varied crostini and delicious desserts. ⊠ *Via Sesto di Ponte a Moriano 1748,* ☎ *0583/406402. AE, DC, MC, V. Closed Wed. and Oct. 10–30.*

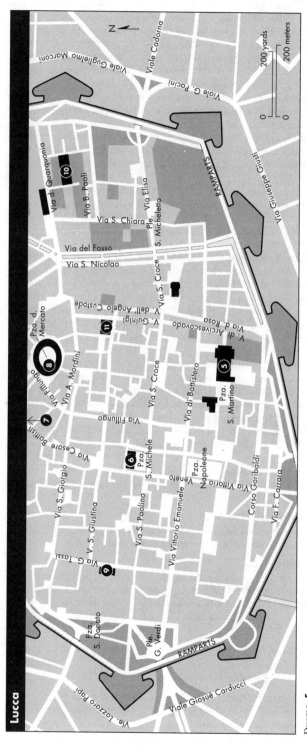

69

Lucca

Duomo, **5**
Museo Nazionale, **10**
Palazzo Guinigi, **11**
Piazza del Mercato, **8**
Pinacoteca
Nazionale, **9**
San Frediano, **7**
San Michele, **6**

$$ ✕ **Buca di Sant'Antonio.** The specialties at this rustic former inn near the church of San Michele are local dishes, some unfamiliar but well worth trying, such as ravioli *di ricotta alle zucchine* (cheese ravioli with zucchini) and roast *capretto* (kid) or agnello with savory herb seasoning. ✉ *Via della Cervia 3,* ☎ *0583/55881. AE, DC, MC, V. Closed Mon. and last 3 wks in July. No dinner Sun.*

$$ ✕ **Il Giglio.** Just off Piazza Napoleone, this restaurant has quiet, turn-of-the-century charm and classic cuisine. It's a place for all seasons, with a big fireplace and an outdoor terrace in summer. Among the local specialties are *farro garfagnino* (a thick soup made with grain and beans), and *coniglio con olive* (rabbit stew with olives). ✉ *Piazza del Giglio 3,* ☎ *0583/494508. AE, DC, MC, V. Closed Wed. No dinner Tues.*

$$$$ ▥ **Principessa Elisa.** An intimate Relais et Châteaux hotel in a neoclassical villa, this deluxe spin-off of the adjacent Villa La Principessa (☞ *below*) is a notch higher on the scale of style and comfort. ✉ *Massa Pisana,* ☎ *0583/379737,* ℻ *0583/379019. 10 suites with bath. Restaurant, bar, pool. AE, DC, MC, V. Closed Jan. 6–Feb. 6.*

$$$ ▥ **Villa La Principessa.** Just outside Lucca, only 3 kilometers (2 miles) from town, this is an exquisitely decorated 19th-century country mansion. Some rooms have beamed ceilings, and doors are individually decorated; antique furniture and portraits give an aura of gracious living. The grounds are well manicured, the pool large and inviting. ✉ *Massa Pisana,* ☎ *0583/370037,* ℻ *0583/379136. 40 rooms and suites with bath. Restaurant (closed Sun.), pool. AE, DC, MC, V. Closed Nov. 1–Mar. 31.*

$$ ▥ **La Luna.** On a quiet, airy courtyard close to historic Piazza del Mercato, this family-run hotel occupies two freshly renovated wings of an old building. The desk and lounge look new, and the bathrooms are modern, but some of the rooms still have the atmosphere of Old Lucca. A parking lot for guests is a bonus. ✉ *Corte Compagni 12 (corner of Via Fillungo),* ☎ *0583/493634,* ℻ *0583/490021. 30 rooms with bath. AE, DC, MC, V. Closed last 3 wks in Jan.*

$ ▥ **Ilaria.** Rooms are small but fresh and functional in this family-run hotel beside a minuscule canal within easy walking distance of the main sights. ✉ *Via del Fosso 20,* ☎ *0583/47558. 17 rooms, 12 with bath. AE, DC, MC, V.*

Nightlife and the Arts

The **Estate Musicale Lucchese,** one of many music festivals throughout Tuscany, runs throughout the summer in Lucca.

Shopping

Lucca's olive oil, available throughout the city, is exported throughout the world; you'll find it at any food store. On the second Sunday of the month, there's a **flea market** in Piazza San Martino.

Pisa

⑫ *22 km (14 mi) southwest of Lucca, 75 km (46 mi) south of La Spezia, 22 km (14 mi) north of Livorno, 64 km (40 mi) northwest of Volterra, 77 km (48 mi) west of Florence.*

There is more to Pisa than its Leaning Tower—but not much more. The city offers surprisingly little temptation after the tower and its companion pieces: the Duomo, the Battistero (Baptistry) and the Camposanto. Nearby Lucca (☞ *above*) is more deserving of your attention.

Pisa's main attraction, situated at the northwestern edge of town, is the **Piazza del Duomo,** also known, appropriately, as the Campo dei Miracoli (Field of Miracles). On it stand the Duomo, the baptistery, and the famous Leaning Tower.

The **Leaning Tower** was begun in 1174, the last of the three structures to be built, and the lopsided settling began when construction reached the third story. The tower's architects attempted to compensate by making the remaining floors slightly taller on the leaning side, but the extra weight only made the problem worse. The settling has continued, and a few years ago it accelerated to a point that led many to fear it would simply topple over, despite all efforts to prop the structure up. Now it has been firmly anchored to the earth. Legend holds that Galileo conducted an experiment on the nature of gravity by dropping metal balls from the top of the 187-foot-high tower; historians say this legend has no basis in fact (which is not quite to say that it is false). ⊠ *Campo dei Miracoli. Closed for restoration.*

The **Duomo** was the first building to use the horizontal marble stripe motif (borrowed from Moorish architecture in the 11th century) so common to Tuscan cathedrals. It is famous for the Romanesque panels on the transept door facing the tower, which depict the life of Christ, and for its beautifully carved 13th-century pulpit, by Giovanni Pisano. The lovely Gothic **baptistery,** which stands across from the Duomo's facade, is best known for the pulpit carved by Giovanni's father, Nicola, in 1260. ⊠ *Campo du Miracoli.* 🎫 *Duomo: 2,000 lire, Nov.–Mar. free.* ☉ *Apr.–Oct., Mon.–Sat. 10–5, Sun. 1–5; Nov.–Mar. 10–12:30 and 3–5:30.* 🎫 *Baptistery: 10,000 lire for baptistery and 1 other attraction; 15,000 lire for baptistery and all 3 attractions (☞ below).* ☉ *Apr.–Oct., daily 8–7:30; Nov.–Mar., daily 10–12:30 and 3–5:30.*

The walled area on the northern side of the Campo dei Miracoli is the **Camposanto** (cemetery), which is filled, according to legend, with earth brought back from the Holy Land during the Crusades. Its galleries contain numerous frescoes, notably *The Drunkenness of Noah,* by Renaissance artist Benozzo Gozzoli, and the disturbing *Triumph of Death* (14th century), whose authorship is disputed, but whose subject matter shows what was on people's minds in a century that saw the ravages of the Black Death. ⊠ *Camposanto,* ☎ *050/560547.* 🎫 *10,000 lire.* ☉ *Apr.–Oct., daily 8–7:30; Nov.–Mar., daily 9–5:30.*

At the southeast corner of the Campo dei Miracoli, the **Museo dell'-Opera del Duomo** holds a wealth of medieval sculptures and the ancient Roman sarcophagi that inspired Nicola Pisano's figures. The well-arranged **Museo delle Sinopie** across the street, on the south side of the square, holds the *sinopie,* or preparatory drawings, for the Camposanto frescoes and is of limited interest to most tourists. ⊠ *Museo dell'Opera del Duomo: Via Arcivescovado,* ☎ *050/560547.* 🎫 *10,000 lire.* ☉ *Apr.–Oct., daily 9–7:30; Nov.–Mar., daily 9–5:30. Museo delle Sinopie:* ⊠ *Piazza del Duomo,* ☎ *050/560547.* 🎫 *10,000 lire.* ☉ *Apr.–Oct., daily 8–7:30; Nov.–Mar., daily 9–5:30.* 🎫 *Combined admission to baptistery, Camposanto, and museums: 10,000 lire for any 2 attractions, 15,000 lire for all 4.*

In the center of town, **Piazza dei Cavalieri** possesses some fine Renaissance buildings: the **Palazzo dei Cavalieri,** the **Palazzo dell'Orologio** and the church of **Santo Stefano dei Cavalieri.** The square was laid out by Giorgio Vasari in about 1560. Vasari was better known for the chronicles of the lives of Renaissance artists that made him the first art historian.

Along the northern side of the Arno, the **Museo di San Matteo** contains some incisive examples of local Romanesque and Gothic art. ⊠ *Lungarno Mediceo,* ☎ *050/541865.* ⊡ *8,000 lire.* ☉ *Tues.–Sat. 9–7, Sun. 9–1.*

OFF THE BEATEN PATH

FORTE DEI MARMI – Tuscany's most exclusive beach resort is a favorite of moneyed Tuscans and Milanese, whose villas are neatly laid out in an extensive pine wood. It's 35 kilometers (22 miles) northwest of Lucca and 65 kilometers (30 miles) northwest of Florence. In summer, a beachcomber's bonanza takes place on Wednesday mornings, when everything from fake designer sunglasses to plastic sandals and terry-cloth towels goes on sale.

Forte dei Marmi is also near the marble-producing towns of **Carrara** (where Michelangelo quarried his stone), **Seravezza,** and **Pietrasanta.**

OFF THE BEATEN PATH

ELBA – The largest island in the Tuscan archipelago, Elba is an hour by ferry or a half hour by Hovercraft from Piombino, or a short hop by air from Pisa. Its main port is **Portoferraio,** fortified in the 16th century by the Medici Grand Duke Cosimo I. Victor Hugo spent his boyhood here, and Napoléon his famous exile in 1814–15, when he built (out of two windmills) the **Palazzina Napoleonica dei Mulini** and (a few miles outside town) the **Villa San Martino.**

The island's main attractions, however, are its rough landscape and pristine beaches offering a full array of sports. Portoferraio, the liveliest town and a transportation hub, is the best base for exploring the island. Good beaches can be found at Biodola, Procchio, and Marina di Campo. From Elba, private visits can be arranged to the other islands in the archipelago, including **Montecristo,** which inspired Alexander Dumas's 19th-century best-seller *The Count of Monte Cristo* and is now a wildlife refuge. Elba's restaurants offer excellent seafood, to be sampled with the local Moscato and Aleatico wines. ⊠ *Palazzina Napoleonica and Villa San Martino,* ☎ *0565/915846.* ⊡ *6,000 lire for both if visited on same day.* ☉ *Tues.–Sat. 9–1:30, Sun. 9–1.*

Dining and Lodging

$$ ✕ **Bruno.** A pleasant restaurant, with beamed ceilings and the look of a country inn, Bruno is just outside the old city walls, a short walk from the bell tower and cathedral. Dine on classic Tuscan dishes, from *zuppa alla pisana* (a thick vegetable soup) to *baccalà* (cod) with leeks. ⊠ *Via Luigi Bianchi 12,* ☎ *050/560818. AE, DC, MC, V. Closed Tues. No dinner Mon.*

$$ ✕ **La Pergoletta.** In a medieval tower in the heart of the old town, on a street named for its "beautiful towers," this restaurant is small and simple and has a shady garden for outdoor dining. The signora who is the owner-cook offers traditional Tuscan minestra di farro and *grigliata* (grilled beef, veal, or lamb). ⊠ *Via delle Belle Torri 36,* ☎ *050/542458. Reservations advised. MC, V. Closed Tues. and Aug.*

$$ ✕ **Osteria dei Cavalieri.** Just off the beautiful old Piazza dei Cavalieri, this popular tavern and wine cellar in a centuries-old tower offers one-course lunch menus, as well as fixed-price menus, of either seafood, meat, or vegetarian dishes, including freshly made *tagliolini* (noodles) and *tagliata di manzo* (sliced beefsteak, usually served with mushrooms). ⊠ *Via San Frediano 16,* ☎ *050/580858. AE, DC, MC, V. Closed Sun. and Aug. No lunch Sat.*

$$$ ▦ **Cavalieri.** Opposite the railway station, in an unremarkable 1950s building, this Jolly Group hotel offers functional, modern comforts in completely soundproof and air-conditioned rooms, all with color TV and minibar. The restaurant specializes in homemade pasta and seafood and is open every day. ✉ *Piazza della Stazione 2,* ☎ *050/43290,* FAX *050/502242. 100 rooms with bath or shower. Bar. AE, DC, MC, V.*

$$ ⊡ **Royal Victoria.** In a pleasant palazzo facing the Arno, a 10-minute walk from the Campo dei Miracoli, this hotel is about as close as Pisa comes to Old World ambience. It's comfortably furnished, featuring antiques and reproductions in the lobby and in some rooms, whose style ranges from the 1800s, complete with frescoes, to the 1920s. ✉ *Lungarno Pacinotti 12,* ☎ *050/940111,* FAX *050/940180. 48 rooms, 40 with bath. AE, DC, MC, V.*

TUSCAN HILL TOWNS
The Quintessential Tuscany

This area of rustic small cities and towns south of Florence has three distinct subdivisions. The first, directly south of Florence, is the Chianti district, Italy's most famous wine-producing area; its hill towns, olive groves, and vineyards comprise the quintessential Tuscany. Many British and northern Europeans have relocated here, drawn by the unhurried life, balmy climate, and picturesque villages; there are so many Britons, in fact, that the area has been nicknamed Chiantishire. Still, it remains strongly Tuscan in character and is sparsely populated. Marking the southernmost extremity of the Chianti region is the second subregion—Siena, a force unto itself; there's nowhere else in Italy where medieval strength and the elegance of the Renaissance are in such perfect balance. Farther south is the third area, where soft green olive groves give way to a blanket of oak and rich dark green cypress forests and reddish brown earth; here and there throughout this area are the vineyards that produce Brunello di Montalcino. Here, the towns are the size of the roads—small—and as old as the hills.

From Florence, there are two basic routes to Siena. The speedy modern S2 is good if you're making a day trip from Florence; to really experience the countryside, take the narrower and more meandering S222, known as the Strada Chiantigiana because it runs through the heart of the wine-producing region. Its most scenic section connects **Strada in Chianti,** 16 kilometers (10 miles) south of Florence, and **Greve in Chianti,** 11 kilometers (7 miles) farther south, whose triangular central piazza is surrounded by restaurants and vintners offering *degustazioni* (wine tastings).

Volterra

⑬ *64 km (40 mi) southwest of Pisa, 50 km (31 mi) west of Siena.*

D. H. Lawrence, in his *Etruscan Places,* sang the praises of Volterra, "standing somber and chilly alone on her rock." The town has long been known for its alabaster, which has been mined since Etruscan times; today the Volterrans use it to make ornaments and souvenirs sold all over town. **Piazza dei Priori,** where the 13th-century Palazzo dei Priori is emblazoned with heraldic emblems, is one of Tuscany's quintessential medieval squares.

A magnificent collection of small alabaster funerary urns that once held the ashes of deceased Etruscans (along with many other Etruscan artifacts) may be seen at the **Museo Etrusco Guarnacci** (✉ Via Don Minzoni). Later art can be found in the **Duomo**, at the **Pinacoteca** (✉ Palazzo Minucci-Solaini, Via dei Sarti 1), and at the **Museo di Arte Sacra** (✉ Via Roma; ☉ Daily 9–12:30). The town's best-known Renaissance works are the 15th-century frescoes in the Duomo by Benozzo Gozzoli and the 16th-century *Deposition* by Rosso Fiorentino in the Pinacoteca. ✎ *Combined admission to Museo Etrusco Guarnacci, Pinacoteca, and Museo di Arte Sacra: 10,000 lire.* ☉ *Mar. 16–Oct. 14, daily 9:30–6:30 (Museo Etrusco Guarnacci closes 1–3); Oct. 15–Mar. 15, daily 9:30–1 (Museo Etrusco Guarnacci 9–2).*

The walls of Volterra also harbor one of the few pieces of Etruscan architecture that escaped Roman destruction: the **Arco Etrusco,** with its weatherworn Etruscan heads, at the Porta all'Arco.

Dining and Lodging

$$ ✕ **Etruria.** Turn-of-the-century frescoes on the walls and outdoor dining in the warm weather are among the attractions at this restaurant on the town's main square. An array of local game is used in such specialties as *pappardelle alla lepre* (broad noodles in hare sauce) and *cinghiale alla maremmana* (roast boar). ✉ *Piazza dei Priori 8,* ☎ *0588/86064. AE, DC, MC, V. Closed Thurs.*

$$ ⌸ **San Lino.** Located in a former convent, this hotel has modern comforts, a swimming pool, and its own regional restaurant. On top of that, it's within the town walls, 10 minutes' walk from the main piazza. ✉ *Via San Lino 26,* ☎ *0588/85250,* ℻ *0588/80620. 43 rooms with bath. Restaurant, pool. AE, DC, MC, V.*

Shopping

SPECIALTY ITEMS

Volterra has a number of shops that sell boxes, jewelry, and other objects made of alabaster. For information and directions, contact **Cooperativa Artieri Alabastro** (✉ Piazza dei Priori 2, ☎ 0588/87590).

En Route   Travel 88 kilometers (55 miles) northeast of Siena. (You may want to break the drive halfway with a rest stop at **Monte San Savino,** a prosperous-looking small town, with the tiny nearby fortified village of **Gargonza** that has been carefully restored into a vacation resort; (☞ Dining and Lodging, *below.*) Then proceed on to Arezzo.

San Gimignano

★ ⑭   *27 km (17 mi) east of Volterra, 57 km (35 mi) southwest of Florence, 31 km (20 mi) northwest of Siena.*

Time seems to have stood still since the Middle Ages in this most remarkable of all Tuscan hill towns, and it still lives up to its original name, San Gimignano-of-the-Beautiful-Towers. Its high walls and narrow streets are typical of Tuscan hill towns, but it is the surviving medieval "skyscrapers" that set the town apart from its neighbors and give the town a uniquely photogenic silhouette. Today 14 towers remain, but at the height of the Guelph-Ghibelline conflict, a forest of more than 70 such towers dominated the city. The towers were built partly for defensive purposes—they were a safe refuge and useful for pouring boiling oil on attacking enemies—and partly to bolster the egos of their owners, who competed with deadly seriousness to build the highest tower in town.

Many of the town's most important medieval buildings are clustered around the central **Piazza del Duomo.** They include the **Palazzo del Podestà,** with its imposing tower, the **Torre Grossa;** the **Palazzo del Popolo,** now the Museo Civico (municipal museum), displaying Sienese and Renaissance paintings; and the Romanesque **Collegiata**, containing fine 15th-century frescoes by Domenico Ghirlandaio in the **Chapel of Santa Fina**. ◰ *A combined ticket (16,000 lire) is valid for all San Gimignano museums and the Chapel of Santa Fina. Museo Civico: 7,000 lire; ⊙ Apr.–Sept., Tues.–Sun. 9:30–7:30; Oct. and Mar., Tues.–Sun. 9:30–6; Nov.–Feb., Tues.–Sun. 9:30–1:30 and 2:30–4:30. Torre Grossa: 7,000 lire. ⊙ as Museo Civico (above); combined ticket for museum and tower (12,000) lire available only Apr.–Sept., Tues.–Sun. 12:30–3 and 6–7:30; Oct.–Mar., Tues.–Sun. 12:30–2:30. Chapel of Santa Fina: ◰ 3,000 lire. ⊙ Apr.–Sept., Tues.–Sun. 9–12:30 and 3–6; Oct.–Mar., Tues.–Sun. 9:30–12:30 and 3–5:30.*

Before leaving San Gimignano, be sure to see its most famous work of art, at the northern end of town, in the church of **Sant'Agostino**: Benozzo Gozzoli's utterly beautiful 15th-century fresco cycle depicting the life of St. Augustine. Also try a taste of Vernaccia, the local dry white wine.

Dining and Lodging

$$–$$$ ✕ **Bel Soggiorno.** On the top floor of a 100-year-old inn, this rustic restaurant has a wall of windows from which to view the landscape. Tuscan specialties include *zuppa del granduca* (a medieval soup of mushrooms, grain, and potatoes) and *sorpresa in crosta* (spicy rabbit stew with a bread crust). ⊠ *Via San Giovanni 91,* ☎ *0577/940375. AE, DC, MC, V. Closed Mon. and Jan. 7–Feb. 28.*

$$–$$$ ✕ **Le Terrazze.** This restaurant in a time-honored inn in the heart of San Gimignano has a charming view of rooftops and countryside and an ample menu featuring Tuscan dishes in seasonal variations. The specialties are served *alla sangimignanese* (baked in the oven). ⊠ *Piazza della Cisterna 23,* ☎ *0577/940328. AE, DC, MC, V. Closed Nov. 1– Mar. 9. No lunch Tues. and Wed.*

$$ ✕ **Stella.** At this rustic, upscale trattoria, between the main church and that of Sant Agostino, prices are more moderate than at places with a view. The owner prides himself on farm-fresh vegetables and his own olive oil. The specialty of the house is grilled meat, including beef, lamb, and pork. ⊠ *Via San Matteo 77,* ☎ *0577/940444. AE, DC, MC, V. Closed Wed. and Jan. 6–Feb. 15.*

$$ ▦ **Pescille.** This is a rambling farmhouse 4 kilometers (2 ½ miles) out-
★ side San Gimignano that has been converted into a handsome hotel, in which restrained contemporary and country classic decors blend well. ⊠ *Località Pescille, Strada Castel San Gimignano,* ☎ *0577/940186,* ℻ *0577/943165. 40 rooms with bath. Pool, tennis court. AE, DC, MC, V. Closed Nov.–Feb.*

Monteriggioni

20 km (12 mi) southeast of San Gimignano, 93 km (58 mi) southeast of Pisa, 55 km (34 mi) south of Florence.

On your way north from Siena toward Colle Val d'Elsa, San Gimignano, and Volterra, be sure to visit this tiny hamlet, which sits on a rise within a circle of formidable 13th-century walls. Its 14 square towers, which Dante likened to giants, were Siena's northernmost defense against Florence. Take time to make the lengthy detour around Colle Val d'Elsa's workaday lower town up to the ridge, where the medieval center remains practically intact.

Dining

$$ ✕ **Il Pozzo.** On the village square, this rustic tavern serves hearty Tuscan country cooking, including *maltagliati al sugo di* agnello (with fresh pasta in a tomato sauce) and *cinghiale in dolce forte* (boar with a tangy sauce). The desserts are homemade. ⊠ *Piazza Roma 2,* ☎ *0577/304127. AE, DC, MC, V. Closed Mon., Jan., and 10 days in Aug. No dinner Sun.*

Siena

⓯ *15 km (9 mi) southeast of Montereggioni, 106 km (66 mi) southeast of Pisa, 68 km (42 mi) south of Florence.*

Italy's loveliest medieval city, Siena is the one trip you should make in Tuscany if you make no other. Florence's great historical rival was founded by Augustus around the time of the birth of Christ, although legend holds that it was founded much earlier by Remus, brother of Romulus, the legendary founder of Rome. During the late Middle Ages, the city was both wealthy and powerful (it saw the birth of the world's oldest bank, the Monte dei Paschi, still very much in business). It was bitterly envied by Florence, which in 1254 sent forces that besieged the city for over a year, reducing its population by half and laying waste to the countryside. The city was finally absorbed by the Grand Duchy of Tuscany, ruled by Florence, in 1559.

Unlike Renaissance Florence, Siena is a Gothic city, laid out over the slopes of three steep hills and practically unchanged since medieval times.

★ Its main square, the **Piazza del Campo,** is one of the finest in Italy. Fan shaped, its nine sections of paving represent the 13th-century government of Nine Good Men and, on the widest side, like an ornament, is the Fonte Gaia, so called because it was inaugurated to great jubilation. The bas-reliefs on it are reproductions of the originals by Jacopo della Quercia. Twice a year, on July 2 and August 16, the square explodes in a frenzy of local rivalries as the site of the famous **Palio,** a horse race in which the city's 17 neighborhoods compete to possess the cloth banner that gives the contest its name. Unlike many other such competitions in Italy, the Palio has a mystique in which the townspeople are deeply involved, and the rivalries it generates are taken very seriously.

★ **⓰** Dominating the Piazza del Campo is the **Palazzo Pubblico,** which has served as Siena's Town Hall since the 1300s. It now also contains the **Museo Civico,** its walls covered with pre-Renaissance frescoes, including Simone Martini's early 14th-century *Maestà* and *Portrait of Guidoriccio da Fogliano,* and Ambrogio Lorenzetti's famous *Allegory of Good and Bad Government,* painted from 1327 to 1329 to demonstrate the dangers of tyranny. The original bas-reliefs of the Jacopo della Quercia fountain, moved to protect them from the elements, are also on display. The climb up the palazzo's bell tower is long and steep, but the superb view makes it worth every step. ⊠ *Piazza del Campo,* ☎ *0577/292263.* ⌨ *Bell tower: 5,000 lire.* ☉ *Mar. 15–Nov. 15, daily 10– 1 hr before sunset; Nov. 16–Mar. 14, daily 10–1.* ⌨ *Museo Civico: 6,000 lire.* ☉ *Mar. 15–Nov. 15, Mon.–Sat 9:30–7, Sun. 9–1:30; Nov. 16–Mar. 14, daily 9–1:30.*

NEED A BREAK?

There are several *gelaterie* (ice-cream parlors) on Piazza del Campo, excellent for surveying the piazza while enjoying a refreshing ice cream. More substantial sustenance may be found nearby at **Ristorante Il Verrocchio** (⊠ Logge del Papa 2, closed Wed.), which serves inexpensive Sienese specialties and is a block east of the northern side of the campo.

★ **⑰** Siena's **Duomo,** several blocks west of Piazza del Campo, is beyond question one of the finest Gothic cathedrals in Italy. Its facade, with its multicolored marbles and painted decoration, is typical of the Italian approach to Gothic architecture, lighter and much less austere than the French. The cathedral, as it now stands, was completed in the 14th century, but at the time the Sienese had even bigger plans. They decided to enlarge the building, using the current church as the transepts of the new church, which would have a new nave running toward the southeast. The beginnings of construction of this new nave still stand and may be seen from the steps outside the Duomo's right transept. But in 1348 the Black Death decimated Siena's population, the city fell into decline, funds dried up, and the plans were never carried out.

The Duomo's interior is one of the most striking in Italy and possesses a fine coffered and gilded dome. It is most famous for its unique and magnificent marble floors, which took almost 200 years to complete (beginning around 1370); more than 40 artists contributed to the work, made up of 56 separate compositions depicting biblical scenes, allegories, religious symbols, and civic emblems. The Duomo's carousel pulpit, which is almost as famous as the floors, was carved by Nicola Pisano around 1265; the life of Christ is depicted on the rostrum frieze. In the **Biblioteca Piccolomini,** a room painted by Pinturicchio in 1509, frescoes depict events from the life of native son Aeneas Sylvius Piccolomini, who became Pope Pius II in 1458. The frescoes are in excellent condition and have a freshness rarely seen in work so old. ⊠ *Biblioteca Piccolomini,* ☎ *0577/283048.* ▣ *2,000 lire.* ☉ *Mid-Mar.–Oct. 31, daily 9– 7:30; Nov.–mid-Mar., daily 10–1, 2–5.*

⑱ Next to the Duomo is its museum, the **Museo dell'Opera del Duomo,** occupying part of the unfinished new cathedral's nave and containing a small collection of Sienese art and the cathedral treasury. Its masterpiece is unquestionably Duccio's *Maestà,* painted around 1310 and magnificently displayed in a room devoted entirely to Duccio's work. ⊠ *Piazza del Duomo,* ☎ *0577/283048.* ▣ *5,000 lire.* ☉ *Mar. 12– Sept. 30, daily 9–7:30; Oct. 1–Oct. 31, daily 9–6:30; Nov. 1–Dec. 31, daily 9–1:30; Jan. 2–Mar. 11, daily 9–1:30.*

Steps between the cathedral and its museum lead to the **Battistero** (baptistery), with its 15th-century frescoes. Its large bronze baptismal font (also 15th century) was designed by Jacopo della Quercia and is adorned with bas-reliefs by various artists, including two by Renaissance masters: Lorenzo Ghiberti (*The Baptism of Christ*) and Donatello (*Herod Presented with the Head of St. John*).

⑲ Chief among Siena's other attractions is the **Pinacoteca Nazionale,** several blocks southeast of the entrance to the Duomo; it contains a superb collection of Sienese art, including Ambrogio Lorenzetti's 14th-century depiction of a castle that is generally considered the first nonreligious painting—the first pure landscape—of the Christian era. ⊠ *Via San Pietro 29,* ☎ *0577/281161.* ▣ *8,000 lire.* ☉ *Apr.–Sept., Tues.–Sat. 8–6; Oct.–Mar., Tues.–Sat. 8:30–1:30, Sun. 8:30–1.*

⑳ Northwest of the Duomo is the church of **San Domenico;** its **Cappella di Santa Caterina** displays frescoes by Il Sodoma portraying scenes from the life of St. Catherine.

NEED A BREAK? Not far from the church of San Domenico, the **Enoteca Italica** is a fantastically stocked wine cellar in the bastions of the Medici fortress. Here you can taste wines from all over Italy and have a snack, too. ⊠ *Fortezza Medicea, Viale Maccari,* ☎ *0577/288497.* ☉ *3 PM–midnight.*

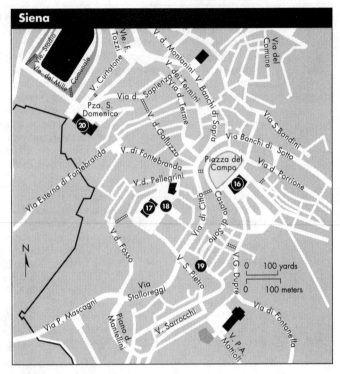

Dining and Lodging

$$ ✕ **Al Marsili.** Located between Piazza del Campo and the cathedral,
★ this 900-year-old wine cellar is an elegant place to dine, under broad,
brick-vaulted ceilings. The menu offers Tuscan and Italian specialties,
among them homemade pastas such as *tortelloni burro e salvia* (large
cheese-filled ravioli with butter and sage). Various meat dishes are cooked
in wine, and the wine list features the finest Tuscan and Italian labels,
including many from the nearby Chianti country. ✉ *Via del Castoro
3,* ☎ *0577/47154. AE, DC, MC, V. Closed Mon.*

$$ ✕ **Le Logge.** Near Piazza del Campo, this typically Sienese trattoria has
★ rustic dining rooms on two levels and tables outdoors from June to
October. The menu features Tuscan dishes, such as *malfatti all'osteria*
(ricotta and spinach dumplings in a cream sauce) and *coniglio con pig-
noli* (rabbit with pine nuts). ✉ *Via del Porrione 33,* ☎ *0577/48013.
MC, V. Closed Sun. and 2 wks in June and Nov.*

$$ ✕ **Tullio Tre Cristi.** This is a typical and historic neighborhood tratto-
ria, long ago discovered by tourists and still reliable. The paintings on
the walls are by famous local artists of the 1920s, but the culinary tra-
dition here goes back even further. Try spaghetti *alle briciole,* a poor-
man's dish of pasta with bread-crumbs, tomato, and garlic, or veal
escalopes (cutlets) subtly flavored with *dragoncello* (tarragon). You can
eat outdoors in summer. To find the restaurant, take Via dei Rossi from
Via Banchi di Sopra. ✕ *Vicolo di Provenzano 1,* ☎ *0577/280608. MC,
V. Closed Mon. and mid-Jan–mid-Feb. No dinner Sun.*

$$$–$$$$ ✕⌑ **La Suvera.** This luxurious estate in the lovely valley of the River
Elsa, 28 kilometers (17 miles) west of Siena and 56 kilometers (35 miles)
south of Florence, was once owned by Pope Julius II. The papal villa
and adjacent buildings have been restored to accommodate guests in

rooms and suites that are magnificently furnished with antiques and appointed with the latest comforts. With drawing rooms, a library, Italian garden, park, pool, and the Oliviera restaurant (serving estate wines) to enjoy, guests find it hard to tear themselves away, though there is plenty to see in the vicinity. ⌧ *Pievescola (Casola d'Elsa), off S541,* ☏ *0577/960300,* FAX *0577/960220. 19 rooms and 13 suites with bath. Restaurant, bar, pool, sauna, tennis court, horseback riding, meeting rooms, helipad. AE, DC, MC, V.* ☺ *Apr. 1–Oct. 31.*

$$$$ 🏨 **Certosa di Maggiano.** A former 14th-century monastery converted
★ into an exquisite country hotel, this haven of gracious living is a little more than a mile from the center of Siena. The atmosphere is that of an exclusive retreat in which a select number of guests enjoy the style and comfort of an aristocratic villa. ⌧ *Via Certosa 82,* ☏ *0577/288180,* FAX *0577/288189. 18 rooms with bath. Restaurant, pool, tennis court. AE, DC, MC, V.*

$$$$ 🏨 **Park.** Set among olive groves and gardens on a hillside just outside the city walls, this hotel offers solid comfort and spacious rooms with views of the grounds and countryside, which also includes a 6-hole practice golf course. A historic 16th-century villa, it has the easy elegance and antique charm of patrician Tuscan country life. The Olivo restaurant is known for fine regional cuisine. ⌧ *Via Marciano 18,* ☏ *0577/ 44803,* FAX *0577/49020. 80 double rooms with bath or shower. Restaurant, bar, pool, 2 tennis courts. AE, DC, MC, V.*

$–$$ 🏨 **Antica Torre.** A restored 17th-century tower within the town walls in the southeast corner of Siena, Antica Torre is a 10-minute walk from Piazza del Campo. It is the work of a cordial couple who have created the atmosphere of a private home, furnished simply but in good taste and with only eight guest rooms. The old stone staircase, wooden beams, and original brick vaults here and there are reminders of the building's august age. ⌧ *Via Fieravecchia 7,* ☏ FAX *0577/222255. 8 rooms with bath. AE, MC, V.*

$–$$ 🏨 **Chiusarelli.** A handy location—near the long-distance bus terminal and a parking area and only a 10-minute walk from the main sights— makes this hotel a good choice. In a well-kept neoclassic villa, built in the early 1900s complete with caryatids, it has functional rooms that are airy and reasonably quiet. There is a small garden and a downstairs restaurant that caters to tour groups. ⌧ *Viale Curtatone 9,* ☏ *0577/280562,* FAX *0577/271177. 50 rooms with bath. MC, V.*

$–$$ 🏨 **Duomo.** Occupying the top floor of a 300-year-old building in the center of Siena, near Piazza del Campo, the hotel is quiet and is furnished in a neat contemporary style, with traces of the past showing in the artfully exposed brickwork in the breakfast room. Many bedrooms have superb views of the city's towers and the hilly countryside. Two rooms are endowed with balconies. ⌧ *Via Stalloreggi 38,* ☏ *0577/289088,* FAX *0577/43043. 23 rooms with bath. AE, DC, MC, V.*

Nightlife and the Arts

In late July and August, Siena hosts the **Settimane Musicali Senesi,** a series of alfresco concerts of local and other music.

Shopping

The city is known for a variety of medieval desserts—*cavallucci, panforti,* and *ricciarelli*—as well as for ceramics.

Abbey of Monte Oliveto Maggiore

㉑ *37 km (23 mi) southeast of Siena.*

This **Benedictine abbey,** Tuscany's most visited, is an oasis of olive and cypress trees amid the harsh landscape of a zone known as the *crete*, where erosion has sculpted the hills starkly, laying open gashes of barren rock in lush farmland. Secluded amid thick woodlands in the deep-cut hills south of Siena, it is accessible by car but not easily by bus.

Olivetans, or "White Benedectines," founded it in 1313; this breakaway group sought to return to the simple ideals of the early Benedictines. The monastery's mellow brick buildings, restored in the last century and set in one of Tuscany's most striking landscapes, hold a treasure or two. Only the main cloister, the church, and portions of the park are open to the public. In the church, the wooden choir, with exquisite inlay designs, is an understated work of art that dates from 1503.

In the main cloister of the abbey, the frescoes by Luca Signorelli and Il Sodoma on the walls of the portico relate the life of St. Benedict with earthy realism, a quality that came naturally to Il Sodoma, described by Vasari as "a merry and licentious man . . . of scant chastity." 🖃 *Free.* 🕑 *Daily 9:15–12, 3:15–5:45.*

Dining

$–$$ ✕ **La Torre.** This pleasant restaurant and café in the massive tower at the abbey's entrance provide more than adequate sustenance to visitors. The local specialties—served in a cozy dining room in winter or on an attractive terrace under tall cypresses in fair weather—include tagliatelle *ai funghi* (with mushroom sauce) or *zuppa di funghi* (mushroom soup). The wine list is excellent, and the tourist menu is a good value. ☎ *0577/707022. AE, MC, V. Closed Tues.*

Montalcino

㉒ *25 km (15.5 mi) south of the Abbey of Monte Oliveto Maggiore, 24 km (15 mi) west of Pienza, 41 km (25 mi) south of Siena.*

Another medieval hill town with a special claim to fame, Montalcino is home to Brunello di Montalcino, one of Italy's best red wines. You can sample it in wine cellars in town or visit a nearby winery for a free guided tour and tasting. One such winery is the Fattoria dei Barbi (☞ Dining, *below*).

Dining

$$$ ✕ **Poggio Antico.** One of Italy's renowned gourmet chefs, Roberto Minnetti, abandoned his highly successful restaurant in Rome a few years ago and moved to the country, about 2 miles outside Montalcino. Now he and his wife, Patrizia—who is also Poggio Antico's hostess—serve fine Tuscan cuisine, masterfully interpreted by Roberto, in a relaxed but elegant dining room replete with arches and beamed ceilings. Among the specialties are *paté di fegatini al moscadello* (liver paté flavored with wine) and *piccione ripieno in slasa d'agretto* (stuffed pigeon in a tangy sauce). ⊠ *Località I Poggi (2½ mi outside Montalcino on road to Grossetto).* ☎ *0577/849200. AE, DC. Closed Mon. and 20 days in Jan.*

$$ ✕ **La Cucina di Edgardo.** This tiny restaurant on Montalcino's main street has three charming dining rooms in a former wine cellar with dark wooden beams, a fireplace, and terra-cotta floors. The specialties of the house, on a menu featuring creative versions of Tuscan food, are *ravioli di magro al basilico e noci* (cheese ravioli with basil and walnuts) and *brasato al Brunello* (beef braised in the local Brunello wine). ⊠ *Via Soccorsi Saloni 21,* ☎ *0577/848232. MC, V. Closed Wed. and Jan. 8–Feb. 8.*

$$ ✕ **Taverna dei Barbi.** A meal at this delightful tavern, set among vine-
★ yards and mellow brick buildings on a wine-producing country es-
tate (Fattoria dei Barbi), may well be a highlight of your journey
through this part of Tuscany. The rustic dining room features a
beamed ceiling, huge stone fireplace, and arched windows. The es-
tate farm produces practically all the ingredients used in such tradi-
tional specialties as *scottiglia di pollo* (browned chicken served with
garlic bread) and a dessert called *ricotta montata* (farm-fresh ricotta
whipped with vin santo, sugar, and vanilla). The estate-produced
Brunello is excellent, and other wines with the Barbi label are avail-
able. ✉ *Fattoria dei Barbi,* ☎ *0577/849357. Reservations essential.
AE, DC, MC, V. Closed Wed., Jan. 15–31, and July 1–15. No din-
ner Tues.* ☼ *Winery (English-speaking guides) open weekdays 9–1
and 3–6, weekends 2:30–6.*

Abbey of Sant'Antimo

10 km (6 mi) south of Montalcino, 31 km (19 mi) south of Siena.

It's well worth your while to visit this **abbey,** a medieval gem of pale
stone set in the silvery green of an olive grove. The exterior and in-
terior sculpture is outstanding, particularly the nave capitals, a com-
bination of French, Lombard, and even Spanish influences. The
sacristy (rarely open) forms part of the primitive Carolingian church
(founded in 781 AD), its entrance flanked by 9th-century pilasters.
The small **vaulted crypt** dates from the same period. Above the nave
runs a *matroneum* (women's gallery), an unusual feature once used
to separate the congregation. Equally unusual is the ambulatory,
whose three radiating chapels (rare in Italian churches) were prob-
ably copied from the French model. ☼ *Daily 9–12 and 2–7 (winter
10–12 and 2–4).* 🎟 *Free.*

Pienza

❷❸ *10 km (6 mi) northeast of the Abbey of Sant' Antimo.*

Pienza owes its appearance to Pope Pius II, who had grand plans to
transform his home village of **Corsignano**—the town's former name—
into a model Renaissance town. The man entrusted with the trans-
formation was Bernardo Rossellini, a protegé of the great Renaissance
architectural theorist Leon Battista Alberti. His mandate was to cre-
ate a cathedral, a papal palace, and a town hall (plus miscellaneous
buildings) that adhered to the vainglorious pope's principles. Gothic
and Renaissance styles were fused, and the buildings were decorated
with Sienese and Florentine paintings. The net result was a project that
expressed Renaissance ideals of art, architecture, and civilized good
living in a single scheme: It stands as an exquisite example of the ar-
chitectural canons that Alberti formulated in the early Renaissance and
which were utilized by later architects, including Brunelleschi and
Michelangelo, in designing many of Italy's finest buildings and piaz-
zas. Today the cool grandeur of Pienza's center seems almost surreal
in this otherwise unpretentious village, known locally for *pienzino,* also
called *cacio,* a smooth sheep's-milk cheese.

Montepulciano

❷❹ *12 km (7 mi) east of Pienza, 13 km (8 mi) west of the A1, 65 km (40
mi) south of Florence.*

Perched high on a hilltop, Montepulciano is made up of a pyramid of
redbrick buildings set within a circle of cypress trees. At an altitude of
almost 2,000 feet, it is cool in summer and chilled in winter by biting

winds that sweep its spiraling streets. The town has an unusually harmonious look, the result of the work of three architects, Sangallo il Vecchio, Vignola, and Michelozzo, who endowed it with fine palaces and churches in an attempt to impose Renaissance architectural ideals on an ancient Tuscan hill-town. The town's showpiece is the beau-

★ tiful **Piazza Grande.** Montepulciano's many wine cellars and antiques dealers and a few trendy shops and cafés hint that this otherwise sleepy town gets its share of tourists, especially during an international arts festival in July and August. On the hillside below the town walls is the church of **San Biagio,** designed by Sangallo, a paragon of Renaissance architectural perfection that is considered his masterpiece.

Dining and Lodging

$$ 🏠 **Il Marzocco.** A 16th-century building within the town walls, it is furnished in 19th-century style, complete with dignified, old-fashioned parlors and a billiard room. Many bedrooms have large terraces overlooking the countryside, and many rooms are large enough to accommodate extra beds; they are furnished in heavy turn-of-the-century style or in spindly white wood. ⊠ *Piazza Savonarola 18,* ☎ *0578/757262,* FAX *0578/757530. 18 rooms, 13 with bath or shower. Restaurant (closed Wed.). AE, DC, MC, V. Closed Nov. 20–Dec. 5.*

$$$$ ✕🏠 **Locanda dell'Amorosa.** A medieval hamlet set in Tuscan farmland
★ has become a rustic retreat for jaded city folk, who reserve ahead for a meal or weekend in the country only a half hour by car from Siena or Arezzo and even less from Montepulciano, Cortona, and Monte Oliveto Maggiore. The stone and brick buildings have been tastefully adapted to their current use, and the restaurant serves regional dishes that seem to taste even better in such apt surroundings. You can take home estate-produced wines and preserves as a souvenir of your stay. ⊠ *Località Amorosa, Sinalunga, 10 km (6 mi) from the Valdichiana exit of A1,* ☎ *0577/679497,* FAX *0577/632001. 17 rooms with bath. Restaurant, pool. AE, DC, MC, V. Restaurant closed Mon. and Tues. lunch and Jan. 8–Mar. 7).*

$ ✕🏠 **La Bandita.** This attractive old farmhouse has been converted into a hotel by the Fiorini family. It has great charm, with terra-cotta floors throughout, lace curtains and antiques in the bedrooms, and a fireplace and grandfather's 19th-century Tuscan provincial furniture in a large, brick-vaulted living room. Some rooms can accommodate an extra bed, there is a garden, and meals are available. ⊠ *Via Bandita 72, Bettolle, 1 km (.6 mi) from Valdichiana exit of A1 autostrada,* ☎ *0577/624649,* FAX *0577/624649. 8 rooms with bath. Restaurant (closed Tues.).MC, V.*

Nightlife and the Arts

The **Cantiere Internazionale d'Arte,** held in July and August, is a multifaceted festival of figurative art, music, and theater, ending with a major theatrical production in Piazza Grande.

En Route   The road leading to Chianciano climbs and dips, winding through woods of evergreens and oaks and affording glimpses of the vineyards that are the pride of this part of Tuscany. Two of Italy's best wines—Brunello di Montalcino and Vino Nobile di Montepulciano—originate here and bear the names of the towns where they are made.

Chianciano

9 km (5.5 mi) south of Montepulciano.

This small medieval town, surrounded by walls, has billboards proclaiming that Chianciano's restorative waters are indispensable for a *fegato sano* (a healthy liver). It's a modern spa with neat parks and a host of hotels.

Chiusi

11 km (7 mi) east of Chianciano, 2.5 km (1.5 mi) east of the AI, 126 km (78 mi) south of Florence.

Known for the frescoed tombs that date from the 5th century BC in its necropolis, Chiusi was one of the most powerful of the 12 ancient cities in the Etruscan federation, and is a transportation hub accessible from either the main north–south rail line or by car or bus from the A1 autostrada.

Cortona

🟡 *46 km (28.5 mi) northeast of Chiusi.*

This is one of Tuscany's prettiest hill-towns. Magnificently situated, with olives and vineyards creeping up to its walls, it commands sweeping views over Lake Trasimeno and the plain of the Valdichiana. Its two fine galleries and scattering of churches are relatively unvisited, while its delightful medieval streets are a pleasure to wander for their own sake.

Cortona may be one of Italy's oldest towns—"Mother of Troy and Grandmother of Rome," in popular speech. Tradition claims that it was founded by Dardanus, the founder of Troy (after whom the Daradanelles are named). He was fighting a local tribe, so the story goes, when he lost his helmet (*corythos* in Greek) on Cortona's hill. In time a town grew up that took its name (Corito) from the missing headgear. By the 4th century BC the Etruscans had built the first set of town walls, whose cyclopedean traces can still be seen in the 2-mile sweep of the present fortifications. As a member of the Etruscans' 12-city Dodecapolis, it became one of the federation's leading northern cities. An important consular road, the Via Cassia, which passed the foot of its hill, maintained the town's importance under the Romans. Medieval fortunes waned, however, as the plain below reverted to marsh. After holding out against neighbors like Perugia, Arezzo, and Siena, the *comune* was captured by King Ladislas of Naples in 1409 and sold to the Florentines two years later.

The heart of Cortona is formed by **Piazza della Repubblica** and the adjacent **Piazza Signorelli.** Wander into the courtyard of the picturesque **Palazzo Pretorio,** and, if you want to see a representative collection of Etruscan bronzes, climb its centuries-old stone staircase to the **Museo dell'Accademia Etrusca** (Gallery of Etruscan Art). ⊠ *Piazza Signorelli 9,* ☎ *0575/630415.* 🎟 *5,000 lire.* ⊙ *Apr.–Sept., Tues.–Sun. 10–1, 4–7; Oct.–Mar., Tues.–Sun. 9–1, 3–5.*

The **Museo Diocesano** (Diocesan Museum) houses an impressive number of large and splendid paintings by native son Luca Signorelli, as well as a beautiful *Annunciation* by Fra Angelico, a delightful surprise to find in this small, eclectic town. ⊠ *Piazza del Duomo 1,* ☎ *0575/ 62830.* 🎟 *5,000 lire.* ⊙ *Apr.–Sept., Tues.–Sun. 9–1, 3–6:30; Oct.–Mar., Tues.–Sun. 9–1, 3–5.*

Dining and Lodging

$$ ✕ **La Loggetta.** Above Cortona's main medieval square, this attractive restaurant occupies a 16th-century wine cellar. In fair weather you can eat outdoors, overlooking the 13th-century town hall, dining on regional dishes and such specialties as cannelloni, here filled with spinach and ricotta, and tagliata. The owners pride themselves on their selection of Tuscan wines. ⊠ *Piazza Pescheria 3,* ☎ *0575/630575. AE, DC, MC, V. Closed Mon., Jan. 7–23, 2 wks in Mar.*

$$ ✕ **Tonino.** Deservedly well known and popular with locals and visitors alike, this large modern establishment can be noisy and crowded on holiday weekends. But it is very satisfactory indeed at all other times, when you can enjoy the view of the Chiana valley and feast on host Tonino's own *antipastissimo,* an incredible variety of delectables. This is the place to taste Chianina beefsteak. ⊠ *Piazza Garibaldi,* ☎ *0575/630500. AE, DC, MC, V. Closed Tues. No dinner Mon.*

$$$ ✕⌦ **Il Falconiere.** A charming old villa less than 3½ kilometers (2 miles) outside Cortona, it once belonged to an early 19th-century poet and has been lovingly restored and impeccably furnished in the local style as an upscale inn. The winter garden and terrace have been transformed into a restaurant that features Tuscan dishes and seasonal specialties. ⊠ *Località San Martino,* ☎ *0575/612679,* ℻ *0575/612927. 12 rooms with bath. Restaurant, bar, pool. AE, DC, MC, V.*

Arezzo

㉖ *29 km (18 mi) north of Cortona, 81 km (50 mi) southeast of Florence.*

The birthplace of the poet Petrarch, of the Renaissance artist and art historian Giorgio Vasari, and of Guido d'Arezzo, the inventor of musical notation, is today best known for the magnificent, but very faint,
★ Piero della Francesca frescoes in the church of **San Francesco,** on Via Cavour in the center of town. Painted between 1452 and 1466, they depict *The Legend of the True Cross* on three walls of the choir. What Sir Kenneth Clark called "the most perfect morning light in all Renaissance painting" may be seen in the lowest section of the right wall, where the troops of the Emperor Maxentius flee before the sign of the cross. Unfortunately, part of the frescoes may be hidden from view while restoration work takes place.

With its irregular shape and sloping brick pavement, framed by buildings of assorted centuries, Arezzo's **Piazza Grande** echoes Siena's Piazza del Campo. Though not so grand, it is lively enough during the outdoor antiques fair every first Sunday of the month and when the **Joust of the Saracen,** featuring medieval costumes and competition, is held there on the first Sunday of September. The curving, tiered apse on Piazza Grande belongs to **Santa Maria della Pieve,** one of Tuscany's finest Romanesque churches. And Arezzo's medieval cathedral at the top of the hill harbors an eye-level fresco of a tender Magdalen by Piero della Francesca; look for it next to the large marble tomb near the organ.

There are several other attractions in Arezzo as well. The church of **San Domenico,** north of Piazza Grande at Piazza Fossombroni (just inside the walls) houses a 13th-century crucifix by Cimabue. The **Giorgio Vasari** house was designed and decorated by the region's leading Mannerist artist in 1540 for his own use. It's just west of San Domenico. The **Museo Archeologico** boasts a fine collection of Etruscan bronzes. ⊠ *Vasari house: Via XX Settembre 55,* ☎ *0575/300301.* 🎫 *Free.* ☼ *Tues.–Sat. 9–7, Sun. 9–1.* ⊠ *Museo Archeologico: Via Margaritone 10,* ☎ *0575/20882.* 🎫 *8,000 lire.* ☼ *Tues.–Sat. 9–2, Sun. 9–1.*

Dining and Lodging

$$ ✕ **Buca di San Francesco.** A frescoed cellar restaurant in a historic building next to the church of San Francesco, this "buca" (literally "hole," figuratively "cellar") has a medieval atmosphere and serves straightforward local specialties, including *ribollita.* Meat eaters will find the lean Chianina beef and the *saporita di Bonconte* (a selection of several meats) succulent treats. ⊠ *Piazza San Francesco 1,* ☎ *0575/23271. AE, DC, MC, V. Closed Tues., and July. No dinner Mon.*

$$ ✕ **Tastevin.** Close to San Francesco and to the central Piazza Guido Monaco, Tastevin has introduced creative cooking styles in Arezzo but serves traditional dishes as well, in three attractive dining rooms, two in warm Tuscan provincial style, one in more sophisticated bistro style. At the small bar the talented owner plays and sings show tunes and Sinatra songs in the evening; there is a 15% cover charge for music. The restaurant's specialties are penne Tastevin (with cream of truffles) and seafood or meat carpaccio. ⊠ *Via dei Cenci 9,* ☎ *0575/28304. AE, MC, V. Closed Mon. (Sun. in summer) and Aug. 1–25.*

$ ✕ **Spiedo d'Oro.** Cheery red-and-white tablecloths add a bright note to this large, reliable trattoria near the archeological museum. This is your chance to try authentic Tuscan home-style specialties, such as *zuppa di pane* (bread soup), *pappardelle all'ocio* (noodles with duck sauce), and osso buco *all'aretina* (sautéed veal shank). ⊠ *Via Crispi 12,* ☎ *0575/22873. No credit cards. Closed Thurs. and July 1–18.*

$$ ✕🏠 **Castello di Gargonza.** A tiny 13th-century hamlet with a castle, church, and cobbled streets offers something unusual as hostelries go. All its houses—cottages and apartments, really—are for rent by the week, and rooms can be had by the night. This enchanting spot in the countryside between Siena and Arezzo, part of the fiefdom of the aristocratic Florentine Guicciardini family, was restored by the modern Count Roberto Guicciardini as a way to rescue a dying village. The houses have one to six rooms each, sleep two to seven people, and have as many as four baths. La Torre restaurant serves local specialties. ⊠ *52048 Monte San Savino,* ☎ *0575/847021,* 🖷 *0575/847054. 18 houses with bath. Restaurant (closed Tues.). AE, MC, V. Closed Jan. 10–Feb. 10.*

$$ 🏠 **Continental.** Centrally located near the train station and within walking distance of all major sights, the Continental has been a reliable and convenient place to stay since it opened in the 1950s. Recently refurbished, it now has bright white furnishings with yellow accents, gleaming new bathrooms complete with hair dryers, and a pleasant roof garden. Rates are at the low end of the $$ category. ⊠ *Piazza Guido Monaco 7,* ☎ *0575/20251,* 🖷 *0575/350485. 74 rooms with bath or shower. Restaurant (closed Mon., no dinner Sun.). AE, DC, MC, V.*

Outdoor Activities and Sports

A popular horseback riding site is **Rendola Riding** (⊠ Rendola Valdarno, Arezzo, ☎ 0575/987045).

Shopping

Arezzo is known for its production of gold, as well as a burgeoning cottage knitwear industry. For sweaters, try **Maglierie** (⊠ Piazza Grande).

The first Sunday of each month, a colorful **flea market** selling antiques and not-so-antiques takes place in the **Piazza Grande.**

TUSCANY A TO Z

Arriving and Departing

By Car

The Autostrada del Sole (A1), connects Florence with Bologna, 105 km (65 miles) north, and Rome, 277 kilometers (172 miles) south, and passes close to Arezzo.

By Plane
The largest airports in the region are Pisa's **Galileo Galilei Airport** (☎ 050/500707) and Florence's **Peretola Airport** (☎ 055/373498).

By Train
The coastal line from Rome to Genoa passes through Pisa and all the beach resorts. The main line from Rome to Bologna passes through Arezzo, Florence, and Prato.

Getting Around

By Boat
Boat services link the islands of Tuscany's archipelago with the mainland; passenger and car ferries leave from Piombino for Elba: **Navarma Line** (⊠ Via Pisacane 110, ☎ 0565/225211); **Elba Ferries** (⊠ Piazzale Premuda, ☎ 0565/220956); **Toremar** (⊠ Piazzale Premuda 13, ☎ 0565/31100). The ferry to Giglio leaves from Porto Santo Stefano on the Argentario peninsula (☞ Toremar, *above*).

By Bus
Tuscany is crisscrossed by bus lines that connect the smaller towns and cities on the autostrade and superhighways. They are a good choice for touring the hill towns around Siena, such as San Gimignano; you can then take a Tra-In or Lazzi bus from Siena to Arezzo and get back onto the main Rome-Florence train line. From Chiusi on the main train line you can get a bus to Montepulciano. Buses connect Florence and Siena with Volterra.

By Car
The best way to see Tuscany, making it possible to explore the tiny towns and country restaurants that are so much a part of the region's charm, is by car. A11 leads west from Florence and meets the coastal A12 between Viareggio and Livorno. The A1 autostrada links Florence with Arezzo and Chiusi (where you turn off for Montepulciano). A toll-free superstrada links Florence with Siena. Drivers should be prepared to navigate through bewildering suburban sprawls around Tuscan cities; to reach the historic sections where most of the sights are located, look for the CENTRO STORICO signs.

By Train
Italy's main rail line, which runs from Milan to Calabria, links Florence and Arezzo in Tuscany and runs past Chiusi and Cortona on its way south. Another main line extends through our Tuscan Gateway towns, connecting Florence with Pisa by way of Prato, Pistoia, and Lucca. There are a few other local lines.

Contacts and Resources

Car Rentals
Cars are for rent at the airports and in the larger cities in Tuscany; Alitalia may offer economical fly/drive packages with discounts on car rentals and hotels.

Avis has offices at Peretola Airport in Florence (☎ 055/372588), Arezzo (⊠ Piazza della Repubblica 1/a, ☎ 0575/354232), Lucca (⊠ Via Castracane 1217, ☎ 0583/490383), and Sinea (⊠ Via Simone Martini, 36 ☎ 0577/270305). **Hertz** has offices at Galileo Galilei Airport in Pisa (☎ 050/49187), Prato (⊠ c/o Autonoleggio Europa, Viale Vittorio Veneto 57, ☎ 0574/21055), and in Siena (⊠ Via San Marco 96, ☎ 0577/41148).

Emergencies
Police, fire (☎ 113). **Ambulance** or medical emergency (☎ 118).

Fishing

For a license, contact the **Federazione Italiana della Pesca Sportiva** (✉ Via dei Neri 6, Firenze).

Guided Tours

From Florence, **American Express** (✉ Via Guicciardini 49/r, ☎ 055/288751) operates one-day excursions to Siena and San Gimignano and can arrange for cars, drivers, and guides for special-interest tours in Tuscany. **CIT** (✉ Via Cavour 56, ☎ 055/294306) has a three-day Carosello bus tour from Rome to Florence, Siena, and San Gimignano, as well as a five-day tour that also takes in Venice.

Horseback Riding

Rifugio Prategiano (✉ Montieri, Grosseto, ☎ 0566/997703), **Le Cannelle** (✉ Parco dell'Uccellina, Talamone, Grosseto, ☎ 0564/887020). For more information, contact the **Federazione Italiana Sport Equestre** (✉ Via Paoletti 54, Firenze, ☎ 055/480039).

Sailing

Charters in Tuscany are available through the **Centro Nautico Italiano** (✉ Piazza della Signoria 31/r, Firenze, ☎ 055/287045); **Mario Lorenzoni** (✉ Via degli Alfani 105/r, Firenze, ☎ 055/284790); and **Renato Lessi** (✉ Località Porto, Castiglione della Pescaia, Grosseto, ☎ 0564/922793). For more information, contact the **Federazione Italiana Vela** (✉ CP 49, Marina di Carrara, ☎ 0585/57323) or the **Federazione Italiana Motonautica** (✉ Via Goldora 16, 55044 Marina di Pietrasanta, ☎ 0584/20963).

Skiing

For information, contact the **Federazione Italiana Sport Invernali** (✉ Viale Matteotti 15, Firenze, ☎ 055/576987).

Travel Agencies

In Florence: **American Express** (✉ Via Guicciardini 49/r, ☎ 055/288751); **CIT** (✉ Via Cavour 56, ☎ 055/294306); or **Thomas Cook** (✉ c/o World Vision, Via Cavour 154/r, ☎ 055/579294).

Visitor Information

REGIONAL INFORMATION

Stop in **Florence** (✉ Via di Novoli, ☎ 055/439311).

LOCAL INFORMATION

There are tourist offices, generally open 9–12:30, 3:30–7:30, in **Arezzo** (✉ Piazza della Repubblica 28, ☎ 0575/377678); **Cortona** (✉ Via Nazionale 72, ☎ 0575/630352); **Lucca** (✉ Piazzale Verdi, ☎ 0583/419689); **Pisa** (✉ Piazza Duomo 8, ☎ 050/560464); **Pistoia** (✉ Palazzo dei Vescovi, ☎ 0573/21622); **Prato** (✉ Via Cairoli 48, ☎ 0574/24112); **San Gimignano** (✉ Piazza del Duomo, ☎ 0577/940008); **Siena** (✉ Via di Città 43, ☎ 0577/42209; ✉ Piazza del Campo 55, ☎ 0577/280551); **Volterra** (✉ Via Turazza 2, ☎ 0588/86150).

4 Umbria and the Marches

Perugia, Assisi, Urbino, Spoleto, and Orvieto

Legends linger in this mystical, ethereal birthplace of the saints, a region where medieval enclaves wear their ancient histories lightly. Here, you'll find Gothic treasures—Giotto's frescoes at Assisi's Basilica di San Francesco and Orvieto's awe-inspiring cathedral— while more urbane pleasures await at Spoleto's Festival of Two Worlds. To the east lies the timeless city of Urbino. A visit there reveals more about the artistic energy of the Renaissance than dozens of history books.

By Robert
Andrews

BIRTHPLACE OF SAINTS AND CONDOTTIERI, Umbria has remained true to its name: "land of shadows." The hills, olive groves, and terraced vineyards of this mystic province are often wrapped in a bluish haze that gives its landscape an ethereal painted look—a landscape often recognized in the frescoes of its celebrated local artists, even when they were decorating churches far from their native soil. Blessed with steep, austere hills, deep valleys, and fast-flowing rivers, the region—roughly halfway between Florence and Rome—has not yet been swamped by tourism and has escaped the unplanned industrial expansion that afflicts much of central Italy. No town in Umbria boasts the extravagant wealth of art and architecture of Florence, Rome, or Venice, but this works in your favor. Cities can be experienced whole, rather than as a series of museums and churches, forced marches through 2,000 years of Western culture; in Umbria the visitor comes to know the towns as people live in them today.

This is not to suggest that the cultural cupboard is bare—far from it. Perugia, the capital of the region, and Assisi, Umbria's most famous city, are rich in art and architecture, as are Orvieto, Todi, and Spoleto. Virtually every small town in the region has a castle, church, or museum worth a stop.

The earliest inhabitants of Umbria, the Umbri, were thought by the Romans to be the most ancient inhabitants of Italy. Little is known about them, since with the coming of Etruscan culture, the tribe fled into the mountains in the eastern portion of the region. The Etruscans, who founded some of the great cities of Umbria, were in turn supplanted by the Romans. Unlike Tuscany and other regions of central Italy, Umbria had few powerful medieval families to exert control over the cities in the Middle Ages—its proximity to Rome ensured that Umbria would always be more or less under papal domination.

The relative political stability of the region did not mean that Umbria was left in peace. Located in the center of the country, it has for much of its history been a battlefield where armies from north and south clashed. Hannibal destroyed a Roman army on the shores of Lake Trasimeno, and the full and bloody course of the interminable Guelph-Ghibelline conflict of the Middle Ages was played out in Umbria. Dante considered it the most violent place in Italy. Trophies of war still decorate the facade of the Palazzo dei Priori in Perugia, and the little town of Gubbio continues a warlike rivalry begun in the Middle Ages—every year it challenges the Tuscan town of Sansepolcro to a crossbow tournament. Today, of course, the bowmen shoot at targets, but neither side has forgotten that 500 years ago its ancestors shot at each other.

In spite of—or perhaps because of—this bloodshed, Umbria has produced more than its share of Christian saints. The most famous is Saint Francis, the decidedly unmartial saint whose life shaped the Church and the history of his time. His great shrine at Assisi is visited by hundreds of thousands of pilgrims each year. Saint Clare, his devoted follower, was Umbria-born, as were Saint Benedict, Saint Rita of Cascia, and, ironically, the shadowy patron saint of lovers, Saint Valentine.

East of Umbria, the Marches—or Marche, in Italian—stretch between the hills of the southern Apennines down to the Adriatic sea. It is a scenic region of mountains and valleys, with great turreted castles standing on high peaks defending passes and roads—silent testament to the region's warlike past. The Marches have passed through numerous hands. First the Romans supplanted the native civilizations; then Charlemagne supplanted the Romans (and gave the region its name: it was divided into "marks," or provinces, under the rule of the Holy Roman Emperor); then began the seemingly never-ending struggle between popes and local lords. Cesare Borgia succeeded in wresting control of the Marches from the local suzerains, annexing the region to the papacy of his father, Alexander VI.

Despite all this martial tussling, it was in the lonely mountain town of Urbino that the Renaissance came to its fullest flower; that small town became a haven of culture and learning that rivaled the greater, richer, and more powerful city of Florence, and even Rome itself.

Pleasures and Pastimes

Dining

Umbria is mountainous, and the cuisine of the region is typical of mountain people everywhere. The food is hearty and straightforward, with a stick-to-the-ribs quality that sees hard-working farmers and artisans through a long day's work and helps them make the steep climb home at night. Italians are generally thought not to eat much meat, but this is untrue of Italy in general and of Umbria in particular. Novelist Anthony Burgess once observed that a beefsteak in Italy is never "*una bistecca*" but always "*una bella bistecca*"—a beautiful steak—and a simple steak in Umbria is almost always *bella*.

The region has made several important contributions to Italian cuisine. Particularly prized are black truffles from the area around Spoleto (signs warning against unlicensed truffle hunting are posted at the base of the grand Ponte delle Torri) and from the hills around the tiny town of Norcia. Norcia, in fact, exports truffles to France and hosts a truffle festival every year in November. Many regional dishes are given a grating of truffle before serving; unless the truffle is a really good one, however, its subtle taste may not come through. The local pasta specialty—thick, handmade spaghetti called *ciriole* or *strengozzi*—is good *al tartufo,* with a dressing of excellent local olive oil and truffles.

In addition, Norcia's pork products—especially sausages, salami, and *arista* (bone marrow of pig)—are so famous that pork butchers throughout Italy are called *norcini,* no matter where they hail from, and pork butcher shops are called *norcinerie.*

In the Marches, fish in various forms is the thing to look for. One of the characteristic dishes in Ancona is *brodetto,* a rich fish chowder containing as many as nine types of Adriatic saltwater fish. Ascoli Piceno, inland, is famous for two dishes: olives *ascolane* (stuffed, rolled in batter, and deep fried) and *vincisgrassi* (a local version of lasagna, far richer than you're likely to find elsewhere in Italy). Ascoli Piceno is also the home of the licorice-flavored liqueur anisette.

CATEGORY	COST*
$$$	60,000–85,000 lire
$$	25,000–60,000 lire
$	under 25,000 lire

*per person, including first course, main course, dessert or fruit, and house wine

Lodging

Virtually every historic town in Umbria has some kind of hotel, no matter how small the place may be. In most cases a small city boasts one or two hotels in a high price category and a few smaller, basic hotels in the inexpensive-to-moderate ($–$$) range. The cheaper the hotel,

Your
passport
around
the world.

- Worldwide access
- Operators who speak your language
- Monthly itemized billing

MCI Calling Card

415 555 1234 2244
J.D. SMITH

Use your MCI Card® and these access numbers for an easy way to call when traveling worldwide.

Austria (CC)♦†	022-903-012
Belarus	
From Gomel and Mogilev regions	8-10-800-103
From all other localities	8-800-103
Belgium (CC)♦†	0800-10012
Bulgaria	00800-0001
Croatia (CC)★	99-385-0112
Czech Republic (CC)♦	00-42-000112
Denmark (CC)♦†	8001-0022
Finland (CC)♦†	9800-102-80
France (CC)♦†	0800-99-0019
Germany (CC)†	0130-0012
Greece (CC)♦†	00-800-1211
Hungary (CC)♦	00▼800-01411
Iceland (CC)♦†	800-9002
Ireland (CC)†	1-800-55-1001
Italy (CC)♦†	172-1022
Kazakhstan (CC)	1-800-131-4321
Liechtenstein (CC)♦	155-0222
Luxembourg†	0800-0112
Monaco (CC)♦	800-90-19

Netherlands (CC)♦†	06-022-91-22
Norway (CC)♦†	800-19912
Poland (CC)✛†	00-800-111-21-22
Portugal (CC)✛†	05-017-1234
Romania (CC)✛	01-800-1800
Russia (CC)✛♦	747-3322
For a Russian-speaking operator	747-3320
San Marino (CC)♦	172-1022
Slovak Republic (CC)	00-42-000112
Slovenia	080-8808
Spain (CC)†	900-99-0014
Sweden (CC)♦†	020-795-922
Switzerland (CC)♦†	155-0222
Turkey (CC)♦†	00-8001-1177
Ukraine (CC)✛	8▼10-013
United Kingdom (CC)†	
To call to the U.S. using BT ■	0800-89-0222
To call to the U.S. using Mercury ■	0500-89-0222
Vatican City (CC)†	172-1022

To sign up for the MCI Card, dial the access number of the country you are in and ask to speak with a customer service representative.

http://www.mci.com

(CC) Country-to-country calling available. May not be available to/from all international locations. (Canada, Puerto Rico, and U.S. Virgin Islands are considered Domestic Access locations.) ♦ Public phones may require deposit of coin or phone card for dial tone. † Automation available from most locations. ★ Not available from public pay phones. ▼ Wait for second dial tone. ✛ Limited availability. ■ International communications carrier.

It helps to be pushy in airports.

Introducing the revolutionary new TransPorter™ from American Tourister® It's the first suitcase you can push around without a fight. TransPorter's™ exclusive four-wheel design lets you push it in front of you with almost no effort–the wheels take the weight. Or pull it on two wheels if you choose. You can even stack on other bags and use it like a luggage cart.

Stable 4-wheel design.

TransPorter™ is designed like a dresser, with built-in shelves to organize your belongings. Or collapse the shelves and pack it like a traditional suitcase. Inside, there's a suiter feature to help keep suits and dresses from wrinkling. When push comes to shove, you can't beat a TransPorter™ For more information on how you can be this pushy, call 1-800-542-1300.

Shelves collapse on command.

American Tourister®

Making travel less primitive®

the fewer the services. Most basic hotels offer breakfast, but few have restaurants or bars.

A recent and popular trend is the conversion of old villas and monasteries into first-class hotels. These tend to be outside the towns, in the countryside, and the splendor of the settings often outweighs the problem of getting into town. In all cases, these country hotels are comfortable, often luxurious, and offer a mixture of Old World charm and modern convenience.

Reservations at any hotel are recommended, and traveling in high season to Perugia, Assisi, Spoleto, Todi, or Orvieto without advance bookings is a chancy proposition.

CATEGORY	COST*
$$$$	over 300,000 lire
$$$	160,000–300,000 lire
$$	100,000–160,000 lire
$	under 100,000 lire

All prices are for a standard double room for two, including tax, service, and breakfast.

Hiking

Magnificent scenery makes Umbria fine hiking and mountaineering country. The area around Spoleto is particularly good, and the tourist office for the town (☞ Contacts and Resources *in* Umbria A to Z, *below*) will supply itineraries of walks and climbs to suit all ages and levels of ability.

Shopping

Pottery and wine are the two most famous Umbrian exports, and examples of both commodities are excellent and unique to the region. **Torgiano,** south of Perugia, is one of the best-known centers of wine making, where you can watch the process and buy the product; you can find some of the best ceramics at **Gubbio, Perugia,** and **Assisi.** Those with the most flair are found in **Deruta,** south of Torgiano on S3bis. The red glazes of Gubbio pottery have been famous since medieval times. The secret of the original glaze died with its inventor some 500 years ago, but there are contemporary potters who produce a fair facsimile.

Swimming

Lakes Trasimeno and Piediluco offer safe and clean bathing facilities. **Castiglione del Lago,** on Lake Trasimeno, has a public beach, with no strong undercurrents or hidden depths.

Exploring Umbria and the Marches

The steep hills and deep valleys that make Umbria and the Marches so picturesque also make them difficult to explore. Driving routes must be chosen carefully to avoid tortuous mountain roads; major towns are not necessarily linked to each other by train, bus, or highway. A convenient base for exploring the region might be Perugia, the largest city in Umbria, but to see the region properly you would still need to stay overnight in other towns along the way. Next we head east across the Apennines to the Marches region; we begin exploring it in the hilltop city of Urbino, travel down to the Adriatic coast to visit Ancona, and then climb back west into the hills to Loreto and Ascoli Piceno. Back in Umbria, we concentrate on two memorable towns: Spoleto, site of the famous arts festival, south of Perugia; and Assisi, St. Francis's hometown, just east of Perugia. The final tour centers on Orvieto, built on a huge rock outcropping in western Umbria, southwest of Perugia.

Great Itineraries

The region of Umbria is particularly suited to touring in a limited time. Basing yourself in Perugia, you can see all the major sights in the regional capital in the equivalent of a day, making easy excursions to the hill villages on your other days without feeling stressed out by constant travel.

Numbers in the text correspond to numbers in the margin and on the Umbria and the Marches, Perugia, and Assisi maps.

IF YOU HAVE 3 DAYS

In ⊞ **Perugia** ①–⑤, your main stops will be the refurbished Galleria Nazionale and the Collegio del Cambio, both contained in the atmospheric **Palazzo dei Priori** ③; much of the rest of your time will be spent alternately ambling along Corso Vannucci and toiling up and down the steep lanes on either side. Devote your second day to ⊞ **Assisi** ⑬–⑳, where the spiritual and the material are fused in a place that remains in essence a small medieval Umbrian town. The choice for a third excursion is a tough one, and you won't be disappointed by whichever place you opt for. Consider **Spoleto** ⑫: a tight-knit hill town whose narrow streets abound with evocative views and delightful surprises.

IF YOU HAVE 5 DAYS

Given five days, you will be able to spend a couple of them exploring the neighboring region of Marche. How you enter these rather inaccessible parts will depend on your mode of transport. In any case, start your tour in **Perugia** ①–⑤, and follow the schedule outlined above for your first two days. If you are traveling by public transport, spend your third night in ⊞ **Spoleto** ⑫, from which you can jump on a train bound for ⊞ **Ancona** ⑨, where you can board a bus or a train for Pésaro and **Urbino** ⑧. This hilltop gem retains its proud, self-contained character, almost untouched by ugly 20th-century construction. Looming over the town is the imposing Palazzo Ducale, which will occupy most of the sightseeing you'll want to do here. Calculate at least half a day for reaching Urbino from Spoleto, and it's not much shorter by car, crossing the Marches border from ⊞ **Gubbio** ⑦, where you might spend your third day as an alternative to Spoleto. Gubbio's charm is not hard to fathom, and you can enjoy a very pleasant day and night here, appreciating the views and shops as well as some choice accommodation and dining possibilities.

IF YOU HAVE 7 DAYS

Reserve four days for Umbria and three for the Marches. With greater flexibility you can choose how many nights you want to spend in Umbria's capital, **Perugia** ①–⑤, and how many in the region's smaller centers. More time in Perugia will allow you to explore the city thoroughly, including the archaeological museum, and you might take in the easy excursion to the wine village of **Torgiano** ⑥. ⊞ **Spoleto** ⑫ and ⊞ **Assisi** ⑬–⑳ are essential stops farther afield, where you might lodge for a night in each. Gubbio is also worth overnighting in, whereas **Orvieto** ㉑ can be seen on your way to or from Rome, from which it's only 90 minutes' travel time. The essential sight here is of course the cathedral, though there are also a couple of good museums, a plethora of fine restaurants and some cozy hotels. East of Perugia, the Marches invite leisurely exploring, though also some lengthy rides in between the main points of interest. ⊞ **Urbino** ⑧ is the premier attraction and is worth staying a night in; ⊞ **Ancona** ⑨ has little of interest though it is the biggest city in the region and has accordingly good facilities for eating and sleeping, not to mention banks, car hire agencies, and information offices. Sleep here if you must; otherwise head south for the infinitely preferable inland town of ⊞ **Ascoli Piceno** ⑪, with a small choice of hotels and a slow, enticing atmosphere. There is little in the way of galleries or sophisticated shops here, but the place oozes charm. On the way, or en route back, drop in at the holy sanctuary of **Loreto** ⑩, nestled in the mountains 15 miles south of Ancona. It is a curiosity, even for nonbelievers, attracting pilgrims from all over the world.

When to Tour Umbria and the Marches

Unlike many other regions of Italy, Umbria and the Marches are relatively free of the tourist hordes, even in summer, when you might welcome the lush greenness of these interior tracts. Indeed, in August, much of the population shifts to the Adriatic resorts of the Marches to enjoy their vacation—though there are more enticing places to resort to if you felt like doing the same. At the other end of the year, the predominantly hilly terrain of Umbria and the Marches means that winters can be bitterly cold, and snow is not uncommon. Since many of the places on our itinerary are hilltop towns, including Perugia itself, you should be prepared for harsh conditions if you're traveling at this time of year, and driving can be hazardous. From the point of view of the region's cuisine, however, winter is best: January–April is the season to sample the truffles for which the area around Norcia and Spoleto is famous (though of course truffles are dried and can be had at any time of year), whereas wild mushrooms are picked fresh in October–December. The forested hills of Umbria and the Marches also ensure beguiling colors in the fall and an explosion of greenery in spring, two seasons when the tourist count is especially low and the temperature usually comfortable.

From the practical point of view, unless you are specifically drawn to the festival scene, make a wide berth of Spoleto between June and July, when the *Due Mondi* and jazz festivals take place, and of Gubbio at the end of May, when the crossbow tournament usually entails a similar level of congestion. If you *are* planning to attend these crowd-pulling events, you will need to book accommodations months in advance.

Sightseers and pilgrims throng the streets of Assisi, the most visited city in Umbria, throughout the year, though the religious festivals of Christmas, Easter, and the feast of Saint Francis (October 4), as well as the town's Calendimaggio Festival (May 1), are particularly swarming. At other times, even weekends can be uncomfortable, so you would do well to schedule your visit to Assisi with care.

UMBRIAN HEIGHTS
Perugia to Gubbio

Perugia

❶ *180 km (112 mi) north of Rome, 153 km (96 mi) southeast of Florence, 455 km (284 mi) southeast of Milan.*

Perugia, the largest and richest of Umbria's cities, is an old and elegant place of great charm. Despite a rather grim crust of modern suburbs, Perugia's location on a series of hills high above the suburban plain has ensured that the medieval city remains almost completely intact. Perugia is the best-preserved hill town of its size, and few other places in Italy illustrate better the concept of the self-contained city-state that so shaped the course of Italian history.

The best approach to the city is by train—the station is in the unlovely suburbs, but there are frequent buses running directly to Piazza d'I-

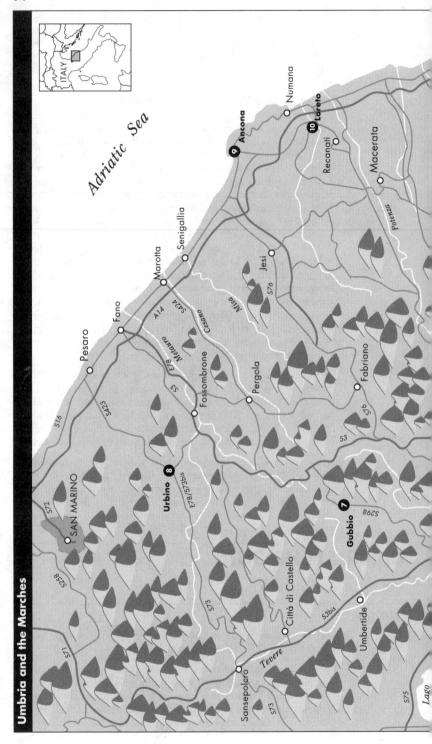

Umbria and the Marches

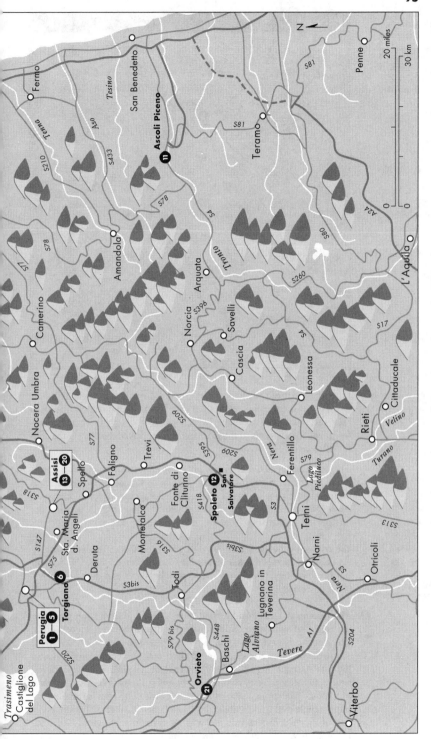

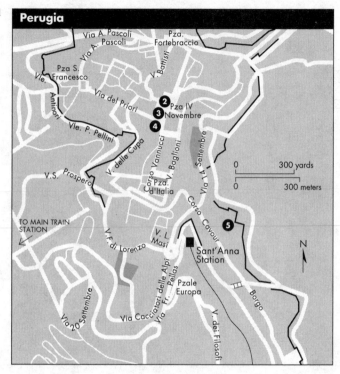

talia, the heart of the old town. If you are driving to Perugia, it is best
to leave your car in one of the parking lots near the station and then
take the bus or the escalator (which passes through fascinating subterranean excavations of the Roman foundations of the city) to the center of town.

The nerve center of the city is the broad, stately **Corso Vannucci,** a pedestrian street that runs from Piazza d'Italia to Piazza IV Novembre. As
evening falls, Corso Vannucci is filled with Perugians out for their evening
passeggiata, a pleasant predinner stroll that may include a pause for
an aperitif at one of the many bars that line the street.

NEED A
BREAK?   You can enjoy the lively comings and goings on Corso Vannucci from
the vantage point of the **Bar Sandri** (⊠ Corso Vannucci 32). This fine old
bar is a 19th-century relic with wood-paneled walls and an elaborately
frescoed ceiling.

---

❷ The **Duomo** is a large and rather plain building dating from the Middle Ages but with many additions from the 15th and 16th centuries.
The interior is vast and echoing, with little in the way of decoration.
There are some elaborately carved choir stalls, executed by Giovanni
Battista Bastone in 1520. The great relic of the church—the wedding
ring of the Virgin Mary that the Perugians stole from the nearby town
of Chiusi—is kept in a chapel in the left aisle. The ring is the size of a
large bangle and is kept under lock (15 locks, actually) and key every
day of the year except July 30, when it is exposed to view. ⊠ *Piazza
IV Novembre.* ☉ *Daily 8–noon, 4–7:30.*

There is a large array of precious objects associated with the cathedral
in the **Museum of the Duomo,** including vestments, vessels, manuscripts,
and gold work, as well as one outstanding piece of artwork, an early

masterpiece by Luca Signorelli, the altarpiece showing the Madonna with Saint John the Baptist, Saint Onophrius, and Saint Lawrence (1484). ⊠ *Piazza IV Novembre.* 🎫 *2,000 lire.* ☉ *Wed.–Fri. 9–noon, Sat. 9–noon and 3:30–5:30, Sun. 3:30–5:30.*

★ ❸ The **Palazzo dei Priori** faces the Duomo across the piazza. It is an imposing building, begun in the 13th century, with an unusual staircase that fans out into the square. The facade is decorated with symbols of Perugia's pride and past power: the griffin is the symbol of the city; the lion denotes Perugia's allegiance to the Guelph (or papal) cause; and both figures support the heavy chains of the gates of Siena, which fell to Perugian forces in 1358.

The fourth floor of the Palazzo dei Priori contains the region's most comprehensive and absorbing art gallery, the **Galleria Nazionale d'Umbria,** recently reopened after a lengthy overhaul. Now enhanced by skillfully lit displays and computers allowing you to focus on details of the works and background information on them, the collection in 33 rooms includes work by native artists—most outstandingly Pinturicchio and Perugino—and others of the Umbrian and Tuscan schools, including Gentile da Fabriano, Duccio, Fra Angelico, Fiorenzo di Lorenzo, and Piero della Francesca. As well as paintings, the gallery has frescoes, sculptures, and some superb crucifixes from the 13th and 14th centuries; other rooms are dedicated to the city of Perugia itself, showing how the medieval city evolved. ⊠ *Corso Vannucci 19,* 🎫 *8,000 lire.* ☉ *Mon.–Sat. 9–7, Sun. 9–1. Closed 1st Mon. of each month.*

★ ❹ Attached to the Palazzo dei Priori, but entered from Corso Vannucci a few doors along from the Galleria Nazionale, is the **Collegio del Cambio,** a series of elaborate rooms that housed the meeting hall and chapel of the guild of bankers and money changers. The walls were frescoed from 1496 to 1500 by the most important Perugian painter of the Renaissance, Pietro Vannucci, better known as Perugino. The decorative program in the Collegio includes common religious themes, like the Nativity and the Transfiguration (on the end walls), but also figures intended to inspire the businessmen who congregated here. On the left wall are female figures representing the virtues, beneath them the heroes and sages of antiquity. On the right wall are the prophets and sibyls—said to have been painted in part by Perugino's most famous pupil, Raphael, whose hand, the experts say, is most apparent in the figure of Fortitude. On one of the pilasters is a remarkably honest self-portrait of Perugino, surmounted by a Latin inscription and contained in a faux frame. ⊠ *Corso Vannucci 25.* 🎫 *5,000 lire.* ☉ *Nov.–Feb., Tues.–Sat. 8–2, Sun. 9–12:30; Mar.–Oct., Mon.–Sat. 9–12:30 and 2:30–5:30, Sun. 9–12:30. During Christmas season (Dec. 20–Jan. 6) museum follows summer timetable.*

❺ A 10-minute walk south of the center along Corso Cavour leads to the **Archaeological Museum of Umbria,** which contains an excellent collection of Etruscan artifacts from throughout the region. Perugia was a flourishing Etruscan site long before it fell under Roman domination in 310 BC. (Other than this collection, little remains of Perugia's mysterious ancestors, although the Gate of Augustus, in Piazza Fortebraccio, the northern entrance to the city, is of Etruscan origin.) ⊠ *Piazza Giordano Bruno.* 🎫 *4,000 lire.* ☉ *Mon.–Sat. 9–1:30 and 2:30–7, Sun. 9–1.*

☾ Umbria's only attraction aimed directly at the younger set is **La Città della Domenica,** a Disney-style playground in the town of Montepulito, 8 kilometers (5 miles) west of Perugia on the secondary road that leads to Corciano. The 500 acres of parkland contain a variety of buildings based on familiar fairy-tale themes—Snow White's House, the Witches' Wood—as well as a reptile house, a medieval museum, an exhibit of shells from all over the world, game rooms, and a choice of restaurants. ⊠ *Località Montepulito.* ☎ *075/505–4941.* ✇ *15,900 lire (16,900 lire Sun. and public holidays).* ⊙ *Mid-Mar.–late-Sept., daily 9–7; late Sept.–Oct., weekends and holidays 9–7; Nov.–mid-Mar. (exhibitions only), Sat. 2–7, Sun. 10–7.*

Dining and Lodging

$$ ✕ **Il Falchetto.** Here you'll find exceptional food at reasonable prices, making this Perugia's best restaurant bargain. The service is smart but relaxed, and the two dining rooms are medieval, with the kitchen and chef on view. The house specialty is *falchetti* (homemade gnocchi with spinach and ricotta cheese). ⊠ *Via Bartolo 20,* ☎ *075/573–1775. Reservations essential. AE, DC, MC, V. Closed Mon.*

$$ ✕ **La Rosetta.** This restaurant, in the hotel of the same name, is a peaceful, elegant place. In the winter you dine inside under medieval vaults; in summer, in the cool courtyard. The cuisine is simple but reliable and flawlessly served. ⊠ *Piazza d'Italia 19,* ☎ *075/572–0841. Reservations essential. AE, DC, MC, V. Closed Mon.*

$$ ✕ **La Taverna.** Next to the Teatro Pavone, off Corso Vannucci, medieval steps lead to this rustic restaurant on two levels, where lots of wine bottles and artful clutter heighten the tavern atmosphere. The menu features regional specialties and better-known Italian dishes. Good choices include *chitarrini* (pasta), with either *funghi* (mushrooms) or *tartufi* (pricier truffles), and grilled meats. ⊠ *Via delle Streghe 8,* ☎ *075/572–4128. Dinner reservations essential. AE, DC, MC, V. Closed Mon.*

$$$$ ▦ **Brufani Hotel.** The two hotels (this one and the Palace Hotel Bellavista; ☞ *below*) in this 19th-century palazzo were once one. The Brufani's public rooms and first-floor guest rooms have high ceilings and are done in the grand style of the Belle Epoque. The second-floor rooms are more modern, and many on both floors have a marvelous view of the Umbrian countryside or the city. ⊠ *Piazza d'Italia 12,* ☎ *075/573–2541,* ℻ *075/572–0210. 24 rooms with bath. Restaurant, bar, air-conditioning, meeting rooms. AE, DC, MC, V.*

$$$ ▦ **Locanda della Posta.** This luxuriously decorated small hotel in the
★ center of Perugia's historic district is a delight to behold, from its faux-marble moldings, paneled doors, and tile bouquets in the baths to the suede-upholstered elevator and fabric-covered walls. Architectural details of the 18th-century palazzo are beautiful, and views of city rooftops from windows and balconies are soothing. Breakfast is included here. ⊠ *Corso Vannucci 97,* ☎ *075/572–8925,* ℻ *075/572–2413. 40 rooms with bath or shower. Breakfast room, lobby lounge. AE, DC, MC, V.*

$$ ▦ **Palace Hotel Bellavista.** The rooms in this hotel are decorated in splendid Belle Epoque grandeur, and many have a view over the hills. The hotel's entrance is unimpressive, but the public rooms are palatial. Weekly rates are available. ⊠ *Piazza d'Italia 12,* ☎ *075/572–0741,* ℻ *075/572–9092. 74 rooms with bath or shower. Bar, meeting rooms. AE, DC, MC, V.*

$$ ▦ **Priori.** On an alley leading off the main Corso Vannucci, this unpretentious but elegant hotel has spacious and cheerful rooms with modern furnishings. There is a panoramic terrace where breakfast (included in the price) is served in summer. The hotel is difficult to find if you're driving, but a car is an encumbrance wherever you are in Perugia's historic center. ⊠ *Via Vermiglioli 3,* ☎ *075/572–3378,* ℻ *075/572–3213. 51 rooms with bath or shower. Bar. No credit cards.*

$ ☎ **Rosalba.** This is a bright and friendly choice on the fringes of Perugia's historic center. Rooms—each equipped with telephone and television—are scrupulously clean, and the ones at the back enjoy a view. Although somewhat out of the way, the hotel is only a matter of minutes from Corso Vannucci by virtue of the nearby escalator stop, saving a good deal of legwork. Parking is easy, too. ⊠ *Via del Circo 7,* ☎ *075/572–8285. 11 rooms with shower. No credit cards.*

Nightlife and the Arts
Summer sees two music festivals in Perugia: the **Jazz Festival of Umbria** (July) and the **Festival of Sacred Music** (September). Event and ticket information for both festivals can be obtained, year-round, from the Perugia Tourist Office (⊠ Piazza IV Novembre 3, ☎ 075/572–3327).

A true devotee of Umbrian music should consider the lengthy trek to the **Chamber Music Festival of Umbria,** which is held every August and September in the town of Città di Castello, about 80 kilometers (49½ miles) north of Perugia on the S3bis. For information, contact the tourist office (⊠ Via R. di Cesare 2/b, ☎ 075/855–4817).

Shopping
Perugia is a well-to-do town, and judging by the array of expensive shops on **Corso Vannucci,** the Perugians are not afraid to part with their money. The main streets of the town are lined with clothing shops selling the best-known Italian designers, either in luxurious boutiques or shops—such as Gucci, Ferragamo, Armani, and Fendi—run by the design firms themselves.

The best and most typical thing to buy in Perugia is, of course, some of the famous and delicious **Perugina chocolate.** *Cioccolato al latte* (milk chocolate) and *fondente* (dark chocolate) are available in tiny jewel-like boxes or in giant gift boxes the size of serving trays. The most famous chocolates made by Perugina are the round chocolate- and nut-filled candies called Baci (kisses), which come wrapped in silver paper and, like fortune cookies, contain romantic sentiments or sayings.

Torgiano

6 *15 km (9 mi) southeast of Perugia.*

Wine lovers are certain to want to visit this home to the famous **Lungarotti winery,** best known for delicious Rubesco Lungarotti, San Giorgio, and chardonnay. The town is also home to a fascinating wine museum, which has a large collection of ancient wine vessels, presses, documents, and tools that tell the story of viticulture in Umbria and beyond. The museum traces the history of wine in all its uses—for drinking at the table, as medicine, and in mythology. You can also pick up one of the winery's award-winning reds and whites to take home. ⊠ *Corso Vittorio Emanuele 11.* ☎ *5,000 lire.* ☉ *Apr.–Sept., daily 9–noon and 3–7; Oct.–Mar., daily 9–1 and 3–6.*

Gubbio

7 *40 km (25 mi) northeast of Perugia.*

The trip from Perugia to **Gubbio** follows S298 through rugged, mountainous terrain. There is something otherworldly about this small jewel of a medieval town tucked away in a mountainous corner of Umbria. Even at the height of summer, the cool serenity and silence of Gubbio's streets remain intact. The town is perched on the slopes of Mt. Ingino, and the streets are dramatically steep.

Gubbio's relatively isolated position has kept it free of hordes of high-season visitors, but even during the busiest times of year the city lives up to its Italian nickname, the City of Silence. Parking in the central Piazza dei Quaranta Martiri (named for 40 hostages murdered by the Nazis in 1944) is easy and secure, and it is wise to leave your car there and explore the narrow streets on foot.

★ Walk up the main street of the town, Via della Repubblica (a steep climb) to Piazza della Signoria. This square is dominated by the magnificent **Palazzo dei Consoli,** a medieval building designed and built by a local architect known as Gattapone—a man still much admired by today's residents (every other hotel, restaurant, and bar has been named after him).

Although the Palazzo dei Consoli is impressive, it is the **piazza** itself that is most striking. When approached from the thicket of medieval streets, the wide and majestic square is an eye-opener. The piazza juts out from the hillside like an enormous terrace, giving wonderful views of the town and surrounding countryside.

The Palazzo dei Consoli houses a small museum, famous chiefly for the **Tavole Eugubine,** bronze tablets written in an ancient Umbrian language. Also in the museum are the **ceri,** three 16-foot-high poles crowned with statues of Saints Ubaldo, George, and Anthony. These heavy pillars are the focal point of the best-known event in Gubbio, the Festival of the Ceri (Candles), held every May 15. On that day, teams of Gubbio's young men, dressed in medieval costumes and carrying the ceri, race up the steep slopes of Mt. Ingino to the Monastery of Saint Ubaldo, high above the town. This festival, enacted faithfully every year since 1151, is a picturesque, if strenuous, way of thanking the patron saints of the town for their assistance in a miraculous Gubbian victory over a league of 11 other towns. ⊠ *Piazza della Signoria.* ▨ *4,000 lire.* ⊙ *Mid-Mar.–Sept., daily 9–12:30 and 3:30–6; Oct.–mid-Mar., daily 9–1 and 3–5.*

The **Duomo** and the Palazzo Ducale face each other across a narrow street on the highest tier of the town. The Duomo dates from the 13th century, with some Baroque additions—in particular, a lavishly decorated bishop's chapel. ⊠ *Via Ducale.* ⊙ *Daily 9–12:30 and 3–5.*

The **Palazzo Ducale** is a scaled-down copy of the Palazzo Ducale in Urbino (Gubbio was once the possession of that city's ruling family, the Montefeltro). Gubbio's palazzo contains a small museum and a fine courtyard. There are magnificent views from some of the public rooms. *Palazzo Ducale.* ⊠ *Via Ducale.* ▨ *4,000 lire.* ⊙ *Mon.–Sat. 9–1:45, Sun. 9–1, also summer 3:30–6:30.*

NEED A
BREAK?   Under the arches that support the Palazzo Ducale is the **Bar del Giardino Pubblico,** a bar set in the tiny public gardens, which seem to hang off the side of the mountain. It is a charming place for a cold drink and a rest after a tiring climb up to the Duomo and Palace. It's open May–September, daily 9–7.

☾ Among the region's historical pageants, Gubbio's costumed **crossbow tournament** is particularly exciting for young and old alike. The *Palio della Balestra* usually takes place on the last Sunday in May; contact the Gubbio tourist agency for details. ⊠ *Piazza Oderisi 6,* ☎ *075/ 922–0693.*

Dining and Lodging

$$ ✕ **Fornace di Mastro Giorgio.** This atmospheric restaurant is in the medieval workshop of a famous master potter, one of Gubbio's most famous sons. The food is lighter than typical Umbrian fare, with the

occasional southern dish, like *tiella barese* (a mixture of rice, mussels, and potatoes), added. ⊠ *Via Mastro Giorgio 2,* ☎ *075/927–5740. Reservations essential in summer. AE, DC, MC, V. Closed Mon. Sept.–June and 2 wks in July. No dinner Sun.*

$$ ✕ **Grotta dell'Angelo.** This rustic trattoria is in the lower part of the Old Town, near the main square and tourist information office. The menu features simple local specialties, including *capocollo* (a type of salami), strengozzi pasta, and lasagna *tartufate* (with truffles). There are a few tables for outdoor dining. Inexpensive guest rooms are available here as well. ⊠ *Via Gioia 47,* ☎ *075/927–3438. Reservations essential. AE, DC, MC, V. Closed Tues. and Jan. 7–Feb. 7.*

$$ ✕ **Taverna del Lupo.** It's one of the best restaurants in the city, as well as one of the largest—it seats 200 people and can get a bit hectic during the high season. Lasagna made in the Gubbian fashion, with ham and truffles, is the best pasta. You'll also find excellent desserts and an extensive wine cellar here. ⊠ *Via G. Ansidei 21,* ☎ *075/927–4368. Reservations essential. AE, DC, MC, V. Closed Mon. Sept.–June and Jan.*

$$ ▦ **Hotel Bosone.** Occupying the old central Palazzo Raffaelli, the Hotel Bosone has many rooms decorated with frescoes from the former palace. The suites furnished with period detail are particularly lavish. ⊠ *Via XX Settembre 22,* ☎ *075/922–0688,* ℻ *075/922–0552. 30 rooms with bath or shower. Restaurant, bar. AE, DC, MC, V.*

$ ▦ **Hotel Gattapone.** Right in the center of town is this hotel with wonderful views of the sea of rooftops. It is casual and family run, with good-size, modern, comfortable rooms, some with well-preserved timber-raftered ceilings. ⊠ *Via Ansidei 6,* ☎ *075/927–2489,* ℻ *075/927–1269. 13 rooms with bath or shower. Closed Jan. AE, DC, MC, V.*

THE MARCHES
Mirror to the Renaissance

An excursion from Umbria into the region of the Marches is recommended for those who want to get off the beaten track and see a part of Italy rarely visited by foreigners. It must be admitted that traveling in the Marches is not as easy as in Umbria or Tuscany. Beyond the narrow coastal plain and away from major towns, the roads are steep and twisting. Train travel in the region is slow, and destinations are limited, although one can reach Ascoli Piceno by rail, and there's an efficient bus service from the coastal town of Pesaro to Urbino, the other principal tourist city of the region.

Urbino

❽ *170 km (106 mi) northeast of Perugia, 190 km (119 mi) east of Florence, 30 km (19 mi) southwest of Pésaro.*

Urbino is a majestic city, sitting atop a steep hill, with a skyline of towers and domes. It is something of a surprise to come upon it—the location is remote—and it is even stranger to reflect that this quiet country town was once a center of learning and culture almost without rival in western Europe. The town looks much as it did in the glory days of the 15th century, a cluster of warm brick and pale stone buildings, all topped with russet-colored tiled roofs. The focal point is the immense and beautiful Ducal Palace.

The tradition of learning in Urbino continues to this day. The city is the home of a small but prestigious Italian state university—one of the oldest in the world—and during term time the streets are filled with

hordes of noisy students. It is very much a college town, with the usual
array of bookshops, record stores, bars, and coffeehouses. During the
summer, the Italian student population is replaced by foreigners who
come to study Italian language and arts at several prestigious private
fine-arts academies.

Urbino's fame rests on the reputation of three of its native sons: Duke
Federico da Montefeltro, the enlightened warrior-patron who built the
Ducal Palace; Raphael, one of the most influential painters in history
and an embodiment of the spirit of the Renaissance; and the architect
Donato Bramante, who translated the philosophy of the Renaissance
into buildings of grace and beauty. Why three of the greatest men of
the age should have been born within a generation of one another in
this remote town has never been explained. Oddly enough, there is little work by either Bramante or Raphael in the city, but the duke's influence can still be felt strongly, even now, some 500 years after his
death.

★ The **Ducal Palace** holds the place of honor in the city, and in no other
palace of its era are the principles of the Renaissance stated quite so clearly.
If the Renaissance was, in ideal form, a celebration of the nobility of man
and his works, of the light and purity of the soul, then there is no place
in Italy, the birthplace of the Renaissance, where these tenets are better
illustrated. From the moment you enter the peaceful courtyard, you
know that you are in a place of grace and beauty, the harmony of the
building reflecting the high ideals of the men who built it.

Today the palace houses the **National Museum of the Marches,** with
a superb collection of paintings, sculpture, and other objets d'art, well
arranged and properly lit. It would be hard to mention all the great
works in this collection—some originally the possessions of the Montefeltro family, others brought to the museum from churches and
palaces throughout the region—but there are a few that must be sin-
gled out. Of these, perhaps the most famous is Piero della Francesca's
enigmatic work, long known as *The Flagellation of Christ.* Much has
been written about this painting, and few experts agree on its meaning. Legend had it that the three figures in the foreground represented
a murdered member of the Montefeltro family (the barefoot young man)
and his two murderers. Others claimed the painting was a heavily veiled
criticism of certain parts of Christian Europe—the iconography is ob-
scure and the history extremely complicated. Recently, however, Sir John
Pope-Hennessy—the preeminent scholar of Italian Renaissance art—
has proved that it represents the arcane subject of the Vision of Saint
Lawrence. All the experts have always agreed that the painting is one
of Piero della Francesca's masterpieces. Piero himself thought so. It is
one of the few works he signed (on the lowest step supporting the throne).

Other masterworks in the collection are Paolo Uccello's *Profanation
of the Host,* Piero della Francesca's *Madonna of Senigallia,* and Titian's
Resurrection and *Last Supper.* Duke Federico's study is an astonish-
ingly elaborate but tiny room decorated with inlaid wood, said to be
the work of Botticelli. ✉ *Piazza Duca Federico,* ☎ *0722/2760.* 🎟 *8,000
lire.* ☉ *Aug.–Oct., Mon. 9–2, Tues.–Sun. 9–7; Nov.–July, daily 9–2.*

The **house of the painter Raphael** really is the house in which he was
born and in which he took his first steps in painting (under the direc-
tion of his artist father). There is some debate about the fresco of the
Madonna that adorns the house. Some say it is by Raphael, whereas
others attribute it to the father—with Raphael's mother and the young
painter himself standing in as models for the Madonna and Child. Either way, it's an interesting picture. ✉ *Via Raffaello.* 🎟 *5,000 lire.* ☉

Apr.–Sept., Tues.–Sat. 9–1 and 3–7, Sun. 9–1; Oct.–Mar., Thurs.–Sat. and Mon.–Tues. 9–2, Sun. 9–1.:

Dining and Lodging

$$ ✕ **La Vecchia Fornarina.** These two small rooms just down from Urbino's central Piazza della Repubblica are often filled to capacity. The trattoria specializes in meaty country fare, such as rabbit and *vitello alle noci* (veal cooked with nuts) or *ai porcini* (with mushrooms). There is also a good range of pasta dishes. ⊠ *Via Mazzini 14,* ☎ *0722/320007. Reservations essential. AE, DC, MC, V. Closed Wed.*

$ 🏨 **Hotel San Giovanni.** This hotel is in the Old Town and is housed in a renovated medieval building. The rooms are basic, clean, and comfortable—with a wonderful view from Nos. 18–21 and 24–31—and there is a handy restaurant–pizzeria below. ⊠ *Via Barocci 13,* ☎ *0722/2827. 33 rooms, 21 with shower. No credit cards. Closed July and Christmas wk.*

En Route To reach Ancona, on the Adriatic coast, from Urbino, take the E78 or S3 to the superhighway A14, which runs along the coast but inland by a kilometer (half mile) or so. The coast road, S16, is a congested two-lane highway with little to recommend it.

Ancona

9 *87 km (54 mi) southeast of Urbino, 60 km (37½ mi) southeast of Pésaro, 139 km (87 mi) northeast of Perugia, 262 km (164 mi) east of Florence, 286 km (179 mi) northeast of Rome.*

Ancona was probably once a lovely city. It is set on an elbow-shape bluff (hence its name; *ankon* is Greek for "elbow") that juts out into the Adriatic. But Ancona was the object of serious aerial bombing during World War II—it was, and is, an important port city—and was reduced to rubble. The city has been rebuilt in the unfortunate postwar poured-concrete style, practical and inexpensive but certainly not pleasing. Unless you are taking a ferry to Venice, there is little reason to visit the city—with a few exceptions. Once in a while there are glimpses of the old architecture, as in the Duomo San Ciriaco and the Loggia dei Mercanti. In addition, Ancona can be the base for an excursion to Loreto or to Ascoli Piceno, farther down the Adriatic coast.

Dining and Lodging

$$ ✕ **La Moretta.** This family-run trattoria is on the central Piazza del Plebiscito. In summer there is dining outside in the square, which has a fine view of the Baroque church of San Domenico. Among the specialties of La Moretta are tagliatelle *in salsa di ostriche* (in an oyster sauce) and the famous brodetto fish stew. ⊠ *Piazza del Plebiscito 52,* ☎ *071/202317. Reservations advised. AE, DC, MC, V. Closed Sun. and Dec. 25–Jan. 6.*

$$$ 🏨 **Grand Hotel Palace.** In the center of town, near the entrance to the port of Ancona, and widely held to be the best in town, this is an old-fashioned place well run by a courteous staff. ⊠ *Lungomare Vanvitelli 24,* ☎ *071/201813,* 🆕 *071/207–4832. 41 rooms with bath. Bar. AE, DC, MC, V.*

$$ 🏨 **Hotel Roma e Pace.** The only two reasons to stay in this hotel are the location and price. The rooms are ugly and cramped, and those facing the street are noisy (choose inward-facing ones). A historical note: In 1907 a Russian named Josef Dzhugashvili applied for a job here and was refused. He later found better-paying employment as supreme head of the Soviet Union under the name Stalin. ⊠ *Via Leopardi 1,* ☎

071/202007, ☎ 071/207–4736. *73 rooms with bath or shower. Restaurant, bar. AE, DC, MC, V.*

Loreto

⑩   *24 km (24 mi) south of Ancona on A14.*

★   **Loreto** is famous for one of the best-loved shrines in the world, that of the **house of the Virgin Mary.** The legend is that angels moved the house from Nazareth, where the Virgin was living at the time of the Annunciation, to this hilltop in 1295. The reason for this sudden and divinely inspired move was that Nazareth had fallen into the hands of Muslim invaders, not suitable landlords, the angelic hosts felt. More recently, following archaeological excavations made at the behest of the Church, evidence has come to light proving that the house did once stand elsewhere and was brought to the hilltop by human means around the time the angels are said to have done the job.

The house itself consists of three rough stone walls contained within an elaborate marble tabernacle; built around this centerpiece is the giant basilica of the Holy House, which dominates the town. Millions of visitors come to the site every year (particularly at Easter and on the Feast of the Holy House, December 10), and the little town of Loreto can become uncomfortably crowded with pilgrims. Many great Italian architects, including Bramante, Sangallo, and Sansovino, contributed to the design of the basilica. Inside are a great many mediocre 19th- and 20th-century paintings but also some fine works by Renaissance masters such as Luca Signorelli and Melozzo da Forlì.

Nervous air travelers may take comfort in the fact that the Holy Virgin of Loreto is the patroness of air travelers and that Pope John Paul II has composed a prayer for a safe flight—available in the church in a half-dozen languages.

Ascoli Piceno

⑪   *105 km (65 mi) south of Ancona.*

Ascoli Piceno is not a hill town; rather, it sits in a valley ringed by steep hills and cut by the fast-racing Tronto River. The town is almost unique in Italy, in that it seems to have its traffic problems—in the historic center, at any rate—pretty much under control; you can drive *around* the picturesque part of the city, but driving *through* it is most difficult. This feature makes Ascoli Piceno one of the most pleasant large towns in the country for exploring on foot. True, there is traffic, but you are not constantly assaulted by jams, noise, and exhaust fumes the way you are in other Italian cities.

★   The heart of the town is the majestic **Piazza del Popolo,** dominated by the Gothic church of San Francesco and the Palazzo del Popolo, a 13th-century town hall that contains a graceful Renaissance courtyard. The square itself functions as the living room of the entire city. At dusk each evening the piazza is packed with people standing in small groups, exchanging news and gossip as if at a cocktail party.

NEED A   Ascoli Piceno is indelibly associated with the Meletti distillery situated on
BREAK?   the outskirts of town. You can sample their famous aniseed spirits at the
wood-paneled **Bar Centrale,** a small and cozy establishment that dates from the turn of the century, at Piazza del Popolo No. 9. For a light lunch or snack, pick up some delicious sandwiches and homemade pastries across the square at the **Pasticceria Angelini.**

🕐 Ascoli Piceno's **Giostra della Quintana** takes place on the first Sunday in August. Children should love this medieval-style joust and the richly caparisoned processions that wind through the streets of the old town. Contact Ascoli's tourist office for details (⊠ Piazza del Popolo, ☎ 0736/257288).

Dining and Lodging

$$ ✕ **Ristorante Tornasacco.** In this attractive family-run restaurant with
★ rustic decor and vaulted brick ceilings, you can sample Ascoli's spe-
cialties, like olives ascolane (here, stuffed with minced meat), as well
as *maccheroncini alla contadina* (a homemade pasta in a thick meat
sauce). ⊠ *Piazza del Popolo 36*, ☎ *0736/254151. AE, DC, MC, V.
Closed Fri. and June 15–30.*

$ 🏨 **Cantina dell'Arte.** This recently renovated hotel is one of the few lodg-
ings in the center of the Old Town. Although the service can be sloppy,
the rooms are clean and well equipped with TV and telephone, repre-
senting excellent value for the money. There is a boisterous and inex-
pensive restaurant run by the same management across the road. ⊠ *Rua
della Lupa 8,* ☎ *0736/255744. 11 rooms with shower. No credit cards.*

En Route The 175-kilometer (108-mile) drive to Spoleto takes you out of the
Marches and back into Umbria. The route—S4 southwest to Rieti, then
S79 north to Terni, then S3 into Spoleto—is roundabout but vastly prefer-
able to a series of winding mountain roads that connect Ascoli Piceno
with Umbria.

SPOLETO AND ASSISI, BIRTHPLACE OF SAINT FRANCIS

Spoleto and Assisi are two of the most popular towns in all of Italy,
but for very different reasons. The delightful medieval town of Spo-
leto hosts Italy's most prestigious international arts festival, the *Festi-
val dei Due Mondi* (Festival of Two Worlds), while Assisi is the
birthplace of one of Christianity's most beloved saints, St. Francis.

Spoleto

★ ⑫ *50 kilometers (30 miles) south of Perugia, 35 kilometers (20 miles) south
of Assisi.*

Spoleto is an enchanting town perfectly situated in wooded country-
side. "A little bit of heaven fallen to earth" it was once called, and it
is not hard to understand the sentiment. "Quaint" may be an overused
term, but it is the most appropriate word to describe this city, still en-
closed by stout medieval walls. The chief pleasure of Spoleto is that
the city itself is the sight. There is no long tramp through museums
and churches in store for you here; rather, you can enjoy the simple
treat of walking through the maze of twisting streets and up and down
cobbled stairways, enjoying the beauty of the town and its wonderful
peace and quiet.

Quiet, that is, except when Spoleto is hosting the **Festival dei Due Mondi**
(Festival of the Two Worlds), an arts festival, held every year from mid-
June to mid-July. During those two months the sleepy town is swamped
with visitors who come to see world-class plays and operas, to hear
concerts, and to see extensive exhibitions of paintings and sculpture.
Hotels in the city and countryside are filled to overflowing, and the
streets are packed with visitors. It is unwise to arrive during this pe-
riod without confirmed hotel reservations. Furthermore, experiencing
the town itself, rather than the festival, is very difficult during these

months. Those who don't care for crowds are advised to stay away during the festival.

Even in the off-season, parking in the Old City is difficult. If you are traveling by car, it is best to park outside the walls. There is usually ample parking available near Piazza della Vittoria.

Spoleto is dominated by a huge castle that was built in 1359–63 by the Gubbio-born architect Gattapone. It was until recently a high-security prison but has been undergoing restoration and is to become a museum. The castle was built to protect the town's most famous monument, the massive bridge known as the **Ponte delle Torri** (Bridge of the Towers), built by Gattapone on Roman foundations. This massive structure stands 262 feet above the gorge it spans and was built originally as an aqueduct. The bridge is open to pedestrians, and a walk over it affords marvelous views—looking down to the river below is the best way to appreciate the colossal dimensions of the bridge. The central span is actually higher than that of the dome of St. Peter's in Rome.

Spoleto's **Duomo** is set in a lovely sloping square at the bottom of a flight of steps below the castle. The church facade is dourly Romanesque but with the pleasant light addition of a Renaissance loggia and eight rose windows. The contrast between the heavy medieval work and the graceful later embellishments graphically demonstrates the difference, not only in style, but in philosophy, of the two eras. The earlier was strong but ungiving; the later, human and open-minded.

The Duomo's interior boasts the best of the city's art, notably the immaculately restored frescoes in the apse by the great Fra Filippo Lippi, showing the Annunciation, the Nativity, and the Death of Mary, with a marvelous Coronation of the Virgin adorning the dome; be ready with a 500-lire coin to illuminate the masterpiece. Another series of frescoes, including work by Pinturicchio, can be seen in the Eroli chapel off the right aisle. ⊠ *Piazza Duomo.* ☉ *Daily 8–1 and 4–6.*

From Piazza del Duomo make your way to **Piazza del Mercato,** site of the old Roman forum and today the main square of the Old Town.

NEED A
BREAK?

Piazza del Mercato is lined with bars and delicatessens that serve good pastries and coffee. Parked in the square every day except Sunday is the van of a *porchetta* (suckling pig) vendor. These mobile snack bars are common to all central and northern Italy, and they serve only one product—roast pork. The whole pig is roasted on a spit, and slices are carved off to make delicious sandwiches on crusty rolls called *rosette*. The porchetta seller in Piazza del Mercato is particularly cheerful, and his portions are generous.

The **Arch of Drusus,** off the southern end of Piazza del Mercato, was built by the Senate of Spoleto to honor the Roman general Drusus, son of the emperor Tiberius.

Between Piazza del Duomo and Piazza del Mercato, on an extension of the picturesque Via Fontesecca, with its tempting shops selling local pottery and other handicrafts, is the church of **Sant'Eufemia** (in the courtyard of the archbishop's palace), an ancient, austere church built in the 11th century. Its most interesting feature is the gallery above the nave where female worshippers were required to sit—a holdover from the Eastern Church—one of the few such galleries in this part of Italy. ⊠ *Via Saffi.* ☉ *Summer, daily 8–8; winter, daily 8–6.*

At the southern end of Corso Mazzini is a small but well-preserved **Roman theater,** used in summer for performances of Spoleto's arts festival. The theater was the site of one of the town's most macabre incidents. During the Middle Ages, Spoleto took the side of the Holy Roman Emperor in the interminable struggle between Guelph (papal) and Ghibelline (imperial) factions over the question of who would control central and northern Italy. Four hundred of the pope's supporters were massacred in the theater, and their bodies were burned in an enormous pyre. It is not an episode of which Spoleto is proud, and, furthermore, the Guelphs were triumphant in the end. Spoleto was incorporated into the states of the Church in 1354. ☉ *Summer, Mon.–Sat. 9–1:30 and 3–7, Sun. 9–1; winter, Mon.–Sat. 9–1 and 3–5, Sun. 9–1.*

On the outskirts of the city, just off Via Flaminia (S3), is the lovely church of **San Salvatore.** You may already have seen a lot of old churches in Italy, but few are as old as this one. It needed renovation in the 9th century—by that time it was already 600 years old. It is nestled under cypresses and surrounded by Spoleto's cemetery and is quiet, cool, and peaceful. The church was built by Eastern monks in the 4th century, and little has been added (or removed) since its renovation. San Salvatore has an air of timelessness and antiquity rarely found in churches so close to major towns. ✉ *Via della Basilica di San Salvatore.* ☉ *Daily 8–1 and 4–6.*

Dining and Lodging

\$\$ ✕ **Il Pentagramma.** Just off the central Piazza della Libertà, this restaurant features such local dishes as *coda di bue alla spoletina* (oxtail) and lamb in a truffle sauce. ✉ *Via Martani 4,* ☏ *0743/223141. Reservations essential during the festival and on weekends. DC, MC, V. Closed Mon.*

\$\$ ✕ **Il Tartufo.** Spoleto's most famous restaurant has a smart modern dining room on the second floor and a rustic dining room downstairs—both of which incorporate the ruins of a Roman villa. The traditional cooking is spiced up in summer to appeal to the cosmopolitan crowd that is attending (or performing in) the Festival of Two Worlds. As its name indicates, the restaurant specializes in dishes prepared with truffles, though there is a second menu from which you can choose items not containing this expensive delicacy. ✉ *Piazza Garibaldi 24* ☏ *0743/40236. Reservations esential. AE, DC, MC, V. Closed Wed. and mid-July–1st wk in Aug.*

\$\$ ✕ **Trattoria Panciolle.** In the heart of Spoleto's medieval quarter, this restaurant has one of the most romantic settings you could wish for. Dining outside in summer is a delight in a small piazza filled with lime trees. Specialties include *strangozzi* (pasta) with mushroom sauce and *agnello scottadito* (grilled lamb chops). Seven guest rooms are also available here. ✉ *Via del Duomo 3,* ☏ *0743/45598. Reservations essential. AE, MC, V. Closed Wed.*

\$\$\$ 🏨 **Dei Duchi.** This excellent, well-run hotel is in the center of the town, near the Roman amphitheater. It's a favorite with performers in the Festival of Two Worlds. Some rooms have fine views of the city. ✉ *Viale Matteotti 4,* ☏ *0743/44541,* 𝖥𝖠𝖷 *0743/44543. 49 rooms with bath or shower. Restaurant, bar, meeting rooms, parking. AE, DC, MC, V.*

\$\$\$ 🏨 **Hotel Gattapone.** The tiny four-star Hotel Gattapone is situated at the top of the Old Town, near the Ponte delle Torri, and has wonderful views of the ancient bridge and the wooded slopes of Monteluco. The rooms are well furnished and tastefully decorated. ✉ *Via del Ponte 6,* ☏ *0743/223447,* 𝖥𝖠𝖷 *0743/223448. 14 rooms with bath. Bar. AE, DC, MC, V.*

\$–\$\$ 🏨 **Nuovo Clitunno.** A renovated 18th-century building houses this pleasant hotel, a five-minute walk from the town center. Bedrooms and public rooms, some with lovely timber-beamed ceilings, have a mixture of period as well as less characterful modern furniture. ✉ *Piazza*

Sordini 6, ☎ 0743/223340, FAX 0743/222663. 31 rooms with bath or shower. Restaurant, bar. AE, DC, MC, V.

Nightlife and the Arts

The **Festival of Two Worlds** in Spoleto (mid-June–mid-July) features star names in all branches of the arts—particularly music, opera, and theater—and draws thousands of visitors from all over the world. Tickets for all performances should be ordered in advance from the festival's box office, beginning at the end of April. ⊠ *Teatro Nuovo, ☎ 0743/40265, closed Mon. Information available year-round from the Teatro Nuovo (☎ 0743/44097) or from the festival's Rome office (⊠ Via Beccaria 18, ☎ 06/321–0288).*

OFF THE BEATEN PATH	**VALNERINA** – This is the name of the area east of Umbria, and it is the most beautiful of central Italy's many well-kept secrets. The roads that serve the rugged landscape are poor, but a drive through the region, even with all those time-consuming twists and turns, will be worth it to see forgotten medieval villages and dramatic mountain scenery. The first stop should be the **waterfalls at Marmore,** the highest falls in Europe. You'll find them a few miles east of Terni, on the road to Lake Piediluco and Rieti. The waters are diverted on weekdays to provide hydroelectric power for the town of Terni, so check with the tourist office (⊠ Viale C. Battisti 7/a, ☎ 0744/423048) in Terni before heading there. On summer evenings, when the falls are in full spate, the cascading water is floodlit—and a delightful sight.

Close to the picturesque town of Ferentillo (northeast of Terni on S209) is the outstanding 8th-century abbey of **San Pietro in Valle.** There are fine frescoes in the nave of the church, and the cloister is graceful and peaceful. As a bonus, one of the abbey outbuildings houses a fine restaurant with moderate prices.

Farther east are the towns of Norcia and Cascia; **Norcia** is the most famous town for Umbrian food specialties. It is also the birthplace of Saint Benedict. **Cascia** is the birthplace of the uncrowned patron saint of Italian women, Saint Rita.

Assisi

🔞 *47 km (30 mi) north and west of Spoleto on S3 and S75, 25 km (16 mi) east of Perugia.*

The first sight of **Assisi** is memorable. The hill on which Assisi sits rises dramatically from the flat plain, and the town is dominated at the top of the mount by a medieval castle; on the lower slopes of the hill is the massive basilica of San Francesco, rising majestically on graceful arched supports. From a distance, Saint Francis's birthplace looks—to use an evocative phrase of travel essayist James Reynolds—"calm, white, pure as the fresh-washed wool from the Pascal Lamb."

Except in the depths of the off-season, Assisi, the most famous and most visited city in Umbria, is always thronged with sightseers and pilgrims. Somehow, though, despite the press of visitors, there is an unspoiled quality to the city—Assisi seems to be actually redolent of the sweet personality of its greatest citizen, Saint Francis, who is buried here in the huge 13th-century Basilica on the Hill of Paradise.

Saint Francis was born here in 1181, the son of a well-to-do merchant. He had, by his own account, a riotous youth but forsook the pleasures of the flesh quite early in life, adopting a life of austerity. His mystical approach to poverty, asceticism, and the beauty of man and nature struck a responsive chord in the medieval mind, and he quickly attracted a vast number of followers. He was a humble and unassuming man, and his compassion and humility brought him great love and veneration in his own lifetime. Without actively seeking power, as did many clerics of his day, he amassed great influence and political power, changing the history of the Catholic Church. He was the first person to receive the stigmata (wounds in his hands, feet, and side corresponding to the torments of Christ on the cross), injuries that caused him great pain and suffering, which he bore with characteristic patience. Nonetheless, Saint Francis welcomed the coming of "Sister Death," in 1226. Today the Franciscans are the largest of all the Catholic orders. And among the mass of clergy at Assisi, you can identify the saint's followers by their simple, coarse brown habits bound by sashes of knotted rope.

★ ⑭ The **Basilica of San Francesco** is one of Italy's foremost monuments and was begun shortly after the saint's death. What Saint Francis would have made of a church of such size, wealth, and grandeur—the opposite of all he preached and believed—is hard to imagine. His coffin, unearthed from its secret hiding place in 1818, is on display in the crypt below the lower church and is a place of piety. The basilica is not one church but two huge structures built one over the other. The lower church is dim and full of candlelit shadows, whereas the upper is bright and airy. Both are magnificently decorated artistic treasure houses, however, especially the upper church, where a fresco cycle by Giotto is a milestone in the history of Western art.

Visit the **lower church** first. The first chapel on the left of the nave was decorated by the Sienese master Simone Martini. Frescoed in 1322–26, the paintings show the life of Saint Martin—the sharing of his cloak with the poor man, the saint's knighthood, and his death.

There is some dispute about the paintings in the third chapel on the right. Experts have argued for years as to their authorship, with many saying that they were done by Giotto. The paintings depict the life of Saint Mary Magdalene. There is a similar dispute about the works above the high altar—some say they are by Giotto; others claim them for an anonymous pupil. They depict the marriage of Saint Francis to poverty, chastity, and obedience.

In the right transept are frescoes by Cimabue, a Madonna and saints, one of them Saint Francis himself. In the left transept are some of the best-known works of the Sienese painter Pietro Lorenzetti. They depict the Madonna with Saints John and Francis, a crucifixion, and a descent from the cross.

It is quite a contrast to climb the steps next to the altar and emerge into the bright sunlight and airy grace of the double-arched Renaissance cloister called the **Cloister of the Dead.** A door to the right leads to the treasury of the church and contains relics of Saint Francis and other holy objects associated with the order.

The **upper church** is dominated by Giotto's 28 frescoes, each portraying incidents in the life of Saint Francis. Although the artist was only in his twenties when he painted this cycle, the frescoes show that Giotto was the pivotal artist in the development of Western painting, breaking away from the stiff, unnatural styles of earlier generations and moving toward a realism and grace that reached their peak in the Renaissance. The paintings are viewed left to right, starting in the transept. The most beloved of all the scenes is probably *Saint Francis Preaching to the Birds,* a touching painting that seems to sum up the gentle spirit of the saint. It stands in marked contrast to the scene of the dream of Innocent III.

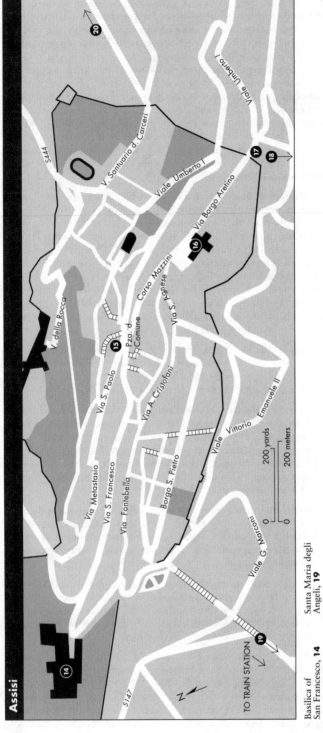

Assisi

Basilica of
San Francesco, **14**
Hermitage of the
Carceri, **20**
Porta Nuova, **17**
San Damiano, **18**
Santa Chiara, **16**

Santa Maria degli
Angeli, **19**
Temple of
Minerva, **15**

The pope dreams of a humble monk who will steady the church. Sure enough, in the panel next to the sleeping pope, you see a strong Francis supporting a church that seems to be on the verge of tumbling down. ✉ *Piazza di San Francesco.* ☉ *Upper and lower churches: Summer, Mon.–Sat. 7 AM–sunset, Sun. 2–sunset; winter, Mon.–Sat. 7–noon and 2–sunset, Sun. 2–sunset.*

The long, central square of the town, Piazza del Comune, holds the
⑮ Temple of Minerva. It is made up of bits and pieces of a Roman temple that dates from the time of Augustus and was later converted into a church. The expectations raised by the perfect classical facade are not met by the interior, subjected to a thorough Baroque assault in the 17th century. ✉ *Piazza del Comune.* ☉ *Daily 7–noon and 2:30– sunset.*

In the southeastern part of Assisi, near the Porta Nuova, the 13th-
⑯ century church of **Santa Chiara is dedicated to Saint Clare, one of the earliest and most fervent of Saint Francis's followers and the founder of the order of the Poor Ladies, or Poor Clares, in imitation of the Franciscans. The church contains the body of the saint, and in the **Chapel of the Crucifix** (on the right) is the cross that spoke to Saint Francis and led him to a life of piety. A heavily veiled member of Saint Clare's order is stationed before the cross in perpetual adoration of the image. To get here from Piazza del Comune, walk down Corso Mazzini past the Pinacoteca. ✉ *Piazza Santa Chiara.* ☉ *Daily 8–noon and 2:30– sunset.*

A little way beyond the church of Santa Chiara, along Via Borgo
⑰ Aretino, the walls of Assisi are cut through by the **Porta Nuova gate.
⑱ From the Porta Nuova, it is a walk of approximately 1 kilometer (½ mile) to reach the church of **San Damiano. It was here that the crucifix spoke to Saint Francis, saying *"Vade, Francisce, et repara domum meam"* ("Go, Francis, and repair my house"). It was also in this church, pleasantly situated in an olive grove, that Saint Francis brought Saint Clare into the religious life. The church became the first home of her order, and it and its convent, simple and austere, give a far better idea of Saint Francis and his movement than the great basilica. ✉ *Località San Damiano.* ☉ *Daily 10–12:30 and 2:30–sunset.*

On the outskirts of the town, on the plain near the train station, is the
⑲ church of **Santa Maria degli Angeli. It is a Baroque building constructed over the **Porziuncola,** a little chapel restored by Saint Francis. The shrine is much venerated because it was here, in the Transito chapel, then a humble cell, that Saint Francis died. ✉ *Località Santa Maria degli Angeli.* ☉ *Daily 9–12:30 and 2:30–sunset.*

⑳ Four kilometers (2½ miles) east of Assisi is the **Hermitage of the Carceri, a monastery set in dense woodlands on the side of Mt. Subasio. In the caves on the slope of the mountain, Francis and his followers established their first home, to which he returned often during his lifetime to pray and meditate. The church and monastery retain the tranquil contemplative air Saint Francis so prized. From a vantage point within the monastery visitors can take in one of the most beautiful vistas over the Umbrian countryside. True to their Franciscan heritage, the friars here are entirely dependent on alms from visitors. ✉ *Eremo degli Carceri.* ☉ *Daily 8 AM–sunset.*

OFF THE
BEATEN PATH   **CANNARA** – A pleasant excursion from Assisi leads to this tiny town; a half-hour walk outside the town are the fields of Pian d'Arca, which legend identifies as the site of Saint Francis's sermon to the birds.

Dining and Lodging

$$ ✕ **Buca di San Francesco.** This central restaurant is Assisi's busiest and most popular. The setting is lovely no matter what the season. In summer you dine outside in a cool green garden; in winter, in the cozy cellars of the restaurant. The food is first-rate, and the *filetto al rubesco* (fillet steak cooked in a hearty red wine) is the specialty of the house. ✉ *Via Brizi 1,* ☎ *075/812204. Reservations essential. AE, DC, MC, V. Closed Mon. and July.*

$$ ✕ **La Fortezza.** Parts of the walls of this modern restaurant were built by the Romans. The service is personable and the kitchen reliable. A particular standout is *anatra al finocchio selvatico* (duck cooked with wild fennel). La Fortezza also has seven simple but clean guest rooms available. ✉ *Vicolo della Fortezza 19/b,* ☎ *075/812418. Reservations essential. AE, DC, MC, V. Closed Thurs. Oct.–July, Feb.*

$ ✕ **La Stalla.** A kilometer or two outside the town proper, this onetime stable has been turned into a simple and rustic restaurant. In summer, lunch and dinner are served outside under a delightful trellis shaded with vines and flowers. In keeping with the decor, the food is hearty country cooking. ✉ *Via Eremo delle Carceri 8,* ☎ *075/812317. Reservations essential. No credit cards. Closed Mon.*

$$$ 🏨 **Hotel Subasio.** This hotel, close to the basilica of Saint Francis, has counted Marlene Dietrich and Charlie Chaplin among its guests. It is housed in a converted monastery and has plenty of atmosphere. Some of the rooms remain a little monastic, but the views, comfortable old-fashioned sitting rooms, flowered terraces, and lovely garden more than make up for the simplicity. Ask for a room with a view of the valley. ✉ *Via Frate Elia 2,* ☎ *075/812206,* FAX *075/816691. 61 rooms with bath or shower. Restaurant, bar. AE, DC, MC, V.*

$$ 🏨 **Hotel Umbra.** A 16th-century town house is home to this hotel, which
★ is in a tranquil part of the city, an area closed to traffic, near Piazza del Comune. The rooms are arranged as small apartments, each with a tiny living room and terrace. ✉ *Via degli Archi 6,* ☎ *075/812240,* FAX *075/813653. 32 rooms with bath or shower. Restaurant (closed Tues. and Wed. lunch), bar. Closed mid-Jan.–mid-Mar. and mid-Nov.–mid-Dec. AE, DC, MC, V.*

$$ 🏨 **San Francesco.** This is a centrally located hotel in a renovated 16th-century building. Some of the rooms have a view of the basilica or the valley. ✉ *Via di San Francesco 48,* ☎ *075/812281,* FAX *075/816237. 44 rooms with bath or shower. Restaurant, bar. AE, DC, MC, V.*

En Route The drive to Orvieto on S3bis ("bis" means alternative highway) is a pleasant one that cuts south through the center of the region and takes you through Todi, a lovely hill town. Todi has an extraordinary grouping of Gothic palaces and a medieval cathedral in its central Piazza del Popolo. At Todi, change to S448, which connects with the main north–south autostrada (A1).

Numbers in the margin correspond to points of interest on the Umbria and the Marches map.

Orvieto

㉑ *112 km (70 mi) southwest of Assisi, 86 km (53 mi) south of Perugia, 96 km (60 mi) northwest of Rome, 37 km (23 miles) west of Todi, off A1.*

Commanding a dramatic position on a great square rock, **Orvieto,** one of Umbria's greatest cities, is an amazing sight, dominating the countryside for miles in every direction. This natural fort was first settled by the Etruscans, but not even Orvieto's defenses could withstand the might of the Romans, who attacked, sacked, and destroyed the city in

283 BC. From that time, Orvieto has had close ties with Rome. It was solidly Guelph in the Middle Ages, and for several hundred years popes sought refuge in the city, at some times needing protection from their enemies, at times fleeing from the summer heat of Rome.

★ Orvieto's position on its rock has meant that little new building has ever been done here, giving the town an almost perfect medieval character. The jewel, the centerpiece of Orvieto, is its **Duomo,** set in the wide and airy Piazza del Duomo. The church, built to commemorate the Miracle of Bolsena, was started in 1290 and received the attention of some of the greatest architects and sculptors of the time. It was further embellished inside by great Renaissance artists. The facade is a prodigious work, covered with carvings and mosaics, the latter intricately ornamenting practically every pillar and post and also used in large representations of religious scenes (many of these were restored or redone in the 18th and 19th centuries). The bas-reliefs on the lower parts of the pillars were carved by Maitani, one of the original architects of the building, and show scenes from the Old Testament and some particularly gruesome renderings of the Last Judgment and Hell, as well as a more tranquil Paradise. (They have been covered with Plexiglas following some vandalizing in the 1960s.)

The vast interior of the cathedral is famous chiefly for the frescoes in the **Cappella Nuova** (the last chapel on the right, nearest the high altar). The earliest works here are above the altar and are by Fra Angelico. They show Christ in Glory and the prophets. The major works in the chapel, however, are by Luca Signorelli and show a very graphic Last Judgment. The walls seem to be filled with muscular, writhing figures, and most critics draw a direct connection between these figures and the later Last Judgment of Michelangelo on the wall of the Sistine Chapel. Leonardo da Vinci, however, was less than impressed. He said that the figures, with their rippling muscles, reminded him of sacks "stuffed full of nuts."

Across the nave of the cathedral from the Cappella Nuova is the **Cappella del Corporale.** It houses the relics of the Miracle of Bolsena, the raison d'être for the Duomo. A priest in the nearby town of Bolsena suddenly found himself assailed by doubts about the transubstantiation—he could not bring himself to believe that the body of Christ was contained in the consecrated communion host. His doubts were put to rest, however, when a wafer he had just blessed suddenly started to drip blood. Drops of blood fell onto the linen covering the altar, and this cloth and the host itself are the principal relics of the miracle. They are contained in a sumptuous gold-and-enamel reliquary on the altar of this chapel and are displayed on the Feast of Corpus Christi and at Easter. ⊠ *Piazza Duomo.* ☉ *Daily 7–1 and 3–sunset.*

To the right of the Duomo is the medieval **Palazzo dei Papi,** once the summer residence of popes, which contains the Archaeological Museum. ▨ *4,000 lire.* ☉ *May–Oct., Mon.–Sat. 9–1:30 and 3–7, Sun. 9–1; Nov.–Apr., Mon.–Sat. 9–1:30 and 2:30–6, Sun. 9–1.*

NEED A BREAK?   Orvieto is known for its wines, particularly the whites. Some of the finest wines in Umbria are produced here (Signorelli, when painting the Duomo, asked that part of his contract be paid in wine), and the rock on which the town sits is honeycombed with caves used to ferment the Trebbiano grapes that are used in making Orvieto vintages. Taking a glass of wine, therefore, at the **wine cellar** at No. 2, Piazza del Duomo, is as much a cultural experience as a refreshment stop. You'll find a good selection of sandwiches and snacks there as well.

Dining and Lodging

$$ ★ ✕ Le Grotte del Funaro. This restaurant has an extraordinary location, deep in a series of caves within the volcanic rock beneath Orvieto. Once you have negotiated the steep steps, typical Umbrian specialties, like tagliatelle *al vino rosso* (with red wine sauce) and grilled beef with truffles, await. Sample the fine Orvieto wines, either the whites or the lesser-known reds. ⊠ *Via Ripa Serancia 41,* ☎ *0763/43276. Reservations essential. Sept.–May. AE, DC, MC, V. Closed Mon.*

$$ ★ ✕ Maurizio. In the heart of Orvieto, just opposite the cathedral, this warm and welcoming restaurant gets its share of tourists and has a local clientele as well. The decor is unusual, with wood sculptures by Orvieto craftsman Michelangeli. The menu offers hearty soups and home-made pastas such as *tronchetti* (a pasta roll with spinach and ricotta filling). ⊠ *Via del Duomo 78,* ☎ *0763/41114. Reservations essential in summer. AE, MC, V. Closed Tues. and 3 wks in Jan.*

$$$ 🏨 Hotel La Badia. This is one of the best-known country hotels in Umbria. The 700-year-old building, a former monastery, is set in rolling parkland that provides wonderful views of the valley and the town of Orvieto in the distance. Facilities include a swimming pool and several tennis courts. The rooms are well appointed. ⊠ *Località La Badia, 8.5 km (3½ mi) south of Orvieto,* ☎ *0763/90359,* 🅵🅰🆇 *0763/92796. 26 rooms with bath or shower. Restaurant, bar, pool, tennis courts, meeting rooms. Closed Jan.–Feb. AE, MC, V.*

$$$ 🏨 Hotel Maitani. The most deluxe hotel in the town of Orvieto itself, the Hotel Maitani is also centrally located. It is set in a 17th-century Baroque palazzo with a garden and a terrace with panoramic views but no restaurant. The rooms are old-fashioned but comfortable. ⊠ *Via Maitani 5,* ☎ *0763/42011,* 🅵🅰🆇 *0763/42012. 40 rooms with bath or shower. Bar, air-conditioning. AE, DC, MC, V.*

$$–$$$ 🏨 Grand Hotel Reale. The best feature of this hotel is its location in the center of Orvieto, across a square that hosts a lively market. Facing the impressive Gothic-Romanesque Palazzo del Popolo, rooms are spacious and adequately furnished, if somewhat old-fashioned. ⊠ *Piazza del Popolo 25,* ☎ *0763/341247,* 🅵🅰🆇 *0763/341247. 32 rooms with bath or shower. Restaurant, bar. MC, V.*

$$–$$$ 🏨 Villa Bellago. This recently opened hotel lies outside the village of Baschi, 12 kilometers (7½ miles) south of Orvieto. In a tranquil setting on a spit of land overlooking Lake Corbara, three farmhouses have been completely overhauled to include well-lighted and spacious guest rooms, a pool, a fully equipped gym, and a fine restaurant specializing in imaginatively prepared Umbrian and Tuscan dishes. Fresh fish is always on the menu. ⊠ *Baschi, 7½ km (4½ mi) south of Orvieto on S448,* ☎ *0744/950521,* 🅵🅰🆇 *0744/950524. 12 rooms with bath. Restaurant (closed Tues.), bar, tennis court. AE, DC, MC, V.*

$$ 🏨 Virgilio. The modest Hotel Virgilio is situated right in Piazza del Duomo, and the rooms with views of the cathedral are wonderful. The rooms are small but well furnished. ⊠ *Piazza del Duomo 5,* ☎ *0763/41882,* 🅵🅰🆇 *0763/43797. 13 rooms with bath or shower. Bar. MC, V.*

Shopping

Orvieto is a center of **woodworking,** particularly fine inlays and veneers. The Corso Cavour has a number of artisan shops specializing in woodwork, the best known being the studio of the Michelangeli family, which is crammed with a variety of imaginatively designed objects ranging in size from a giant *armadio* (wardrobe) to a simple wooden spoon.

Minor arts, such as **embroidery** and **lace making,** flourish in Orvieto as well. One of the best shops for *merletto* (lace) is Duranti (✉ Via del Duomo 10).

Excellent **Orvieto wines** are justly prized throughout Italy and in foreign countries. The whites are fruity, with a tart aftertaste, and are made from the region's Trebbiano grapes. Orvieto also produces its own version of the Tuscan dessert wine *vin santo*. It is darker than its Tuscan cousin and is aged five years before bottling.

En Route   The countryside southeast of Orvieto, as you head toward the town of Narni, is rarely included in most travel itineraries—a pity, since the scenery and rustic charm of the small towns on the route make this one of the most pleasant parts of Umbria. It is also a manageable chunk of country that can be seen in a half day's touring by car.

UMBRIA A TO Z

Arriving and Departing

By Bus

Perugia and Orvieto are served by private bus services, leaving from Rome and Florence.

By Car

On the western edge of the region is the Umbrian section of the Autostrada del Sole (A1), the principal north–south highway in Italy. It links Florence and Rome with the important Umbrian town of Orvieto and passes near Todi and Terni. The S3 intersects with A1 and leads on to Assisi and Urbino. The Adriatica superhighway (A14) runs north–south along the coast, linking the Marches to Bologna and Venice.

By Train

The main rail line from Rome to Ancona passes through Narni, Terni, Spoleto, and Foligno. Travel time from Rome to Spoleto is a little less than 90 minutes on intercity trains. The main Rome–Florence line stops at Orvieto, and, with a change of trains at the small town of Terontola, one can travel by rail from Rome or Florence to Perugia and Assisi.

Getting Around

By Bus

There is good local bus service between all the major and minor towns of Umbria. Some of the routes in rural areas, especially in the Marches, are designed to serve as many destinations as possible and are, therefore, quite roundabout and slow. Schedules often change, so consult with local tourist offices before setting out.

By Car

Umbria has an excellent and modern road network. Central Umbria is served by a major highway, S75bis, which passes along the shore of Lake Trasimeno and ends in Perugia, the principal city of the region. Assisi, the most visited town in the region, is well served by the modern highway S75, which connects to S3 and 3bis, which cover the heart of the region. Major inland routes connect coastal A14 to large towns in the Marches, including Urbino, Jesi, Macerata, and Ascoli Piceno, but inland secondary roads in mountain areas can be tortuous and narrow.

By Train

Branch lines link the central rail hub, Ancona, with the inland towns of Fabriano and Ascoli Piceno. In Umbria, a small, privately owned railway runs from Città di Castello in the north to Terni in the south.

Contacts and Resources

Emergencies

Police: Perugia (✉ Piazza dei Partigiani, ☎ 113); **Assisi** (✉ Piazza Matteotti 3, ☎ 075/812239); **Spoleto** (✉ Viale Trento e Trieste, ☎ 0743/40324); **Orvieto** (✉ Piazza Cahen, ☎ 0763/342476).

Visitor Information

Ancona (✉ Via Thaon De Revel 4, ☎ 071/33249; railway station, Piazza Fratelli Rosselli, ☎ 071/41703). **Ascoli Piceno** (✉ Piazza del Popolo, ☎ 0736/257288). **Assisi** (✉ Piazza del Comune 12, ☎ 075/812534). **Gubbio** (✉ Piazza Oderisi 6, ☎ 075/922–0693). **Loreto** (✉ Via Solari 3, ☎ 071/977139). **Orvieto** (✉ Piazza del Duomo, ☎ 0763/341772). **Perugia:** Umbria's regional tourist office (✉ Corso Vannucci 30, ☎ 075/5041); Perugia's city tourist office (✉ Piazza IV Novembre 3, ☎ 075/572–3327). **Spoleto** (✉ Piazza della Libertà 7, ☎ 0743/220311). **Urbino** (✉ Piazza Duca Federico 35, ☎ 0722/2441).

5 Portrait of Florence, Tuscany, and Umbria

Florence, Tuscany, and Umbria at a Glance: A Chronology

FLORENCE, TUSCANY, AND UMBRIA AT A GLANCE: A CHRONOLOGY

c.1000 BC Etruscans arrive in central Italy.

c. 800 Rise of Etruscan city-states.

510 Foundation of the Roman republic; expulsion of Etruscans from Roman territory.

c. 350 Rome extends rule to Tuscia (Tuscany), the land of the Etruscans.

c. 220 Umbria, the land of the Umbri and later Etruscans, come under Roman sway.

133 Rome rules entire Mediterranean Basin except Egypt.

49 Julius Caesar conquers Gaul.

46 Julian calendar introduced; it remains in use until AD 1582.

44 Julius Caesar is assassinated.

27 Rome's Imperial Age begins; Octavian (now named Augustus) becomes the first emperor and is later deified. The Augustan Age is celebrated in the works of Virgil (70 BC–AD 19), Ovid (43 BC–AD 17), Livy (59 BC–AD 17), and Horace (65 BC–AD 27).

AD 14 Augustus dies.

65 Emperor Nero begins the persecution of Christians in the empire; Saints Peter and Paul are executed.

117 The Roman Empire reaches its apogee.

165 A smallpox epidemic ravages the Empire.

c. 150–200 Christianity gains a foothold within the Empire, with the theological writings of Clement, Tertullian, and Origen.

212 Roman citizenship is conferred on all nonslaves in the Empire.

238 The first wave of Germanic invasions penetrates Italy.

293 Diocletian reorganizes the Empire into West and East.

313 The Edict of Milan grants toleration of Christianity within the Empire.

410 Rome is sacked by Visigoths.

476 The last Roman Emperor, Romulus Augustus, is deposed.

552 Eastern Emperor Justinian (527–565) recovers control of Italy.

570 Lombards gain control of much of Italy, including Rome.

590 Papal power expands under Gregory the Great.

c. 600–750 Lucca is chief city of Tuscany.

774 Frankish ruler Charlemagne invades Italy under papal authority and is crowned Holy Roman Emperor by Pope Leo III (800).

c. 800–900 The breakup of Charlemagne's (Carolingian) realm leads to the rise of Italian city-states.

1077 Pope Gregory VII leads the Holy See into conflict with the Germanic Holy Roman Empire.

1152–1190 Frederick I (Barbarossa) is crowned Holy Roman Emperor (1155); punitive expeditions by his forces (Ghibellines) are countered by the

Guelphs, creators of the powerful Papal States in central Italy. Guelph–Ghibelline conflict becomes a feature of medieval life.

c. 1200 Lucca appears strongest of Tuscan cities. Religious revival in Umbria centers around activities of St. Francis of Assisi and the foundation of the Franciscan order. Umbria takes the lead in art and architecture attracting Pisano, Cimabue, Giotto, Simone Martini, and Lorenzetti.

c. 1250 Florence takes the cultural and financial lead.

1262 Florence bankers issue Europe's first bills of exchange.

1264 Charles I of Anjou invades Italy, intervening in the continuing Guelph–Ghibelline conflict.

1290–1375 Tuscan literary giants Dante Alighieri (1265–1321), Francesco Petrarch (1304–74), and Giovanni Boccaccio (1313–75) form the basis of literature in the modern Italian language.

1309 The pope moves to Avignon in France, under the protection of French kings.

1376 The pope returns to Rome, but rival Avignonese popes stand in opposition, creating the Great Schism until 1417.

c. 1380–1420 Umbrian cities ruled by *condottieri*.

1402 The last German intervention into Italy is repulsed by the Lombards.

1443 Brunelleschi's dome is completed on Florence's Duomo (Cathedral).

1469–92 Lorenzo "Il Magnifico," the Medici patron of the arts, rules in Florence.

1498 Girolamo Savonarola, the austere Dominican friar, is executed for heresy after leading Florence into a drive for moral purification, typified by his burning of books and decorations in the "Bonfire of Vanities" the year before.

1504 Michelangelo's *David* is unveiled in Florence's Piazza della Signoria.

1513 Machiavelli's *The Prince* is published.

1521 The Pope excommunicates Martin Luther of Germany, precipitating the Protestant Reformation.

1540 Pope Paul III consolidates rule of Umbria with other Papal states.

1545–63 The Council of Trent formulates the Catholic response to the Reformation.

1573–1610 Caravaggio pioneers a painting style using violently contrasting light and dark themes.

1720–90 The Great Age of the Grand Tour. Northern Europeans visit Italy and start the vogue for classical studies. Among the famous visitors are Edward Gibbon (1758), Jacques-Louis David (1775), and Johann Wolfgang von Goethe (1786).

1796 Napoléon begins his Italian campaigns, annexing Rome and imprisoning Pope Pius VI four years later.

1801 Tuscany is made kingdom of Etruria within French domain.

1807–1809 Tuscany is a French département.

1808 Umbria annexed to French empire as département of Trasimeno.

1815 Austria controls much of Italy after Napoléon's downfall.

1848 Revolutionary troops under Risorgimento (Unification) leaders Giuseppe Mazzini (1805–72) and Giuseppe Garibaldi (1807–82) establish a republic in Rome.

1849 French troops crush rebellion and restore Pope Pius IX.

1860 Garibaldi and his "Thousand" defeat the Bourbon rulers in Sicily and Naples.

1861 Tuscany and Umbria join Kingdom of Sardinia, which becomes Kingdom of Italy.

1870 Rome finally captured by Risorgimento troops and declared capital of Italy by King Victor Emmanuel II.

1900 King Umberto I is assassinated by an anarchist; he is succeeded by King Victor Emmanuel III.

1915 Italy enters World War I on the side of the Allies.

1922 Fascist "black shirts" under Benito Mussolini march on Rome; Mussolini becomes prime minister and later "Duce" (head of Italy).

1929 The Lateran Treaty: Mussolini recognizes Vatican City as a sovereign state, and the Church recognizes Rome as the capital of Italy.

1940–44 In World War II, Italy fights with the Axis powers until its capitulation (1943), when Mussolini flees Rome.

1957 The Treaty of Rome is signed, and Italy becomes a founding member of the European Economic Community.

1966 November flood damages many of Florence's artistic treasures.

1968–79 The growth of left-wing activities leads to the formation of the Red Brigades and provokes right-wing reactions. Bombings and kidnappings culminate in the abduction and murder of Prime Minister Aldo Moro in 1980.

1992 The Christian Democrat Party, in power throughout the postwar period, loses its hold on a relative majority in Parliament.

1993 Italians vote for sweeping reforms after the Tangentopoli (Bribe City) scandal exposes widespread political corruption, including politicians' collusion with organized crime. A bomb outside the Uffizi Gallery in Florence kills five, but spares the museum's most precious artworks; authorities blame the Mafia, flexing its muscles in the face of a crackdown.

1994 A center-right coalition wins the spring elections, and media magnate Silvio Berlusconi becomes premier. Italian politics seem to be evolving into the equivalent of a two party system.

INDEX

NOTES

NOTES

NOTES

NOTES

NOTES

NOTES

NOTES

NOTES

NOTES

Fodor's Travel Publications

Available at bookstores everywhere, or call 1–800–533–6478, 24 hours a day.

Gold Guides
U.S.

Alaska

Arizona

Boston

California

Cape Cod, Martha's Vineyard, Nantucket

The Carolinas & the Georgia Coast

Chicago

Colorado

Florida

Hawai'i

Las Vegas, Reno, Tahoe

Los Angeles

Maine, Vermont, New Hampshire

Maui & Lāna'i

Miami & the Keys

New England

New Orleans

New York City

Pacific North Coast

Philadelphia & the Pennsylvania Dutch Country

The Rockies

San Diego

San Francisco

Santa Fe, Taos, Albuquerque

Seattle & Vancouver

The South

U.S. & British Virgin Islands

USA

Virginia & Maryland

Washington, D.C.

Foreign

Australia

Austria

The Bahamas

Belize & Guatemala

Bermuda

Canada

Cancún, Cozumel, Yucatán Peninsula

Caribbean

China

Costa Rica

Cuba

The Czech Republic & Slovakia

Eastern & Central Europe

Europe

Florence, Tuscany & Umbria

France

Germany

Great Britain

Greece

Hong Kong

India

Ireland

Israel

Italy

Japan

London

Madrid & Barcelona

Mexico

Montréal & Québec City

Moscow, St. Petersburg, Kiev

The Netherlands, Belgium & Luxembourg

New Zealand

Norway

Nova Scotia, New Brunswick, Prince Edward Island

Paris

Portugal

Provence & the Riviera

Scandinavia

Scotland

Singapore

South Africa

South America

Southeast Asia

Spain

Sweden

Switzerland

Thailand

Tokyo

Toronto

Turkey

Vienna & the Danube

Fodor's Special-Interest Guides

Caribbean Ports of Call

The Complete Guide to America's National Parks

Family Adventures

Gay Guide to the USA

Halliday's New England Food Explorer

Halliday's New Orleans Food Explorer

Healthy Escapes

Kodak Guide to Shooting Great Travel Pictures

Net Travel

Nights to Imagine

Rock & Roll Traveler USA

Sunday in New York

Sunday in San Francisco

Walt Disney World, Universal Studios and Orlando

Walt Disney World for Adults

Where Should We Take the Kids? California

Where Should We Take the Kids? Northeast

Worldwide Cruises and Ports of Call

Special Series

Affordables
Caribbean
Europe
Florida
France
Germany
Great Britain
Italy
London
Paris

Fodor's Bed & Breakfasts and Country Inns
America
California
The Mid-Atlantic
New England
The Pacific Northwest
The South
The Southwest
The Upper Great Lakes

The Berkeley Guides
California
Central America
Eastern Europe
Europe
France
Germany & Austria
Great Britain & Ireland
Italy
London
Mexico
New York City
Pacific Northwest & Alaska
Paris
San Francisco

Compass American Guides
Arizona
Canada
Chicago
Colorado
Hawaii
Idaho
Hollywood
Las Vegas
Maine
Manhattan
Montana
New Mexico
New Orleans
Oregon
San Francisco
Santa Fe
South Carolina
South Dakota
Southwest
Texas
Utah
Virginia
Washington
Wine Country
Wisconsin
Wyoming

Fodor's Citypacks
Atlanta
Hong Kong
London
New York City
Paris
Rome
San Francisco
Washington, D.C.

Fodor's Español
California
Caribe Occidental
Caribe Oriental
Gran Bretaña
Londres
Mexico
Nueva York
Paris

Fodor's Exploring Guides
Australia
Boston & New England
Britain
California
Caribbean
China
Egypt
Florence & Tuscany
Florida
France
Germany
Ireland
Israel
Italy
Japan
London
Mexico
Moscow & St. Petersburg
New York City
Paris
Prague
Provence
Rome
San Francisco
Scotland
Singapore & Malaysia
Spain
Thailand
Turkey
Venice

Fodor's Flashmaps
Boston
New York
San Francisco
Washington, D.C.

Fodor's Pocket Guides
Acapulco
Atlanta
Barbados
Jamaica
London
New York City
Paris
Prague
Puerto Rico
Rome
San Francisco
Washington, D.C.

Mobil Travel Guides
America's Best Hotels & Restaurants
California & the West
Frequent Traveler's Guide to Major Cities
Great Lakes
Mid-Atlantic
Northeast
Northwest & Great Plains
Southeast
Southwest & South Central

Rivages Guides
Bed and Breakfasts of Character and Charm in France
Hotels and Country Inns of Character and Charm in France
Hotels and Country Inns of Character and Charm in Italy
Hotels and Country Inns of Character and Charm in Paris
Hotels and Country Inns of Character and Charm in Portugal
Hotels and Country Inns of Character and Charm in Spain

Short Escapes
Britain
France
New England
Near New York City

Fodor's Sports
Golf Digest's Best Places to Play
Skiing USA
USA Today The Complete Four Sport Stadium Guide

Fodor's Vacation Planners
Great American Learning Vacations
Great American Sports & Adventure Vacations
Great American Vacations
Great American Vacations for Travelers with Disabilities
National Parks and Seashores of the East
National Parks of the West